PULSE OF THE NATION

PULSE OF THE NATION

GAA 140 YEARS RANKINGS, RATINGS, TALES AND DRAMA

MARTIN BREHENY & DONAL KEENAN

HACHETTE
BOOKS
IRELAND

Copyright © 2024 Martin Breheny and Donal Keenan

The right of Martin Breheny and Donal Keenan to be identified as the authors of the work has been asserted by them in accordance with the Copyright, Designs and Patents Act 1988.

First published in Ireland in 2024 by HACHETTE BOOKS IRELAND

1

All rights reserved. No part of this publication may be reproduced, stored in a retrieval system, or transmitted, in any form or by any means without the prior written permission of the publisher, nor be otherwise circulated in any form of binding or cover other than that in which it is published and without a similar condition being imposed on the subsequent purchaser.

Permission has been granted from GAA to include associated photos in the book. Sportsfile, Inpho Photography and GAA Museum have granted permission for specific photos. Shirt motif: sobahus surur/Shutterstock ©

Cataloguing in Publication Data is available from the British Library.

ISBN 9781399734653

Cover design: Cathal O'Gara; Slick Fish Design. Front cover images: Christy Ring: Connolly Collection/Sportsfile, Cora Staunton: Piaras Ó Mídheach/Sportsfile, Peter Canavan: Brendan Moran/Sportsfile, Joe Canning: Ramsey Cardy/Sportsfile, Jack O'Shea: Ray McManus/Sportsfile, Angela Downey: Ray McManus/Sportsfile, Henry Shefflin: Damien Eagers/Sportsfile, Stephen Cluxton: Piaras Ó Mídheach/Sportsfile. Back cover image: GAA Museum.

All efforts have been made to trace holders of copyright of images used within the book. For queries, please contact info@hhgi.ie.

Typeset in Garamond Premier Pro by Bookends Publishing Services, Dublin
Printed and bound in Great Britain by Clays Ltd, Elcograf S.p.A.

Hachette Books Ireland policy is to use papers that are natural, renewable and recyclable products and made from wood grown in sustainable forests. The logging and manufacturing processes are expected to conform to the environmental regulations of the country of origin.

Hachette Books Ireland
8 Castlecourt Centre
Castleknock
Dublin 15, Ireland

A division of Hachette UK Ltd
Carmelite House, 50 Victoria Embankment, London EC4Y 0DZ

www.hachettebooksireland.ie

CONTENTS

Foreword by Jarlath Burns, GAA President   vii
Authors' Introduction   x

1   Football's Greatest: Position by Position   1

2   Hurling's Greatest: Position by Position   58

3   Dual Jewels   113

4   Our Greatest Days: County by County   138

5   Championships and Change   257

6   By Order of Management   278

7   A Touch of Controversy   292

8   Threats and Challenges   319

9   Congress Clippings   339

10   From Pastime to Big Time   356

11   Trailblazers   371

12   GAA Goes Global   383

Acknowledgements   396

FOREWORD

Jarlath Burns, GAA President

Is cúis mhór áthais dom fáilte a chur roimh fhoilsiú an leabhair ghalánta seo agus Cumann Lúthchleas Gael ag ceiliúradh 140 ar an bhfód i mbliana.

For many of us, it is hard to imagine an Ireland with no GAA and no Gaelic games.

The games provide a rhythm to our lives, a sense of order and a cycle that far outstrips the presentation of cups and the passing of seasons.

One hundred and forty years ago, in Hayes Hotel in Thurles, people of vision – and no doubt some degree of uncertainty – helped the GAA to take its first steps, hardly for one moment dreaming about what it was they were about to unfurl on Irish society.

The emergence of an institution followed – not in a predictable, straightforward manner, but one that, in its early years, ebbed and flowed, mirroring the story and fortunes of the nation.

At its core was something of real substance, something that enabled it to navigate early turbulence to ensure a safe passage for the establishment of codified versions of our native games.

In so doing, they gave the exponents of those same games a sense of identity and a pride in place that, combined, would enable the fledgling organisation to put down roots – roots that permeate Irish society to this day and that are detectable everywhere Irish people are found globally.

To that end, it is right and proper that we laud the landmark year that is 140 and welcome the publication of Pulse of the Nation to mark it.

Martin Breheny and Donal Keenan, two of the most experienced GAA journalists to cover the beat, cast an eye back over the best players to play our games in both codes and highlight the great days enjoyed on a county-by-county basis.

They examine the phenomenon that was the inter-county dual player and the role of the manager, and they chart the changes to our championship structures of recent years after so many years of straight knockout games based on the provincial system.

In addition to charting the rise and fortunes of both LGFA and camogie, they also look at the global growth of the games, the big stories – some of which they covered – from GAA congresses and, of course, the headline generators for the organisation down through the years.

In many ways, this is an invaluable reference point for followers of our games and activities, a catch-all, whistle-stop tour down through the decades, connecting young and old alike through the prism of our games.

It will serve as a useful reference guide evoking memories and introducing younger readers to tales of the past for the first time.

I wish Donal, Martin and everyone involved with the project every success and look forward to digesting its contents in the weeks and months ahead.

Rath Dé ar an obair

Iarlaith Ó Broin
Uachtarán, Cumann Lúthchleas Gael

INTRODUCTION

When Maurice Davin, an athlete of international renown, strode into the billiard room in Hayes Hotel in Thurles shortly after 1p.m. on Saturday, 1 November 1884, he was taken aback. Just six other men, including Michael Cusack, who had organised the meeting of like-minded sports enthusiasts, were present.

'He must have felt some disappointment that so few had come,' his biographer and former GAA president Séamus O'Riain observed.

Davin and Cusack hid their disappointment well and proceeded with the meeting to organise what they called the Gaelic Athletic Association. The other five men in the room, according to O'Riain and based on research by the early-twentieth-century historian Thomas F. O'Sullivan, were John Wyse Power, John McKay, James K. Bracken, Joseph O'Ryan and Thomas St George McCarthy.

Davin, who became first GAA president, was a man renowned for his passion and optimism but had many reasons to worry about the future of the new association in the early days as internal wrangling, opposition from political leaders, the police and even some elements of the clergy threatened to derail his plans.

He could not have imagined that the games, for which he devised the first official sets of playing rules, and the association that he founded would, 140 years later, be such a massive movement, its tentacles spreading across the world.

Surviving early obstacles – the Civil War, War of Independence, the growing pains of a new Republic, financial strife and mass emigration – the GAA grew to become the biggest sporting and cultural movement on the island of Ireland.

Davin's vision for the new association in 1884 was outlined by Séamus O'Riain. 'He saw it as the instrument to revive and encourage the sports and pastimes characteristic of the Irish people, including athletics, hurling and Irish football.'

The GAA became the beating heart of every parish. It provided an outlet for the people to express themselves; it developed facilities in which communities could come together for sport and recreation.

And it provided the games and the championships that engaged the people like nothing else. It found heroes in the players who became the inspiration for future generations.

To celebrate the 140th anniversary of the GAA, we have focused on those heroes and, for the first time, ranked the top ten footballers and hurlers in each of the fifteen positions, going back to the beginning of the championships. Our judgement is based on almost half a century watching the games in stadiums all over the country, while relying on reportage and various histories of the games and players for earlier times.

The question may arise as to why there are no similar rankings for ladies football and camogie. The answer is simple.

We have covered very little of either sport and so didn't feel we could make credible assessments on players' merits. Nor is there much historical material to work from, given that media coverage of ladies football and camogie was, up to fairly recently, quite limited. It was different for hurling and football, which have enjoyed extensive reportage and analysis from their earliest days. In addition, there are detailed records, player profiles, award schemes and other data to work from. All of these, plus our personal opinions, made the football and hurling rankings possible – even if, no doubt, many will disagree with various choices.

This book is based essentially on 2024 being the 140th anniversary of the founding of the GAA. Though the Camogie Association and Ladies Gaelic Football Association have always had a good relationship with the GAA, the three organisations are independent of one another. Of course, this may not be the case for much longer as detailed work is underway for full integration, with 2027 as the target date for completion of the process.

That will change the landscape considerably for the better as the three organisations work together more closely to provide a streamlined operation for the entire community. With coverage of ladies football and camogie increasing rapidly year by year, a ranking exercise will, no doubt, be possible at some point in the future.

We would have liked to delve into camogie and ladies football – and handball and rounders, the other sports championed by the GAA – to the same degree as hurling and football, but it wasn't just possible, not only from a knowledge perspective, but also because there was so much to cover in the many facets of the GAA's 140-year story.

We have examined all the major developments that have made the GAA what it is today, including the changes, the controversies, the threats and challenges, the developments in competitive structures, the evolution of the role of team manager, the increasing role of women in the games and the association as a whole, and the GAA's growth internationally.

We have also chosen the greatest highlights in the 140 years on the field of play for all thirty-two counties, as well as London and New York. And there's more too in an extensive work that provides a fascinating insight into how the GAA has become such a massive movement at home and abroad.

This book will provoke discussion, debate and also attract criticism – all essential elements in the enduring story of an association created by a visionary group who dreamed a dream and invited others to share in it.

1 FOOTBALL'S GREATEST POSITION BY POSITION

Never underestimate the power of dreams and the influence of the human spirit. We are all the same in this notion. The potential for greatness lives within each of us.
Wilma Rudolph, who in Rome in 1960 became the first American female athlete to win three gold medals in a single Olympic Games.

Who is the greatest? It's a question that has intrigued sports fans down through the ages, with opinions as varied as the numbers answering.

Whether adjudicating on current or past players, or a mixture of both, answering is a highly subjective matter, especially when teams are involved. Even in an individual sport, like athletics where performances are measurable, it's impossible to be definitive when comparing athletes from different eras.

World records continue to tumble, but are the athletes individually better than their predecessors?

Roger Bannister's achievement in breaking the four-minute barrier for the mile in 1954 will always be feted, but a similar run now would leave an athlete a long way behind the winner.

At face value, that puts the modern generation of athletes – and indeed all those who improved on that sub-four-minute over the past seventy years – ahead of Bannister, but it's not that straightforward.

Professionalism, better training methods and equipment, improved body conditioning and nutrition, more friendly-running tracks, psychological advances, plus other aids have all combined to help athletes run faster. What if those advantages could be superimposed on Bannister's natural talent? Would he be quicker than all the rest right up to today? The same applies to other sports, including Gaelic games.

Assessing players from different generations creates two camps. A younger generation tends to look at the past as largely crude and unsophisticated by comparison with modern times. Whereas an older generation assert that there was more substance – certainly in Gaelic football – to games in the past and that it has been replaced by a robotic structure, high on organisation and imitation, and low on individualism, head-to-head contests, risk-raking and excitement.

In all probability, the truth rests in between the two.

Requirements for players have certainly changed over the years, but the basic texture of football and hurling has remained the same. It's still about goals and points – scoring as many as possible and conceding as few as possible.

The means of achieving both objectives have evolved and

changed, but top players would be good in any era. So how to compare and evaluate them?

For the purpose of this exercise, we drew on our own experiences of watching games for over half a century. Of course, that wasn't enough in an organisation that is 140 years old.

In order to bring players from as far back as possible into the mix, we also drew on the opinions of the media correspondents who covered the games.

Given that media coverage of Gaelic games was sketchy and haphazard for many years, it's all but impossible to find reliable guides to player prowess for the association's earlier years. However, as coverage expanded, more emphasis was placed on highlighting individual excellence.

We absorbed as much of the earlier coverage as we could and mixed it with the ever-increasing analysis from the 1930s onwards – we rely on our own opinions for the past fifty years. Pulling all the strands together, we have come up with a one-to-ten ranking across each position in football and hurling.

Given that we have watched all the players for the past half-century, there may be a leaning towards that timespan but, in as far as was possible, we have been mindful of what went before – we have not neglected the early years.

The manner in which football in particular has changed made comparisons from different eras very difficult. For instance, prior to 1960, goalkeepers fouled the ball if they touched it on the ground in the square. It called for a different skillset to what followed when that rule was abolished.

The requirements for outfield players have changed over the

years too. The demands on a modern-day full-back are completely different to what it was even twenty years ago. Back then – and previously too – a player needed to be big, strong and assertive. Aerial bombardments were frequent so the full-back needed to have an imposing presence, capable of making high, spectacular catches, while also repelling ground offensives.

Right throughout the field, individual battles waged. It was largely fourteen versus fourteen outfield contests, unlike today when, to a large degree, systems and structures supersede individual expertise. We have tried to take all that into account when compiling our rankings.

Another factor, which added to the challenge, involved versatility and the ability of players to excel in a variety of areas.

Many played in several positions in defence or attack; others switched from defence to attack, or vice versa, during their careers, while midfielders have always had a wide range of qualities.

The most versatile performer is at a disadvantage in positional rankings. It's a tribute to their adaptability, but they tend to lose out when compared with those whose entire careers were spent in one position.

But then, this is not an exact science. It is an attempt to put the comparative talents of players in some order. Restricting it to ten in each position made it all the more difficult – suffice to say, many great exponents of football and hurling have been omitted.

As for those who made the lists, their status as players whose standards reached incredible heights is unquestionable.

🎽 GOALKEEPER

1. Stephen Cluxton (Dublin)
Who would have thought when he made his senior championship debut against Longford in the 2001 Leinster quarter-final that Cluxton would become one of the most enduring and inspiring players in GAA history? His influence goes way beyond basic goalkeeping techniques, which he took to a new level, and extends to preparation, leadership, application and mental toughness. Add to all that a longevity that few achieve in any sport, local or international.

2. Dan O'Keeffe (Kerry)
Born in Cork, it was Kerry's good fortune that the O'Keeffe family moved to Tralee while Dan was still a child. 'Danno' went on to become one of the best goalkeepers in GAA history during a career that saw him win seven All-Ireland senior titles between 1931 and 1946, and fifteen Munster titles between 1931 and 1948. He was chosen on the GAA's Team of the Century in 1984 and the Team of the Millennium in 2000.

3. Martin Furlong (Offaly)
An All-Ireland minor winner in 1964, Furlong's talents took him through a remarkable career, highlighted by winning All-Ireland titles in 1971, 1972 and 1982. It leaves him with the distinction of being the only Offaly footballer with three All-Ireland senior medals as a member of the starting fifteen. A superb shot-stopper,

he was also expert at timing runs off his line to avert danger. He won the first of four All-Star awards in 1972 and added three more in 1981, 1982 and 1983, and was Footballer of the Year in 1982.

4. John O'Leary (Dublin)

At the age of nineteen, John O'Leary was promoted to the Dublin team for the 1980 Leinster final, despite not having been on the panel earlier in the campaign. He went on to play seventy successive championship games over the next seventeen years, at the end of which he had won two All-Ireland titles, one as captain in 1995. He won five All-Star awards, a goalkeeping achievement surpassed only by Stephen Cluxton. His average goal concession rate in the championship was an impressive 0.7 per game.

5. Johnny Geraghty (Galway)

An inspiring figure in Galway's All-Ireland three-in-a-row success of 1964, 1965 and 1966, Geraghty's agility and athleticism launched an evolutionary period in goalkeeping. Inspired by Gordon Banks, England's legendary keeper, Geraghty was a keen student of how soccer goalkeepers went about their business. Indeed, his excellence drew the attention of three soccer clubs – Manchester United, Fulham and Leicester – but the Kilkerrin man wasn't tempted by the approaches.

6. Billy Morgan (Cork)

Morgan's remarkable consistency in a career that spanned three decades – from 1966 to 1981 – was underlined by being nominated for an All-Star award ten times in eleven seasons. Rather surprisingly, he won only one award, in 1973 – a year in which he captained Cork to their first All-Ireland title since 1945 and was the Texaco Footballer of the Year, the first goalkeeper to win the award in a scheme introduced in 1958.

7. Paddy Cullen (Dublin)

Did Cullen's penalty save from Galway's Liam Sammon in the 1974 All-Ireland final change the course of Dublin football history? They went on to win the game, a success that led to a whole new era for the county, which also won two of the next three All-Ireland titles. Cullen, whose career extended from 1967 to 1979, was a pivotal figure in the dramatic change of fortunes. He won four All-Star awards and was nominated six times.

8. Aidan Brady (Roscommon)

Brady's status as a special talent was emphasised in 1984 – the GAA's centenary year – when he was chosen on a team drawn from players who hadn't won All-Ireland senior medals. His only real opportunity to achieve that huge ambition came in 1962 when Roscommon reached the final for the first time since 1946, but they lost to Kerry. He won four Connacht championship medals and featured regularly on the provincial team between 1954 and 1963.

9. David Clarke (Mayo)

Like so many other top Mayo players of his era, Clarke's career ended without an All-Ireland senior medal, but he can still look back with huge satisfaction on his efforts to end the county's long drought. Gifted with superb reflexes, his shot-stopping ability changed the course of many games in Mayo's favour. He beat off strong opposition to win All-Star awards in 2016 and 2017 and was nominated for the Footballer of the Year award in 2017.

10. Brian McAlinden (Armagh)
McAlinden won no All-Ireland titles and no All-Star awards (despite being nominated four times) but that in no way detracts from his stature in a fifteen-year career that started in the mid-1970s. He was remarkably consistent, even at times when Armagh weren't going particularly well, a fact recognised by his selection on a 1980s team comprised of players who hadn't won All-Star awards.

2. RIGHT FULL-BACK

1. Enda Colleran (Galway)
Colleran's star quality was first spotted in 1960 as a member of a minor team that won that year's All-Ireland title. Several of the team went on to feature in Galway's triple senior success in 1964, 1965 and 1966. Colleran was captain for the 1965 and 1966 seasons when his leadership qualities were very much in evidence. His excellence was recognised in 1984 when he was chosen on the Team of the Century and, in 2000, when he was selected on the Team of the Millennium.

2. Robbie O'Malley (Meath)

Given their role as security experts, rather than flashy, front-of-house performers, corner-backs rarely win the Footballer of the Year award, but so impressive was O'Malley in 1988 that he was rewarded with the ultimate individual honour. It was well-deserved. He delivered some powerful performances in Meath's drive to the All-Ireland two-in-a-row (1987 and 1988), especially in the drawn and replayed final against Cork in 1988. He won three All-Star awards in 1987, 1988 and 1990, and captained the Irish International Rules team in 1990.

3. Páidí Ó Sé (Kerry)

Where to place Ó Sé? Right half-back, where he played for several years, or right full-back where he moved at the start of 1983? He was equally effective in both positions in a glorious Kingdom era from 1975 to 1986 when they won eight All-Ireland titles. He played in all eight finals, as well as two which Kerry lost in 1976 and 1982. His five All-Star awards were split three to two in favour of the right full-back position.

4. Marc Ó Sé (Kerry)

Hugely versatile – similar to his uncle Páidí – it was at right-corner back that Marc Ó Sé enjoyed his best days, topped in 2007 when he won Footballer of the Year. He won five All-Ireland medals, ten Munster titles and All-Star awards in 2006, 2007 and 2011. He was often tasked with marking the best forward on opposing teams, a challenge to which he invariably rose. His intelligent reading of the game was important in solidifying Kerry's resistance. The bigger the occasion, the more he thrived.

5. Harry Keegan (Roscommon)

Harry Keegan holds the record as the Roscommon player with the most All-Star awards, having been selected three times in 1978, 1980 and 1986. This was quite an achievement as Roscommon won no All-Ireland titles during his lengthy career, which started in 1972 and, as history shows, most All-Star awards go to All-Ireland winners. He played in one final when Roscommon lost to Kerry in 1980. Strong, powerful and ultra-determined, he ticked all the boxes in the corner-back requirement manual.

6. Donie O'Sullivan (Kerry)

It takes a lot to be recognised as one of Kerry's finest, but Donie O'Sullivan achieved this in 2000 when he was chosen on the best Kingdom team of the previous fifty years. He was also named on the Munster Team of the Millennium. It was worthy recognition for excellence in a thirteen-year career – the high point of which came in 1970 when he captained Kerry to All-Ireland success, one of his four All-Ireland medals. A year later, he was chosen as the county's first All-Star, a feat he repeated in 1972.

7. Jimmy Deenihan (Kerry)

Kerry supporters still believe that if Jimmy Deenihan hadn't picked up a serious leg injury during the summer of 1982, the All-Ireland five-in-a-row would have been completed. Instead, Kerry lost the final by a point to Offaly. Before his injury, Deenihan had been a defiant presence in the Kingdom defence for nine years. As well as winning five All-Ireland medals, he also won one All-Star award and was nominated six times.

8. Willie Casey (Mayo)

A sub on the Mayo team in 1951 – when the county won a second consecutive All-Ireland title – Willie Casey went on to have a brilliant career before departing the scene after the defeat to Galway in the 1964 Connacht final. Mayo endured many lean years during his time, but he remained a consistent driving force, invariably rising to the challenge against top-ranked opponents.

9. Paddy McCormack (Offaly)

The 'Iron Man From Rhode' was an imposing figure at full-back when Offaly won the All-Ireland title for the first time in 1971 and when they won again a year later – his experience from a lengthy career played a crucial role in both successes. He won an All-Star award in 1972. He had spent much of his earlier career at right full-back, including in 1961 and 1969 when Offaly reached the All-Ireland final, losing to Down and Kerry respectively.

10. Gabriel Kelly (Cavan)

One influencing factor in assessing a player's quality over the past fifty years has been the number of All-Star awards he has won. The scheme was launched in 1971 but an unofficial version ran for part of the 1960s, during which Gabriel Kelly was selected at right full-back three times. He never got to play in an All-Ireland final, but won four Ulster championships with Cavan in 1962, 1964, 1967 and 1969. He was a regular on Ulster's Railway Cup teams in the 1960s, winning four titles.

⟨3⟩ FULL-BACK

1. John O'Keeffe (Kerry)
It said much about his maturity that, aged nineteen, John O'Keeffe was at centre-back when Kerry won the All-Ireland title in 1970. Two years later, he was at midfield when they lost to Offaly in a replayed final. These experiences broadened his knowledge, and he adapted well when he relocated to full-back as Kerry embarked on a history-making run under Mick O'Dwyer in 1975. O'Keeffe brought style and guile to the many demands of the position at a time when its role was evolving. He won four All-Star awards at full-back and one at midfield.

2. Paddy O'Brien (Meath)
Meath's capacity to produce superb full-backs started in the late 1940s when Paddy O'Brien launched himself into the public consciousness. He developed into one of the best in GAA history and was chosen on the GAA's Team of the Century in 1984. Affectionately known as 'Hands', he was an exceptionally high fielder, a talent that played a huge part in Meath's All-Ireland wins in 1949 and 1954.

3. Joe Keohane (Kerry)
In choosing Joe Keohane on the GAA's Team of the Millennium, the selection panel paid tribute to his excellence in a senior inter-

county career that started as an eighteen-year-old in 1937. His debut season was crowned with the first of his five All-Ireland titles, which included a three-in-a-row in 1939, 1940 and 1941. Apart from being high fielders, full-backs of his era also had to be exceptionally strong and, in addition to their own duties, were expected to protect their goalkeepers from marauding attackers. Keohane excelled on all fronts.

4. Noel Tierney (Galway)

Tierney's high fielding and driving runs away from goal as he repelled another opposition challenge were consistent features of Galway's greatest championship era when the county won successive All-Ireland titles in 1964, 1965 and 1966. The solidity of their defensive line was brought home by their conceding only one goal in three All-Ireland semi-finals and three finals, games in which they beat Kerry and Meath twice each, Down and Cork. Tierney, a major influence in them all, was chosen as Footballer of the Year in 1964.

5. Jack Quinn (Meath)

Jack Quinn's name has always been synonymous with heroic full-back exploits – but then, he was a gifted performer, with a wide range of talents that enabled him to play in a number of different positions. The high point of a senior career that extended from 1963 to 1976 came in 1967 when Meath won the All-Ireland title. Later that year, he was named at full-back on an unofficial All-Star team, an honour he had also gained in 1966.

6. Darren Fay (Meath)

As part of his team-building in a period of transition, manager Seán Boylan took a major leap of faith in 1996 by promoting a twenty-year-old to the demanding full-back position. He need not have worried. Darren Fay, whose potential had been well flagged, settled in quickly and, as the season progressed, it became apparent that he was a special talent. By September, he was an All-Ireland medal winner, and he added a second in 1999. He won All-Star awards in 1996, 1999 and 2001.

7. Paddy Prendergast (Mayo)

The Ballintubber man's inter-county career started with Donegal, where he was based as a garda, before he returned to Mayo in 1948. This coincided with the start of a glorious era, during which the county won two All-Irelands (1950 and 1951) and four Connacht titles in a row (1948–1951), as well as a fifth Connacht title in 1955. Paddy Prendergast's powerful presence at full-back played a big part in all those successes.

8. Mick Lyons (Meath)

Lyons experienced good and bad times with Meath, having started out in the late 1970s at a time when they were struggling, something that continued well into the 1980s. Gradually, the county's fortunes improved, with Lyons a dominant figure in a surge that saw them win successive All-Ireland titles in 1987, when he was captain, and 1988. An uncompromising sentry in front of goal, there was much more to his game than power and he also possessed a sharp football intellect.

9. Steven O'Brien (Cork)

Hugely versatile, Steven O'Brien was comfortable in any defensive position – as underlined by an All-Star haul which saw him win awards at full-back in 1990, centre half-back in 1994 and left half-back in 1995. He won two All-Ireland medals at full-back in 1989 and 1990 when Cork won successive All-Irelands for the first time. His commanding presence in front of goal was an important element in that achievement.

10. Eddie Boyle (Louth)

Regarded as one of Louth's greatest footballers, Eddie Boyle's two Leinster titles in 1943 and 1948 were the highest peaks of his senior inter-county career. These titles helped build a glowing reputation, which was enhanced by his exploits with Leinster in the Railway Cup, a competition that enjoyed real status during his time. He won five titles with Leinster in 1935, 1939, 1940, 1944 and 1945. As part of the GAA's centenary celebrations in 1984, he was named at full-back on a team comprised of players who hadn't won All-Ireland medals.

LEFT FULL-BACK

1. Seán Flanagan (Mayo)

Chosen at left full-back on the GAA's Team of the Century in 1984 and on the Team of the Millennium in 2000, Seán Flanagan's reputation as a defender of outstanding ability was based on a career that saw him captain Mayo to successive All-Ireland titles in 1950 and 1951. His influence on team affairs extended beyond playing, having also taken a significant role in training the squad and match-day tactics. Clearly, he was a man ahead of his time.

2. Keith Higgins (Mayo)

The only gap on Higgins' football CV is an All-Ireland senior title, a target he did more than most to try to hit during a sixteen-year career that began in 2005. He played in six All-Ireland finals, losing five (three by a point) and drawing one. The absence of an All-Ireland title from his long list of achievements in no way lowers his status, as his consistency during all those years was quite remarkable. He won four All-Star awards in 2012, 2013, 2014 and 2017, and was nominated seven times.

3. Robbie Kelleher (Dublin)

In four seasons (1970–1973), Dublin played only seven championship games, recording just two wins. In the six subsequent seasons (1974–1979), they played thirty-two championship games, losing only three – all to Kerry. Robbie Kelleher and several others were aboard for the bad and good times. It was a remarkable transformation, yielding three All-Ireland and six successive Leinster titles. Kelleher won four All-Star awards in that period, one more than any other Dublin player.

4. Michael Fitzsimons (Dublin)

Michael Fitzsimons' arrival on the scene in 2010 came a year before Dublin ended a sixteen-year wait for an All-Ireland title. He represented a new breed, one that cared little for the past and were determined to build a new empire. He was at left full-back on the team that won the 2011 All-Ireland title and went on to become one of the best man-markers in a number of positions as part of a record-breaking Dublin squad.

5. Tony Scullion (Derry)

The essence of versatility, Tony Scullion could play in most defensive positions, although left full-back was his best. He was a leading driver in the Derry surge in the early 1990s – first when they won the National League in 1992 and, even more crucially, when they were crowned All-Ireland champions for the first time the following year. He won four All-Star awards and also enjoyed great success with Ulster teams, winning six Railway Cup titles.

6. Graham Canty (Cork)

The ultimate in versatility, Canty played in most defensive positions, as well as midfield, in a long career that peaked in 2010 when he captained Cork to their first All-Ireland title for twenty years. He was highly effective wherever he lined out, providing real leadership. He was a triple All-Star winner, having been selected at left full-back in 2007 and centre-back in 2009 and 2010. He was nominated six times.

7. Kevin Kehilly (Cork)

Players like Kevin Kehilly must envy the modern generation of players where opportunities for extended championship runs are plentiful. It wasn't like that in Kehilly's time in the 1970s and 1980s when one defeat ended that year's campaign – and since Cork were up against an exceptional Kerry team, they rarely got out of Munster. None of that takes away from Kehilly's status as a highly intelligent and effective defender. He won All-Star awards at full-back and left full-back.

8. Tom O'Hare (Down)

Down's first All-Ireland title success in 1960, followed by a second a year later, ensured that all the players from that team became part of GAA folklore. Tom O'Hare, who arrived on the scene a few years later, had to wait until 1968 for an All-Ireland win. By then, he was established as a tenacious and ultra-reliable defender, a status he retained up to his departure five years later. He was a regular on Ulster teams for several years.

9. Conor Gormley (Tyrone)

An ability to adapt to whichever position the tactical demands of a game required was a top priority for Tyrone players under Mickey Harte after he took over as manager at the end of 2002. That was especially demanding on defenders but many of them managed it very well, including Conor Gormley, who was effective in a variety of areas. That included left full-back, where he won an All-Star award in 2008. He also won All-Stars at right half-back and centre half-back.

10. John McKnight (Armagh)

An All-Ireland minor championship winner in 1949, McKnight was aboard the senior team that reached the All-Ireland in 1953. Unfortunately for him and Armagh, the dream of a first

All-Ireland title was dashed by Kerry. McKnight remained a consistent presence on Armagh and Ulster teams, winning a Railway Cup medal in 1956. In 1984, he was named at left full-back on a selection that comprised the best players not to win an All-Ireland medal.

[5] RIGHT HALF-BACK

1. Tomás Ó Sé (Kerry)

There wasn't a more encouraging sight for Kerry supporters than Tomás Ó Sé powering upfield from right half-back, soloing the ball with a controlled technique few of his peers could match. Quite often, it ended with him kicking a point. His capacity to make those breaks when his side needed them most was invaluable. He was equally efficient in defensive duties during a career that yielded five All-Ireland senior titles and five All-Star awards between 2000 and 2009.

2. James McCarthy (Dublin)

Many players are position specialists, most comfortable in a defined role where they build a career around the particular requirements needed. Not James McCarthy, whose game has much wider parameters. From the start of his Dublin career in February 2010, he has shown athleticism and adventure, combined with a smart football brain that has left him equally effective as a half-back or midfielder. Add in his driving forward runs and he became a real powerhouse.

3. Lee Keegan (Mayo)

One of Mayo's best players, Lee Keegan brought so much to his game that it was unfortunate his career ended without an All-Ireland senior medal. He played in seven finals (including a replay) between 2012 and 2021, but ultimate glory eluded him. His scoring rate was exceptionally high for a defender but then he was expert at timing his forward runs. He was Footballer of the Year in 2016 and won five All-Star awards.

4. Séamus Moynihan (Kerry)

Séamus Moynihan played at midfield in his debut year (1992), but it was as a defender that he established a deserved reputation as one of the finest talents of his generation. Equally comfortable in all defensive positions, his ability to adapt to whatever challenge confronted him was invaluable for Kerry in a career that lasted fourteen years. It yielded four All-Ireland medals, three All-Stars and a Footballer of the Year award in 2000.

5. Seán Murphy (Kerry)

From 1953 into the early 1960s, Seán Murphy was a formidable presence in the Kerry defence, winning All-Ireland titles in his debut year and again in 1955 and 1959. His excellence in 1959 earned him the Footballer of the Year award in a scheme that had been introduced a year earlier. He was chosen at right half-back on the GAA's Team of the Century in 1984 and Team of the Millennium in 2000.

6. Tommy Drumm (Dublin)

Tommy Drumm's performance as captain and centre-back in Dublin's 1983 All-Ireland final win was one of the highlights of his career. Despite being reduced to twelve men for much of the second half, they beat Galway by two points. Drumm's career started at right half-back where he won three successive All-Stars in 1977, 1978 and 1979 before he moved to number six. He was equally impressive there, winning a fourth All-Star, as well as Footballer of the Year in 1983.

7. Niall Cahalane (Cork)

The epitome of versatility, Cahalane was effective in a variety of defensive positions, a talent that owed much to his athleticism and an ability to read play intelligently. It stood him and Cork well for many years. An influential figure in the most successful period in Cork football history, when, after losing the 1987 and 1988 All-Ireland finals, they won the next two. He won All-Star awards in 1987 and 1988.

8. Paul Curran (Dublin)

Following in the footsteps of his father, Noel, who had won an All-Ireland medal with Meath in 1967, Paul Curran excelled as a defender for Dublin, though he also played at midfield and attack at different stages of his thirteen-year career. He won an All-Ireland senior title in 1995 and All-Star awards in 1992, 1995 and 1996. He was chosen as Footballer of the Year in 1995. His all-round adaptability made him one of the stars of his generation.

9. Brian McEniff (Donegal)

Brian McEniff's central role in managing Donegal when they won the All-Ireland title for the first time in 1992 tends to overshadow his long career as a player. It shouldn't. He was hugely influential in 1972 when Donegal won the Ulster title for the first time, filling the demanding role of player-manager as they broke new frontiers. Later that year, he became Donegal's first All-Star. He was player-manager again when Donegal won the 1974 Ulster title.

10. Eugene Mulligan (Offaly)

The year 1971 was special for Offaly, as they won the All-Ireland title for the first time. It was extra exciting for Eugene Mulligan, whose excellence not only saw him recognised as Footballer of the Year but also as the automatic choice at right half-back on the inaugural All-Stars team – the only position with a single nominee. He won a second All-Ireland title in 1972 and went on to excel until his retirement in 1980.

6. CENTRE HALF-BACK

1. John Joe O'Reilly (Cavan)

Revered in song and story, John Joe O'Reilly's name has an iconic ring – and not just in Cavan, with whom he won two All-Ireland titles in 1947 and 1948 (both as captain). A noted sprinter and basketballer, he brought many of the requirements from those disciplines into his football. His approach to the number-six role was ahead of its time, especially the expertise he brought to tackling. He was chosen on the Teams of the Century (1984) and Team of the Millennium (2000). Sadly, he died in 1952 at the age of thirty-four.

2. Kieran McGeeney (Armagh)

A natural leader, it was appropriate that Kieran McGeeney was captain when Armagh won the All-Ireland title for the first time in 2002. Through his dedication and determination, he was influential in driving the culture that enabled Armagh to emerge as a powerful force at the start of the new millennium before landing the biggest prize of all. His contribution to the 2002 success earned him the Footballer of the Year award. He won All-Star awards in 1999, 2000 and 2002.

3. Gerry O'Malley (Roscommon)

Gerry O'Malley's career spanned three decades (1940s–1960s), underlining his dedication and durability. Unfortunately for him, and despite reaching the final in 1962, it didn't yield an All-Ireland senior medal, but his determined attempts to make it happen took his status nationally to great heights. In 1984, the GAA's centenary year, he was chosen at centre-back on a team comprised of players who hadn't won All-Ireland titles. He was also an accomplished hurler.

4. Glenn Ryan (Kildare)

Mick O'Dwyer, who managed Kildare from 1991 to 1994 and again from 1997 to 2002, described Glenn Ryan as 'the rock, the anchor, the captain and the inspiration' of the team that reached the 1998 All-Ireland final, which they lost to Galway. Earlier that year, Ryan had led Kildare to a first Leinster title for forty-two years, and won another in 2000. The essence of solidity during a sixteen-season career with the Lilywhites, he won All-Star awards in 1997 and 1998.

5. Tim Kennelly (Kerry)

Tim Kennelly made his senior debut in 1974 at the age of twenty, at a time when a new and exciting group of Kerry players were beginning to emerge as special talents. He went on to win five All-Ireland senior titles between 1975 and 1981, a period in which he was twice an All-Star (1979 and 1980). A centre-back of immense stature, 'Horse', as he was affectionately known, revelled in the most demanding physical exchanges.

6. Dan McCartan (Down)

One of four Down players who won All-Ireland medals in 1960, 1961 and 1968, Dan McCartan was at centre-back in 1960 and 1961 and at full-back in 1968. He also won eight Ulster titles and three National League titles. The ease with which he made the transfer from number six to number three highlighted his natural football instinct and it was that, allied to a fiercely competitive nature, that made him a player of immense stature.

7. Karl Lacey (Donegal)

Footballer of the Year in 2012, the year Donegal won their second All-Ireland title, Karl Lacey was a pivotal figure in the rebuild launched by manager Jim McGuinness in 2011. Lacey won All-Star awards at centre-back in 2011 and 2012. He had spent much of the earlier part of his career in the full-back line, where he won All-Star awards on the left in 2006 and on the right in 2009.

8. Bill Casey (Kerry)

A powerhouse defender, Bill Casey was one of the main Kingdom anchors in the latter part of the 1930s and most of the 1940s. His first All-Ireland final ended in disappointment when Kerry lost to Galway in 1938, but he went on to win four titles in 1939, 1940, 1941 and 1946. Bill, whose nephew Brian Mullins enjoyed a great career with Dublin in the 1970s and 1980s, was the centre-back choice on the Munster Team of the Millennium in 2000.

9. Paddy Moriarty (Armagh)

Armagh's first All-Star recipient in 1972, the honour coming at left full-forward, Moriarty was a classy attacker before switching to defence where he developed into an outstanding number six. He and his Armagh colleagues got one shot at All-Ireland glory in 1977 but were beaten by a Dublin team at the peak of its powers. Moriarty was the All-Star centre-back that year. One of football's top all-round performers.

10. Cian O'Sullivan (Dublin)

Cian O'Sullivan's promotion to the Dublin team in 2010 coincided with the beginning of the most remarkable period in the county's history. He won his first All-Ireland medal at right full-back in 2011, but was at his best in the centre half-back area, where his sense of calmness, authority and good judgement resonated with colleagues around him. He was a leading figure in Dublin's glory period and was an All-Star number six in 2013, 2015 and 2017.

7. LEFT HALF-BACK

1. Martin O'Connell (Meath)
Martin O'Connell's career may have featured him in attack at times, but it was at left half-back that he made the biggest impression over many years, including in 1987 and 1988 when Meath won the All-Ireland two-in-a-row. Chosen at number seven on the Team of the Millennium in 2000, O'Connell won All-Star awards in that position in 1988, 1990 and 1991, before adding a fourth at left full-back in 1996, when he was also chosen as Footballer of the Year, having won a third All-Ireland medal.

2. Jack McCaffrey (Dublin)
From the day Jack McCaffrey made his senior debut as a twenty-year-old in 2013, it was obvious that he was a remarkable talent. He arrived on the scene at a time when Dublin had the deepest talent pool in the county's history and he quickly developed into one of the most exciting half-backs the game has seen, with ball-carrying sprints that carried him into opposition territory, often yielding crucial scores. By 2015, he was Footballer of the Year.

3. Philip Jordan (Tyrone)
Peter Canavan (six) and Seán Cavanagh (five) are the only Tyrone men to have more All-Star awards than Philip Jordan (four), which

shows the exalted circles in which he moved during his nine-year career. Relatively few half-backs have won four All-Stars but Jordan's consistent excellence saw him achieve it between 2003 and 2010, a period in which he also won three All-Ireland titles in the most successful era in Tyrone history.

4. Paudie Lynch (Kerry)

Paudie Lynch's long career saw him play in defence, attack and midfield, but then he was such a competent footballer that slotting in wherever management felt he was required came easily to him. It started in the half-forward line, moved to midfield but it was as a defender that he really hit the heights, winning five All-Ireland titles between 1975 and 1981. He won All-Star awards at midfield in 1974, left half-back in 1978 and left full-back in 1981.

5. Stephen White (Louth)

Stephen White was selected on the GAA's Team of the Century in 1984, but lost out to Meath's Martin O'Connell on the Team of the Millennium. He won the first of three Leinster championships in 1948, adding a second in 1950 and a third in 1957, the year in which Louth won the All-Ireland title for the first time since 1912. He won four Railway Cup medals with Leinster – two in attack, one in midfield and one in defence.

6. Colm Boyle (Mayo)

Between 2008 and 2021, Colm Boyle played 120 times for Mayo, testament to his dedication and durability. Unfortunately for him, his career ended without an All-Ireland senior medal, but he will still be remembered as an exceptionally efficient half-back. Indeed, he holds the unusual distinction of having won All-Stars in all three positions, two on the left (2013 and 2014), one in the centre (2016) and one on the right (2017).

7. Jim McDonnell (Cavan)

From the mid-1950s to the mid-1960s, Jim McDonnell was a major presence in Cavan football, primarily at half-back, although he also played at midfield on occasions. Cavan won three Ulster titles in that period (they also lost three finals) but failed to reach an All-Ireland final. That was certainly no fault of McDonnell's, who remained the essence of reliability. He enjoyed many great days with Ulster, playing on teams that won four Railway Cup titles in 1956, 1960, 1963 and 1964.

8. Pat Reynolds (Meath)

From 1964, when he was promoted to the senior team as an eighteen-year-old, to the mid-1970s, Pat Reynolds was a formidable presence on a Meath team that experienced contrasting fortunes – winning an All-Ireland title in 1967, having lost to Galway a year earlier. They also lost to Kerry in the 1970 final. Reynolds was chosen on the Team of the Year in 1967 and was the first Meath man to be selected on the official All-Stars in 1971.

9. Seán Óg de Paor (Galway)

Seán Óg de Paor knew bad and good times with Galway, having done more than most to turn the former into the latter as the

Tribesmen powered their way to All-Ireland glory for the first time in thirty-two years in 1998. He added a second title in 2001. An intelligent reader of the game, his ability to judge accurately when to stay as part of the defensive shape and when to go forward as an attacker made him an invaluable asset. He won two All-Star awards.

10. Jim Reilly (Cavan)

Jim Reilly won no All-Ireland senior medals, no provincial titles and no All-Star awards, but that should not mislead anyone into thinking that he wasn't as good as many of those who accumulated some – or indeed all three – of those big prizes. In truth, he was, but Cavan weren't when his career was at its peak in the 1980s. He enjoyed more success with Ulster, where he had an important input into three Railway Cup successes.

8 & 9 MIDFIELD

1. Jack O'Shea (Kerry)

Jack O'Shea was the complete package: seven All-Ireland senior medals, four Footballer of the Year awards in six seasons, six successive All-Star awards, eleven All-Star nominations and chosen on the GAA's Team of the Century in 1984. That's quite a haul for a man whose inter-county career ran from 1976 to 1992. A superb fielder, an accurate kicker and a smart reader of the game, he also had limitless energy, which he used effectively all over the pitch.

2. Mick O'Connell (Kerry)
It's unfortunate that more footage of Mick O'Connell's exploits aren't available in the archives but since his career ran from the 1950s to the 1970s, there's little enough around. Despite that, he was known everywhere as a real superstar, due mainly to his exceptional fielding skills and accurate kicking. Footballer of the Year in 1962, he won an All-Star award in 1972 and was chosen on both the GAA Team of the Century (1984) and Team of the Millennium (2000).

3. Brian Fenton (Dublin)
Making his debut in 2015, Brian Fenton didn't experience defeat in a championship game until the 2021 All-Ireland semi-final when Dublin lost to Mayo. In between, they won six successive All-Ireland titles. Fenton played a huge role in that record-breaking run, establishing himself as one of the best players in football history as a fielder, distributor and in getting forward to snatch crucial scores.

4. Brian Mullins (Dublin)
The flowing hair ... the high fielding ... the powerful runs ... the sheer determination. They combined to make nineteen-year-old Brian Mullins quite a star in his debut year (1974) as Dublin defied the odds to win the All-Ireland title. Mullins went on to become one of the all-time great midfielders. His career was interrupted by injuries sustained in a car accident but, typical of his commitment, he battled back to full fitness. He won two All-Stars and was nominated six times.

5. Darragh Ó Sé (Kerry)

The Kingdom have always had the knack of producing excellent midfielders and Darragh Ó Sé certainly lived up to the standard. A wonderful fielder and a ferocious competitor, he was a solid anchor in a fifteen-year career that began in the mid-1990s at a time when Kerry were emerging from a slump. The bigger the challenge, the more he revelled in it, a quality that inspired his team-mates. He won six All-Ireland senior titles and was an All-Star midfielder four times.

6. Tommy Murphy (Laois)

Known as the 'Boy Wonder' after making his senior inter-county debut at the age of sixteen, Tommy Murphy arrived on the scene at a time when Laois were doing well in the 1930s. He progressed rapidly and built a career that drew recognition all over the country. Naturally gifted in all the key components required to make a top-class midfielder, he made such a lasting impression that he was named on the GAA's Team of the Millennium in 2000.

7. Seán Cavanagh (Tyrone)

The 2008 Footballer of the Year was a superb midfielder but he could also take his game in other directions too, making him equally comfortable in the half-forward line, where he won two All-Star awards. His other three came at midfield. It all points to a wide array of skills, which he possessed in abundance. His ball-carrying technique made him very difficult to dispossess while his 'dummy' action, prior to lining up a shot, repeatedly confused even the most seasoned defenders.

8. Dermot Earley (Roscommon)

From 1965, when he made his senior debut as a seventeen-year-old, to the day he retired twenty years later, Dermot Earley was central to Roscommon's efforts to land the main prizes. They won most of them but the biggest of all – the All-Ireland – eluded them. His fielding skills, smooth running style, boundless energy and general appreciation of what was required around the middle third made him an exceptional performer. He won two All-Star awards in 1974 and 1979.

9. Paddy Kennedy (Kerry)

Paddy Kennedy attributed his high-fielding skills to long walks and ballroom dancing, two pursuits he enjoyed. Whatever the origins, his leaping ability topped an extensive list of talents that he displayed consistently during a highly successful career. He played in ten All-Ireland senior finals (including replays) between 1937 and 1947 in a historic period for Kerry, who won the three-in-a-row for the second time in 1939, 1940 and 1941.

10. Willie Bryan (Offaly)

There was no more elegant sight in football than Willie Bryan timing his runs to perfection before soaring high to make a spectacular catch. He was a joy to behold for Offaly supporters in the memorable 1971 season, when the county won the All-Ireland title for the first time. Offaly completed the two-in-a-row a year later, in a campaign where Bryan played even better. Later that year, he secured the Footballer of the Year award and picked up a second All-Star.

11. Anthony Tohill (Derry)

After winning an All-Ireland minor medal in 1989, Anthony Tohill went to play for Australian Rules club Melbourne Demons. He came back to Ireland in 1991 after breaking his leg – and became one of the sparks that ignited Derry, who won the 1992 National League title before reaching an even higher peak by winning the All-Ireland title for the first time in 1993. Tohill's powerhouse career continued for another decade, during which he gave outstanding service to Derry and Ireland's International Rules team. He is a four-time All-Star.

12. Pádraig Carney (Mayo)

'The Flying Doctor', as Pádraig Carney was affectionately known after Mayo flew him back from America for the National League semi-final and final in 1954, had an outstanding career, albeit one that ended at the age of twenty-six because of his medical studies in the US. By then, he had established quite a reputation, having played a major part in Mayo's All-Ireland successes in 1950 and 1951. He was equally efficient in midfield or attack.

13. John McDermott (Meath)

John McDermott's introduction to senior championship football in 1991 during Meath's epic four-match encounter with Dublin helped prepare him for the demands of the big time. He learned quickly and went on to become a towering presence. He was central to Seán Boylan's rebuild post-1995, which yielded All-Ireland wins in 1996 and 1999. A superb fielder, strong runner and a reliable finisher, McDermott ticked all the midfield boxes. He was a three-time All-Star in 1996, 1998 and 1999.

14. Jim McKeever (Derry)

Regarded as one of the greatest fielders, Jim McKeever's versatility meant that he played in a number of positions during his long career. But it was as a midfielder that he did best of all, highlighted in 1958 by his performance as captain against Dublin in the All-Ireland final. Derry lost, but McKeever played so well, as indeed he had all season, that he was named as Footballer of the Year in the scheme's inaugural year.

15. Joe Kernan (Armagh)

All-Ireland titles eluded Joe Kernan as a player (he would later achieve them with Crossmaglen Rangers and Armagh as manager), but there's no doubt that he was a real warrior in his seventeen-year inter-county career, during which he won three Ulster championships. He scored two superb goals against Dublin in the 1977 All-Ireland final but Armagh were well beaten by the reigning champions. His performances throughout the season earned him an All-Star award and he won a second in 1982.

16. Gerry McEntee (Meath)

Gerry McEntee was an experienced performer when Seán Boylan took over as Meath manager in 1982 and set about reigniting the Royal fire. It was a slow burn at first, but everything changed in 1986 when they won the Leinster title for the first time since 1970. Successive All-Ireland titles followed in 1987 and 1988. McEntee's forceful personality and relentless determination were crucial features on a team known for its resilience.

17. Kevin Walsh (Galway)

Kevin Walsh enjoyed a spectacular start to life as a Galway footballer, winning an All-Ireland minor medal in 1976. By the time he won his first senior medal twelve years later, he had long established himself as one of the most intelligent midfielders in the game. His basketball experience boosted his skill range, while his ability to read the play was invaluable. He added a second All-Ireland title in 2001 and was a three-time All-Star.

18. Colm McAlarney (Down)

Colm McAlarney holds the distinction of having won Railway Cup medals with Ulster in three decades. He was a rookie in 1968 when he won the first of four medals and won further honours in 1971, 1979 and 1980. In 1968, he produced one of the great All-Ireland performances against Kerry on a day when Down won their third All-Ireland title. He won four Ulster championships, a National League and was All-Star midfielder in 1975 and 1978.

19. Peter McGinnity (Fermanagh)

Peter McGinnity played in only one Ulster senior final and never won a major competition but was rightly recognised as a player of immense talent. He was only sixteen years old when part of the Fermanagh Under-21 team that reached the All-Ireland final in 1970, losing to Cork. He won four Railway Cup medals with Ulster and was Fermanagh's first All-Star in 1982.

20. John Galvin (Limerick)

When he ended his fifteen-year inter-county career in 2015, the *Limerick Leader* described John Galvin as 'the greatest Limerick footballer of all time'. It's a view held by many in the county. He was highly regarded elsewhere too as a midfielder of real substance, who regularly out-played better-known opposition. Major honours eluded him at senior level, the closest call coming in 2004 when Limerick drew with Kerry in the Munster final before losing the replay.

10. RIGHT HALF-FORWARD

1. Seán O'Neill (Down)

During a sixteen-year inter-county career, Seán O'Neill displayed speed, a remarkable range of skills and on-field intelligence that were central to Down's successes. He was right half-forward on the first Down team to win an All-Ireland senior title in 1960 and when they retained it in 1961. They won a third title in 1968, with O'Neill at full-forward, a performance that contributed to his Footballer of the Year award. In addition, he won eight Ulster titles, three National Leagues, eight Railway Cups, plus two All-Star awards.

2. Maurice Fitzgerald (Kerry)

In 1988, at the age of eighteen, Maurice Fitzgerald was thrust into the limelight when he was selected for the Munster final, where he kicked ten points against Cork. It wasn't enough to win the game, but it earned him the first of three All-Star awards. Much of his career coincided with a fallow period for Kerry and he had to wait until 1997 for his first All-Ireland medal; he added a second in 2000. Gifted with sublime skills, he was Footballer of the Year in 1997.

3. Trevor Giles (Meath)
Trevor Giles first came to prominence on the All-Ireland-winning Meath minor team of 1992. It earned him a quick promotion to the senior ranks, and he became a central figure in Seán Boylan's second generation of All-Ireland winners, winning titles in 1996 and 1999. Giles was an All-Star on three occasions and took the Footballer of the Year honour in 1999.

4. Anton O'Toole (Dublin)
Fondly nicknamed the 'Blue Panther', Anton O'Toole was part of Dublin's 'Blue Revolution' of the 1970s that had such an impact on football. A quiet man of enormous influence, he won four All-Ireland senior titles in a career that stretched from 1972 to 1984, during which he played 105 league and championship games, scoring a total of 13–101. A three-time All-Star, he was nominated seven times.

5. Ger Power (Kerry)
Such was Ger Power's versatility as a footballer and athlete that he played in numerous positions in both defence and attack with both club and county. He won eight All-Ireland titles during the Kingdom's golden years between 1975 and 1986, and was captain

in 1980. He won six All-Star awards – two at left half-back and three at right half-forward, and a sixth, in 1986, at left full-forward.

6. Ja Fallon (Galway)

Ja Fallon was a mere youngster when shrewd observers, having watched him with his club Tuam Stars and St Jarlath's College, first predicted that he would be a star in the future. They were right, as he quickly developed into one of Galway's best forwards. He was especially effective throughout 1998, when the Tribesmen ended a thirty-two-year wait for All-Ireland success. They won a ninth title in 2001. He was a two-time All-Star in 1995 and 1998.

7. Paul Mannion (Dublin)

With his career still in full swing, Paul Mannion is one of the youngest players on these lists. He enjoyed a brilliant underage career, winning two All-Ireland Under-21 championships. He graduated to senior status in early 2013 and won his first title the following September at the start of a remarkable Dublin era. He missed the 2015 season due to overseas studies in China, but returned to play a big part in Dublin's history-making six-in-a-row run.

8. Brian Dooher (Tyrone)

From 1996 to 2011, Brian Dooher was one of the most recognisable figures in the game. His incredible workrate was invaluable as Tyrone enjoyed unprecedented success, which included the county's first All-Ireland senior title in 2003. He was appointed captain following the untimely death of Cormac McAnallen in

2004 and led Tyrone to two more All-Ireland successes in 2005 and 2008. He was joint team manager, with Fergal Logan, when Tyrone won the 2021 All-Ireland.

9. Barney Rock (Dublin)

Barney Rock was one of the greatest marksmen the game has ever seen, from play and from frees. He first came to prominence on the Dublin 1979 minor team and was promoted to the senior side a year later. An All-Ireland medal winner in 1983, he was a three-time All-Star during an eleven-year career in which he scored 30–360 in ninety-nine games. His son Dean, who announced his retirement in early 2024, was also an exceptional talent, winning eight All-Ireland medals between 2013 and 2023.

10. Seán O'Connell (Derry)

Seán O'Connell's club career began in 1953 and continued until 1978. During that time, he became one of the most feared forwards in the game. He won his first Ulster title with Derry in 1958 – their first provincial success – and went on to add three more in 1970, 1975 and 1976. A prolific finisher, he was a regular on Ulster Railway Cup teams for many years, winning four Railway Cup medals.

11. CENTRE HALF-FORWARD

1. Seán Purcell (Galway)

When people debate who the greatest footballer of all time is, Seán Purcell's name is always prominent. He was certainly one of the most versatile players. The 'Master', as he was known in Galway, was an outstanding full-back, midfielder and centre half-forward, the position he played when he won his only All-Ireland senior medal in 1956. He won six Connacht championships, a National League in 1957 and three Railway Cup medals with Connacht. He was chosen on both the Team of the Century (1984) and the Team of the Millennium (2000).

2. Larry Tompkins (Kildare and Cork)

Larry Tompkins was just sixteen years old when he played minor, Under-21 and senior football for Kildare in 1980. Lean years followed for the Lilywhites, and he might have been lost to football after heading to New York in 1985, following a falling-out with officials in his native county. However, he returned to play for Cork in 1987 and enjoyed an outstanding career in Rebel colours, which yielded All-Ireland titles in 1989 and 1990 (the latter as captain), six Munster titles and a National League title, plus three All-Star awards.

3. Michael Murphy (Donegal)

Michael Murphy was a seventeen-year-old schoolboy at St Eunan's College in Letterkenny when he first played senior football for Donegal in 2007. Four years later, he was appointed Donegal captain by manager Jim McGuinness, and, in 2012, became only the second player from the county to lift the Sam Maguire Cup after Donegal beat Mayo in the All-Ireland final. A three-time All-Star in three different positions, it underlined his versatility in a career that lasted until 2022.

4. Mattie McDonagh (Galway)

Mattie McDonagh is the only Connacht footballer to hold four All-Ireland senior championship medals. He won his first as a nineteen-year-old in 1956 when he played at midfield against Cork. He later switched to centre half-forward and it was in that position that he helped Galway win three successive All-Ireland titles in 1964, 1965 and 1966 (and he was named Footballer of the Year in 1966). He also played inter-county hurling for Roscommon, the county in which his club was affiliated for hurling.

5. Jimmy 'Jamesie' Murray (Roscommon)

Roscommon was not a fashionable football county in the late 1930s and early 1940s but that did not quell the passion Jimmy Murray had for the game. His determination was evident from an early age and his leadership qualities made him a natural captain. His appointment at the start of 1943 prompted a golden era for Roscommon and he led them to glorious back-to-back All-Irelands in 1943 and 1944. He was joined on that team by his brother Phelim.

6. Eugene McKenna (Tyrone)

Tyrone led the 1986 All-Ireland final against Kerry by 1–8 to 0–4 just after half-time. Nobody in the stadium or watching on television could believe their eyes. Then Eugene McKenna got injured, left the field and everything changed. Tyrone lost their way and Kerry won comfortably. McKenna's career ended without a senior All-Ireland medal, but he was honoured with three All-Star awards in 1984, 1996 and 1989 and he is regarded as one of the greatest Tyrone and Ulster players of all time.

7. Martin McHugh (Donegal)

Relatively small in stature, Martin McHugh was still capable of exerting a massive influence on games, as he did during a long and successful career that included 138 senior games with Donegal. An All-Ireland Under-21 title winner in 1982, he and many of his team-mates graduated to senior level and brought the All-Ireland senior title to Donegal for the first time in 1992. Twice an All-Star (1983 and 1992), he was Footballer of the Year in 1992. He also managed Cavan to Ulster success in 1997.

8. Greg Blaney (Down)

At the age of just sixteen, Greg Blaney was left half-forward on the Down Under-21 team that captured the All-Ireland title in 1979. He also won an Ulster minor medal that year. It was the start of a glorious career, which also included considerable success as a hurler. A centre-forward with vision, strength, passing precision and scoring prowess, he won two All-Ireland senior medals in 1991 and 1994, was an All-Star on three occasions and regularly represented Ireland in the International Rules series.

9. Tony Hanahoe (Dublin)

Tony Hanahoe had the unique distinction of being player, manager and captain of the All-Ireland-winning Dublin team in 1977. It was quite a hat-trick for a man who, prior to 1974, had experienced lean times in a senior career that had started in 1965. That he was able to combine the three roles so successfully in 1977 underlined the deep knowledge and understanding he brought to the game. His different approach to centre-forward play was an important part of Dublin All-Ireland successes in 1974, 1976 and 1977.

10. Declan O'Sullivan (Kerry)

Declan O'Sullivan is one of only eight players in football history to captain his county to back-to-back All-Ireland senior titles. That was achieved in 2006 and 2007 when Kerry beat Mayo and Cork respectively in the finals. In a senior career that began in 2003, he won three other All-Ireland titles, the last as a sub in 2014. Having been troubled by injury for some time, he announced his retirement late in 2014. He was an All-Star in 2007, 2008 and 2009.

👕12 LEFT HALF-FORWARD

1. Pat Spillane (Kerry)

The Spillanes and their extended family were football royalty in Kerry. Pat was 'The King'. Possessed of wonderful natural ability, he had a huge work ethic in games, on the training ground and in the gym. He won the first of eight All-Ireland medals in 1975; the last three were consecutive from 1984 to 1986, and came after he recovered from a career-threatening knee injury. Twice Footballer of the Year in 1978 and 1986, his career as a pundit has been equally successful.

2. Matt Connor (Offaly)

Matt Connor was only twenty-five years old when injuries he sustained in a car accident on Christmas morning in 1984 left him in a wheelchair, but he had already achieved legendary status as one of football's most gifted exponents. In the 1980 All-Ireland semi-final, which Offaly lost to Kerry, he kicked 2–9 – 2–3 from play. Two years later, he scored 0–7 as Offaly won the All-Ireland title. He was an All-Star three times in 1980, 1982 and 1983.

3. Mickey Kearins (Sligo)

It's a testament to his abilities that Mickey Kearins earned national esteem when Sligo operated mostly outside football's upper echelons for much of his career. Through the Railway Cup competition, he found a role on a bigger stage with Connacht, winning interprovincial titles in 1967 and 1969. He was selected on the first All-Star team in 1971 and, four years later, won his only Connacht senior championship medal. He later became a highly respected referee and coach.

4. Michael Donnellan (Galway)

Maintaining a tradition begun by his grandfather, also Michael, in the 1920s and 1930s, and carried on by his father John and Uncle Pat, Michael Donnellan won the first of two All-Ireland senior titles in 1998. He produced some slaloming runs, incisive passes and general play-making that mesmerised his opponents, Kildare. A product of the famed nursery of St Jarlath's College, he added his second championship in 2001. He was a three-time All-Star, in 1998, 2000 and 2001.

5. Ciarán Kilkenny (Dublin)

As gifted a hurler as he is a footballer, Ciarán Kilkenny could also have chosen a career in Australian Rules football (he was on the rookie list with the Hawthorn club). But he chose to return to his native city and concentrate on Gaelic football. It brought spectacular success. His strength and athleticism, allied with scoring power, made him an integral part of the most successful squads in football history.

6. Paddy Doherty (Down)

In 1957, homesickness brought Paddy Doherty back from a potential soccer career in England and ensured he would be part of the emergence of the ground-breaking Down team of the 1960s. He was top scorer as Down won the Sam Maguire for the first time in 1960, won a second title the following year and was still at the peak of his powers when a third title was landed in 1968.

7. Tony McTague (Offaly)

Twice honoured as an All-Star in 1971 and 1972, Tony McTague was one of the greatest free-takers of his, or any, generation, and was equally prolific from play. He emerged as an exceptional talent on the Offaly minor team that won the All-Ireland championship in 1964. He made his senior debut the following year and had an unbroken ten-year career, winning two All-Ireland titles, one as captain in 1972.

8. Séamus Leydon (Galway)

A winner of an All-Ireland Colleges medal with St Jarlath's, Tuam, and an All-Ireland minor medal with Galway in 1960, Séamus Leydon's path to stardom was laid out early. He became one of the permanent figures in the Galway senior team that dominated football in the mid-1960s, winning three consecutive championships. He also won a National League medal in 1965, two Railway Cup medals and was selected on the first All-Star team in 1971.

9. Kevin O'Brien (Wicklow)

The spotlight rarely shines on Wicklow football but when it did, in 1990, Kevin O'Brien took full advantage. The year began with his club, Baltinglass, winning the All-Ireland club championship. Later in the year he also toured Australia with the successful International Rules team. At the end of the year, he became Wicklow's first All-Star and remained one of the most impressive footballers in the country for another decade. A highpoint of his Wicklow career was captaining them to an All-Ireland B title in 1992.

10. Declan Browne (Tipperary)

When Declan Browne made his senior football championship debut in 1996, football was hardly a priority. He was also a member of the Tipperary minor hurling team that won the All-Ireland title that year. Football management persuaded him to stick with the big ball and he won the first of two All-Star awards in 1998. The second came in 2003 when he was also selected for the International Rules team.

🏐 RIGHT FULL-FORWARD

1. David Clifford (Kerry)

The rise of a superstar: in 2016, David Clifford scored 2–5 for St Brendan's, Killarney, in the All-Ireland Colleges final; in 2017, he scored 4–4 for Kerry in the All-Ireland minor final, winning his second medal in the grade. He then moved to the senior grade where he has got better with each passing year. His range of skills seems never-ending and some of his exploits have been breathtaking. He won his fifth All-Star in 2023, at the age of just twenty-four.

2. Mikey Sheehy (Kerry)

As an example of Mikey Sheehy's scoring prowess, take a look at the stats from the 1979 All-Ireland championship. He scored an average of 0–7 in every game, including an incredible 3–5 in the All-Ireland semi-final against Monaghan and 2–6 against Dublin in the final. He scored the most famous goal of all in the 1978 final against Dublin, chipping a free over the stricken keeper, Paddy Cullen, to change the course of the game. He won eight All-Ireland titles, is a seven-time All-Star and was Footballer of the Year in 1979.

3. Colm Cooper (Kerry)

Another Kerryman completes the top three right full-forwards. Colm 'Gooch' Cooper scored twenty-three goals (and 283 points) in an eighty-five-game championship career between 2002 and 2016, the most memorable of which came in the 2004 All-Ireland final against Mayo. A high ball sent in by Eamon Fitzmaurice was fielded by Cooper, who turned and twisted, leaving defenders floundering, before he slipped the ball to the net. He continued to bamboozle defenders for the rest of his career – a career that yielded five All-Ireland titles, eight All-Stars and the Footballer of the Year award in 2004.

4. Colm O'Rourke (Meath)

Colm O'Rourke's career ran from 1976 to 1995, with much of the early part played out at a time when Meath made little impression on the championship. Despite that, he managed to build quite a reputation, which rose to a different level as Meath surged forward in the mid-1980s. By the end of his career, in which he scored 16–105 in the championship, he had won two All-Ireland titles, three All-Stars and a Footballer of the Year award.

5. Alan Brogan (Dublin)

Alan Brogan began his senior inter-county career in 2002 and, over the next thirteen years, he gained a deserved reputation as a forward of immense quality. He won the first of eleven Leinster championships in 2002, an All-Ireland Under-21 title in 2003 and was the recipient of three All-Star awards in 2006, 2007 and 2011, when he shared the stage with his brother Bernard. He won three All-Ireland senior medals, the last in 2015, after which he announced his inter-county retirement. He was Footballer of the Year in 2011.

6. Steven McDonnell (Armagh)

Strength and a natural scoring instinct were the key features of a player who was an essential part of the Armagh team that became one of the best in the country at the start of the new millennium. From play and frees, Steven McDonnell contributed hugely to the All-Ireland breakthrough in 2002. Although Armagh did not retain their title, McDonnell was honoured as Footballer of the

Year by his fellow-players in 2003. He was a regular selection on the International Rules teams.

7. Eugene 'Nudie' Hughes (Monaghan)

A winner of three All-Star awards, one of them at corner-back and the other two at corner-forward, 'Nudie' Hughes was an inspirational figure on the Monaghan team of the late 1970s and 1980s. In 1979, Monaghan won the Ulster title for the first time in forty-one years, and added two more titles in 1985 and 1988. He won Railway Cup medals with Ulster in defence and attack.

8. Charlie Gallagher (Cavan)

Charlie Gallagher was still eligible for the minor grade when he made his senior debut for Cavan in 1955. He had to wait until 1964 to win the first of three Ulster championships but, by then, he was regarded nationally as one of the great marksmen, regularly topping the scoring charts. A regular for Ulster in the Railway Cup series, he was a winner on four occasions.

9. Mickey Linden (Down)

With silky skills, great speed, a sharp footballing brain and an eye for a score, Mickey Linden was central to Down's return to the top of the football summit in the 1990s, when they won two All-Ireland titles (1991 and 1994). His senior career spanned the entire decades of the 1980s and 1990s and continued into the early 2000s. He continued to play with his club, Mayobridge, making his last competitive appearance at the age of fifty-six.

10. Dessie Dolan (Westmeath)

Dessie Dolan's father – Dessie senior – had an excellent career with Westmeath in the 1960s and 1970s, and it was evident from his son's early days that he would be just as good. Dessie junior first experienced the spotlight when Westmeath won the All-Ireland Under-21 title in 1999. He thrived on the public stage and was the star attacker on the team that won the Leinster senior title for the first time in 2004, a year in which he won an All-Star award.

FULL-FORWARD

1. Peter Canavan (Tyrone)

Possessed of all the skills, accompanied by a vision that enabled him to pick out passes most others would not see, and with a natural instinct for scores, Peter Canavan enjoyed a trophy-filled career that lasted fifteen years. He captained Tyrone to two All-Ireland Under-21 titles in 1991 and 1992, and won the first of six All-Star awards in 1994. Despite injury, he was an inspirational figure when captaining Tyrone to their first All-Ireland senior title in 2003 and added a second two years later.

2. Tom Langan (Mayo)

When the Team of the Millennium was selected in 2000, the hottest competition for a place was probably at full-forward. That Tom Langan was chosen, even though it was not always his starting position, says everything about his influence on Gaelic football for more than a decade from the mid-1940s to the mid-1950s. A noted goal-scorer, he won two All-Irelands (1950 and 1951), five Connacht championships, two National Leagues and a Railway Cup title.

3. Pádraic Joyce (Galway)

A product of St Jarlath's College, Tuam, with whom he won an All-Ireland Colleges title in 1994, Pádraic Joyce was later part of a new wave of young players who were central to Galway's march to All-Ireland glory in 1998. They added another title in 2001, beating Meath, when Joyce's second-half performance is regarded as one of the great individual displays in a final. A triple All-Star, he captained Ireland to International Rules success against Australia in 2004.

4. Eoin 'Bomber' Liston (Kerry)

When Mick O'Dwyer, the famed Kerry manager, was planning for the 1978 championship, with an emphasis on matching Dublin, he turned to a big, strong six-foot-five full-forward – 'Bomber' Liston. An All-Ireland Under-21 medal winner in 1977, Liston made an immediate impact at senior level, none more crucial than in 1978 when he scored 3–2 against Dublin in the All-Ireland final. By the time he retired, he had won seven All-Ireland titles and four All-Star awards.

5. Frank Stockwell (Galway)

Amongst his many claims to fame, Frank Stockwell holds the record for the highest-scoring tally in a sixty-minute All-Ireland final. He kicked 2–5 against Cork in 1956 as Galway won by 2–13 to 3–7. Always renowned for his partnership in attack with Seán Purcell, Stockwell was an outstanding individual performer who also won six Connacht championships, a National League and two Railway Cups.

6. Jimmy Keaveney (Dublin)

After a first spell with Dublin (1964–1972) Jimmy Keaveney retired. He had won a Leinster title in 1965, but did not expect to add another. However, he was coaxed back by Kevin Heffernan in 1974 and thoroughly enjoyed his renaissance in a glory period for Dublin, during which they won three All-Ireland titles. Accurate from frees and play, he scored 30–402 in 104 games between 1964 and 1979. He was Footballer of the Year in 1976 and 1977, and an All-Star three times.

7. Con O'Callaghan (Dublin)

A talented hurler who chose to concentrate on football, Con O'Callaghan was a precociously talented underage player who slotted comfortably into the Dublin squad in 2016 when he won his first All-Ireland title. A year later, he was an automatic choice in the starting fifteen and marked his first All-Ireland final appearance when he scored a goal after ninety seconds against Mayo. A new Dublin star had arrived. He was a key figure in Dublin's All-Ireland six-in-a-row run, completed with the 2020 success, and remains one of their main men.

8. Paddy Moclair (Mayo)

Paddy Moclair had a major impact on the style of football played in the 1930s when he operated as a roving full-forward, a tactic that worked well for Mayo when they won six consecutive National League titles between 1934 and 1939. They also won the All-Ireland title for the first time in 1936, with Moclair a lead performer in a strong cast. A big personality, he was honoured as an All-Time All-Star in 1982.

9. Kieran Donaghy (Kerry)

A multi-talented sportsman whose skills as a basketball player complemented his footballing talent, Kieran Donaghy first captured attention on the reality TV show *The Underdogs*, in 2004. He was selected by Kerry a year later, and enjoyed a hugely successful career as both a finisher and provider of crucial scores. Known as 'Star', he won four All-Ireland championships, eight Munster titles and three National League titles. He was an All-Star three times and Footballer of the Year in 2006.

10. Frank McGuigan (Tyrone)

Blessed with a wide array of skills, Frank McGuigan's Tyrone career was curtailed by injury and time spent in the United States. He was still a minor in 1972 when he made his senior championship debut. A year later, at nineteen, he was captain of the team that won the Ulster title. His most famous performance was in the 1984 Ulster final when he scored 0–11 in the win over Armagh. Later that year, he won an All-Star award.

👕15 LEFT FULL-FORWARD

1. Kevin Heffernan (Dublin)

Most famous in modern times as the managerial architect of the dramatic Dublin revival in the mid-1970s, Kevin Heffernan's hugely successful career as a player is sometimes overlooked. It shouldn't be. In a fourteen-year senior career (1948–1962), he played 115 league and championship games with Dublin, scoring 52-226. In addition, his sharp tactical brain brought an added dimension. An All-Ireland winner as Dublin captain in 1958, he was a regular on Leinster teams for a decade, winning seven Railway Cup medals. He was selected on both the Team of the Century (1984) and Team of the Millennium (2000).

2. Mick O'Dwyer (Kerry)

Player, coach, manager and evangelist – 'Micko' was all of those. In an eighteen-year senior career (1956–1974) he established a huge reputation, initially as a defender, later as an attacker, winning four All-Ireland titles, eight National Leagues, twelve Munster titles and a Railway Cup. He won the Footballer of the Year award in 1969 at the age of thirty-three. That was followed by an extraordinary managerial career, during which he led Kerry to eight All-Ireland titles. He later sprinkled his magic in Kildare, Laois and Wicklow.

3. John Egan (Kerry)

The esteem in which John Egan is held – he passed away at the age of fifty-nine in April 2012 – is exemplified by the life-size bronze statue erected in his honour in his native Sneem. A quiet man by nature, Egan was most eloquent on the pitch, where his balance, soloing expertise and eye for goal lit up every arena. He won six All-Ireland titles and was Kerry captain in 1982 when they lost to Offaly. He won five All-Stars in 1975, 1977, 1978, 1981 and 1982.

4. Bernard Brogan Jnr (Dublin)
One of three brothers to play senior football for Dublin, Bernard made his championship debut in 2007 and went on to establish himself as one of the best all-time forwards. He played 113 league and championship games, scoring a total of 36–343. Footballer of the Year in 2010, he won the first of seven All-Ireland titles a year later. A four-time All-Star, he captained the Irish team in the 2015 International Rules series.

5. Stephen O'Neill (Tyrone)
After a hugely successful underage career, winning an All-Ireland minor and two Under-21 titles, Stephen O'Neill made an immediate impact on his elevation to senior status in 2001, winning an Ulster title and the first of three All-Star awards. In 2003, he was an important figure in Tyrone's first All-Ireland senior triumph and enjoyed his greatest year in 2005, when he won a second All-Ireland and was Footballer of the Year. He added a third All-Ireland in 2008.

6. Tony McManus (Roscommon)
Although he never managed to win an All-Ireland senior title – Roscommon lost to Kerry in the 1980 final – Tony McManus was regarded as one of the finest footballers in a career that began in the

mid-1970s and lasted until the early 1990s. Along with his brother, Eamonn, he played in five All-Ireland clubs finals with Clann na nGael, but they lost all five. Somewhat surprisingly, he won only one All-Star award, in 1979.

7. Packie McGarty (Leitrim)

Patrick 'Packie' McGarty had few medals to show at the end of a long career, having playing for Leitrim from 1949 (he made his senior debut as a sixteen-year-old) to 1973, but he had great memories and earned the respect of GAA people everywhere. He played in six Connacht finals, losing five to Galway and one to Mayo. He was a two-time Railway Cup winner with Connacht. In 1984, he was named on the best team never to win an All-Ireland senior medal.

8. Conor McManus (Monaghan)

At the age of thirty-five in July 2023 – and at a time when a hip problem threatened his continuing participation in the sport – Conor McManus produced one of the great displays of his career in the All-Ireland semi-final against Dublin. It wasn't enough to realise his dream of playing in an All-Ireland final, but it consolidated his place in the list of all-time great corner-forwards, thanks to his consistently high strike rate from frees and play.

9. Bernard Flynn (Meath)

One of the best finishers of the 1980s and 1990s, Bernard Flynn compensated for his slight stature with great strength, agility and an alert football brain. Corner-backs everywhere found him a very difficult opponent in a career that yielded All-Ireland titles in 1987 and 1988, and All-Star awards in 1987 and 1991.

10. Matty Forde (Wexford)

Matty Forde defied history and geography when he became the first Wexford footballer to receive an All-Star award in 2004. The honour came at the end of a memorable year for the then twenty-five-year-old. He was top scorer in the National League and later went on to record the great individual feat of scoring 2–10 (2–7 from play) of Wexford's winning total of 2–14 in an All-Ireland qualifier win over Offaly.

2 HURLING'S GREATEST POSITION BY POSITION

Some are born great, some achieve greatness, and some have greatness thrust upon them.
William Shakespeare

Christy Ring or Henry Shefflin? What about Mick Mackey, Lory Meagher, Eddie Keher, D.J. Carey? Those are just some of the names tossed into the mix whenever there's a debate on who was the greatest hurler of all-time.

There never has been – and there never will be – a means of deciding definitively as it would be impossible to get even a broad level of agreement on the criteria because of the different requirement pertaining to each position.

Forwards tend to have an in-built advantage when 'best of' discussions arise – because there's more glamour attached to scoring than stopping. A prolific forward will always have a higher profile than the best goalkeeper, defender or midfielder. It's the same in all team sports.

It's proven in Gaelic games by the Hurler of the Year and Footballer of the Year awards, with the majority going to forwards.

There's no attempt in this book to rank players under a general heading. Instead, it's done on a position-by-position basis. Given the fewer number of hurling counties at the higher level, there's a smaller spread than football, where twenty-six counties are represented.

It's half that in hurling, with Antrim, Clare, Cork, Dublin, Galway, Kilkenny, Laois, Limerick, Offaly, Tipperary, Waterford, Westmeath and Wexford filling all 150 places in the fifteen positions.

Assessing hurlers from different eras is more difficult than football as the game has undergone even more changes, including to the actual hurley itself. Another factor is the impact of pitches, which are now far better than they used to be. The condition of the playing surface is more important in hurling than football.

The skill level among modern-day hurlers is exceptionally high and this is helped greatly by improved pitches. Players from previous generations often had to contend with surfaces that made everything a whole lot more difficult. Still, top-class players would be good in any era.

🎽 GOALKEEPER

1. Tony Reddin (Tipperary & Galway)

Chosen on the Team of the Century (1984) and Team of the Millennium (2000), the Galway native achieved his highest honours with Tipperary, winning All-Ireland titles in 1949, 1950 and 1951. Reddin's dependability between the posts was central to those successes. He also won five Railway Cup medals with Munster between 1950 and 1955. He was an inspiration to aspiring, young goalkeepers, who were encouraged to take up the difficult art after watching his regular heroics.

2. Noel Skehan (Kilkenny)

Noel Skehan's longevity was remarkable. Having had to serve an extended apprenticeship as a sub to Ollie Walsh, his chance finally came in 1972 when he took over the number-one slot and captained Kilkenny to an All-Ireland win. By the time he retired in 1985, he had accumulated a further five All-Ireland medals, bringing his total to nine – six on the team, three as a sub. He also won seven All-Star awards – a record for a goalkeeper – and was Hurler of the Year in 1982.

3. Ger Cunningham (Cork)

Hurler of the year in 1986, Ger Cunningham also won four All-Star awards – three consecutively in 1984, 1985 and 1986 and another in 1990 – though he was nominated eleven times between 1981 and 1992. His reliability over a twenty-year inter-county career at minor, Under-21 and senior level was instrumental in many Cork successes, including three All-Ireland senior titles in 1984, 1986 and 1990. He was chosen on the Cork Team of the Millennium in 2000.

4. Brendan Cummins (Tipperary)

Brendan Cummins' senior career extended from 1995 until 2013, during which he established himself as a goalkeeper of exceptional quality. He brought real flamboyance to his game, which added to his popularity among Tipperary supporters and drew admiration from the rest of the country. He played a big part in Tipperary's All-Ireland wins in 2001 and 2010, while his consistency over such a long period won him five All-Star awards in 2000, 2001, 2003, 2008 and 2010.

5. Davy Fitzgerald (Clare)

Davy Fitzgerald's outstanding save from Tipperary's John Leahy late in the 1997 All-Ireland final almost certainly ensured that Clare became champions. It was a standout moment in a great career. Fitzgerald's bubbly personality combined with his incredible reflexes were major influences in Clare's return to the top table in 1995 when they won their first All-Ireland title in eighty-one years. He won three All-Star awards and was nominated eight times. In a very successful career in management, he guided Clare to All-Ireland success in 2013. He also managed Waterford (2010) and Wexford (2019) to provincial titles.

6. Ollie Walsh (Kilkenny)

Ollie Walsh's senior career spanned three decades (1956–1972), underlining a remarkable capacity to stay at the top of his game in an era when goalkeepers weren't afforded anything like the protection they enjoy today. Walsh overcame all that to become one of the all-time greats in a career that yielded five All-Ireland senior titles in 1957, 1963, 1967, 1969 and 1972, the latter as a sub. He was chosen as Hurler of the Year in 1967, becoming the first goalkeeper to win the prestigious award.

7. Donal Óg Cusack (Cork)

From his earliest days on the senior team, Donal Óg Cusack was an innovative presence. His accurate puck-outs, both short and long, were a significant feature in Cork's strategy as they emerged from a barren period to win the All-Ireland title in 1999, following up with two more in 2004 and 2005. Apart from that part of his game being an added bonus for Cork, he was also excellent on the traditional basics of the goalkeeper. He won two All-Star awards in 1999 and 2006.

8. Damien Fitzhenry (Wexford)

By comparison with other top goalkeepers, Damien Fitzhenry's All-Ireland haul is modest – he won only one title in 1996. However, that doesn't present an accurate depiction of a career where he maintained the highest standards for a very long time. That's borne out by his being nominated for an All-Star award on no fewer than eight occasions. Some of them came in years when Wexford hadn't done particularly well, but Fitzhenry still managed to attract lots of positive attention. He won two All-Star awards.

9. Damien Martin (Offaly)

A senior inter-county career that started as a seventeen-year-old in 1964 and lasted twenty-two years underlines just how good Damien Martin was. Disappointment accompanied him and Offaly for a long time, but everything changed in 1980 when they won the Leinster title for the first time before making the historic All-Ireland breakthrough in 1981. Nominated seven times, Martin holds the distinction of being the first All-Star goalkeeper, having been chosen in 1971, the scheme's inaugural year.

10. Séamus Durack (Clare)

The Clare team of 1977 and 1978 are regarded as one of the best in hurling history not to have won an All-Ireland title. They won successive National League titles but lost out to an exceptional Cork team in both Munster finals. Séamus Durack was one of their top performers during that period, and his excellence recognised by All-Star recognition in 1977 and 1978 and again in 1981. He was nominated every year between 1972 and 1982.

🎽 RIGHT FULL-BACK

1. Bobby Rackard (Wexford)

One of the three famous Rackard brothers who contributed so much to Wexford's greatest era in the 1950s, Bobby was a versatile performer who was equally efficient in a number of defensive positions. The high points of his career came in 1955 and 1956 when Wexford won successive All-Irelands for the first and only time, beating Galway and Cork respectively. He was chosen at right full-back on the Team of the Century (1984) and Team of the Millennium (2000).

2. Phil 'Fan' Larkin (Kilkenny)

'Good things come in small parcels' comes to mind for a man who was smaller than most of the opponents he encountered. Phil Larkin's agility, competitiveness and ability to read play more than compensated in a career in which he won his first All-Ireland senior medal in 1963. After some years off the Kilkenny panel, he returned in the early 1970s and went on to win four more All-Ireland medals as well as four All-Star awards.

3. Michael Kavanagh (Kilkenny)

Michael Kavanagh's senior career started at right half-back, where he spent three seasons, the last being in 1999 when he won the first of eight All-Star nominations. He switched to right full-back in 2000 at a time when Kilkenny were embarking on the most successful period in their history. His intelligent defending made a big contribution to their All-Ireland wins in 2000, 2002, 2003, 2006, 2007, 2008 and 2009, a period in which he won four All-Star awards.

4. Mick 'Rattler' Byrne (Tipperary)

Chosen at right corner-back in 1984 on Tipperary's Team of the Century and in 2000 on their Team of the Millennium (John Doyle was at number four), Mick Byrne's status as a defender of exceptional quality was earned during a career in which he excelled for a long time in the 1940 and 1950s. The high points came in 1949, 1950 and 1951 when the Premier county won three successive All-Ireland titles. He was still aboard for their next All-Ireland win in 1958.

5. Paul Murphy (Kilkenny)

Another high-quality product from Kilkenny's ultra-efficient corner-back production line, Paul Murphy made a big impact in his first championship season in 2011 when the Cats regained the All-Ireland title, having lost to Tipperary a year earlier. By the end of his career, he had won four All-Ireland medals, the last coming in 2015. He also won four All-Star awards, having been nominated six times. He ticked every box in the corner-back requirement manual.

6. Sylvie Linnane (Galway)

Sylvie Linnane's inter-county career started at right half-back where he played when Galway won the All-Ireland title for the first time in fifty-seven years in 1980. He dropped back to right full-back in the mid-1980s and was a hugely important figure in the county's best period, during which they won successive All-Ireland titles in 1987 and 1988 and National League titles in 1987 and 1989. A fierce competitor with indomitable spirit, he won All-Star awards in 1985, 1986 and 1988.

7. Seán Finn (Limerick)

Corner-backs don't get away with many mistakes as they are usually severely punished by ace snipers in opposition colours. It speaks volumes for Seán Finn's intelligent grasp of what's required to play in that position, as well as his capacity to execute it efficiently and consistently, that he was selected on four successive All-Star teams from 2018 to 2021. He is the only right corner-back in the fifty-three-year history of the scheme to achieve such a distinction.

8. Brian Murphy (Cork)

Between 1968, when he enjoyed Colleges success in hurling and football, and 1984, when he was aboard the Nemo Rangers team that won the All-Ireland club football title, Brian Murphy secured at least one major title each year. It was usually more than one in a career that saw him join the small band of players who have won All-Ireland senior hurling and football titles and All-Stars in both codes. He was a tight-marking corner-back on the Cork team that secured the hurling three-in-a-row in 1976, 1977 and 1978.

9. Tom Neville (Wexford)

Tom Neville's senior career ran from 1960 to 1972, during which time he won two All-Ireland medals and was on the losing side three times. He was a first choice on Leinster teams for much of the 1960s. His career ended shortly after the launch of the All-Stars scheme, but he was chosen three times on unofficial 'best of' teams in 1963, 1964 and 1965.

10. Jamesy Kelleher (Cork)

How would a player from the early 1900s fare in today's game? How would a player from the current era fare back then? It's impossible to know. What's beyond question in Jamesy Kelleher's case is that he was an outstanding performer in a variety of positions during a career that ran from 1900 to 1914. His status as one of Cork's earliest superstars was enhanced in 2000 when he was chosen at right corner-back on their Team of the Millennium.

FULL-BACK

1. Nick O'Donnell (Wexford)

Kilkenny's gift to Wexford! Born in Graignamanagh, Nick O'Donnell was on the Kilkenny squad before moving to Wexford, where he established himself as an exceptional full-back in the 1950s and early 1960s. It was the most successful period in Wexford's history, winning All-Irelands in 1955, 1956 and 1960, with O'Donnell as a powerful anchor at number three. Chosen as Hurler of the Year in 1960, his enormous stature in the game was later recognised when he was selected on the Team of the Century (1984) and Team of the Millennium (2000).

2. Pat Hartigan (Limerick)

Would the course of hurling history have been different if Pat Hartigan hadn't sustained a career-ending injury in 1979? Limerick won Munster titles in 1980 and 1981 but lost to Galway in the All-Ireland final and semi-final respectively, games where they badly missed Hartigan's towering presence. His excellence was recognised by the All-Star selectors each year from 1971 to 1975. He remains the only full-back in the fifty-three-year history of the scheme to win five successive awards.

3. Brian Lohan (Clare)

Brian Lohan's red helmet became a symbol of defiance, a warning to opponents that the area in front of the Clare goal was guarded by the tightest of security. He led the resistance with inspiring authority, playing a major role in steering Clare from hopeful contenders to All-Ireland winners in 1995 – their first title since 1914 – and again in 1997. He won three successive All-Star awards in 1995, 1996 and 1997 and added a fourth in 2002.

4. Noel Hickey (Kilkenny)

The first decade of the new millennium was the most successful in Kilkenny's history – they won seven of ten All-Ireland titles. Noel Hickey featured in six of those finals, only missing out in 2009 when he was a sub. He was back at number three when they won the 2011 title and was a sub in 2012, taking his medal haul to nine. He won All-Star awards in 2000, 2003 and 2008 and was nominated eight times.

5. Conor Hayes (Galway)

The 1980s were by far the greatest decade in Galway hurling history, a period in which they won three All-Ireland, two National League and six (representing Connacht) Railway Cup titles. The 1980 All-Ireland win was their first since 1923. Conor Hayes featured in all the successes, including the All-Ireland two-in-a-row in 1987 and 1988 when he was an inspirational captain. He won three successive All-Star awards in 1986, 1987 and 1988 and was nominated seven times.

6. Diarmuid 'The Rock' O'Sullivan (Cork)

For Cork supporters, nothing was more inspiring than the sight of 'The Rock' – whose senior career stretched from 1997 to 2008 – making a spectacular catch, followed by a powerful drive forward to clear his lines. He did it consistently for several years as part of a Leeside surge that yielded All-Ireland wins in 1999, 2004 and 2005. He was the All-Star full-back in all three years, as well as in 2000, and was nominated six times.

7. Tony Brennan (Tipperary & Galway)

A native of Tipperary, Tony Brennan's prowess first became apparent with Galway, where he was based with the army for several years. He played with Galway and Connacht in the late 1930s and early 1940s before returning to his native Tipperary. That's where he enjoyed most success, including winning All-Ireland titles in Tipp's memorable three-in-a-row in 1949, 1950 and 1951. One of the most highly regarded full-backs of his generation, he combined athleticism with skill to present an imposing barrier in front of goal.

8. Eugene Coughlan (Offaly)

Breaking through the psychological barrier attached to trying to win Offaly's first All-Ireland title required players with the toughest of mentalities. Eugene Coughlan was a leader in that category as they powered their way to the summit in 1981. He won a second All-Ireland medal in 1985. Powerful, assured and a smart reader of the game, he typified Offaly's confident advance. An All-Star in 1984 and 1985, he was nominated seven times.

9. Daithi Burke (Galway)

A four-time All-Ireland club football winner with Corofin, Daithi Burke would probably have been a big success with Galway footballers if he'd headed in that direction. Instead, he concentrated on hurling at county level, building a career as an outstanding performer in both defensive lines. Strong under the high ball and fiercely competitive in every facet of play, his consistency levels have remained high over many years. He is a member of the small group of players who have won four successive All-Stars, which he achieved between 2015 and 2018, before adding a fifth in 2020.

10. Austin Flynn (Waterford)

Austin Flynn played for Waterford from 1955 to 1967, with their best years coming between 1957 and 1963, when they won an All-Ireland title (1959), three Munster titles (1957, 1959 and 1963) and one National League title (1963). Flynn's authority at number three was one of the main ingredients in those successes. He was chosen three times on unofficial All-Star teams in 1963, 1965 and 1966 and was also first choice Munster full-back for much of the 1960s.

〔4〕 LEFT FULL-BACK

1. John Doyle (Tipperary)

Promoted to the Tipperary senior team as a nineteen-year-old in 1949, John Doyle established himself as a powerful presence in a career that lasted until 1967, by which time he had amassed eight All-Ireland titles as well as numerous other honours, including the Hurler of the Year in 1964. A strong, imposing figure, he was also more skilful than most corner-backs of his era. He was chosen at left full-back on the Team of the Century (1984) and Team of the Millennium (2000).

2. Jackie Tyrrell (Kilkenny)
A key defensive figure in a golden era for Kilkenny, Jackie Tyrrell's understanding of corner-back requirements and his ability to implement them efficiently made him one of the all-time greats. He finished his career with nine All-Ireland senior medals, seven as a member of the starting fifteen. Four of them were won successively between 2006 and 2009, a period in which he was at his imperious best. He won four successive All-Star awards between 2007 and 2010 and was nominated seven times.

3. John Horgan (Cork)
John Horgan's career spanned three decades from the late 1960s to the early 1980s, during which time he became one of the game's best defenders. His blond hair, eye-catching darts from corner-back and long-range scoring feats, which were rare for corner-backs at that time, made him an instantly recognisable and admired figure all over the country. He won four All-Ireland senior medals – including successive titles in 1976, 1977 and 1978 – and was an All-Star three times in 1974, 1977 and 1978.

4. Ollie Canning (Galway)

One of the best players whose careers ended without an All-Ireland senior inter-county medal, Ollie Canning played in attack in his early senior days in 1999 and part of 2000 before dropping back into defence. Smart and quick, he excelled at number four for many years. He played in two All-Ireland finals in 2001 and 2005 but Galway lost to Tipperary and Cork respectively. He won four All-Star awards and four All-Ireland club medals with Portumna.

5. Brian Corcoran (Cork)

Brian Corcoran spent longer in the half-backs and attack than at number four, but such was his massive impact there in 1992 that it deserves special recognition. He finished the season with All-Star and Hurler of the Year awards, the youngest player to receive the latter honour. It underlined just how effective the nineteen-year-old had been in his debut season. He added two more All-Stars at centre-back (1999), when he also won Hurler of the Year, and full-forward (2004) and finished his career with three All-Ireland senior medals.

6. Martin Hanamy (Offaly)

An automatic choice on the Offaly team for thirteen years, Martin Hanamy brought a remarkable level of consistency to a position that has little room for error. His ability to mark corner-forwards of varying sizes, speed and style was a major contributory factor to many Offaly successes, including All-Ireland wins in 1994 (as captain) and 1998 and Leinster title wins in 1988, 1989, 1990, 1994 and 1995. He won three All-Star awards, in 1988, 1994 and 1998, and was nominated six times.

7. Willie O'Connor (Kilkenny)

Durability, determination and an unflinching spirit were among Willie O'Connor's many assets in a career that yielded three All-Ireland senior medals, the last one coming in 2000 when he captained Kilkenny to their first title since 1993. It was a fitting honour for a man who was equally comfortable in the full-back or half-back lines. He won an All-Star at number seven in 1992 and added three others, two at left full-back (1997 and 2000) and one on the right (1998).

8. Denis Murphy (Cork)

The mid-1950s to the mid-1960s was an usually lean time for Cork senior hurling, a period in which they won no All-Ireland and no Munster championships. It came as a huge relief when both were secured in 1966. Murphy was aboard that team for what was his only All-Ireland success in a career that stretched from 1960 to 1969. Despite Cork's relative lack of success, he built a lasting reputation. He was chosen on the Munster Team of the Millennium in 2000.

9. Pat Fleury (Offaly)

A member of the squad revered in Offaly for bringing the Leinster title to Offaly for the first time (1980), followed by a first All-Ireland title a year later, Pat Fleury brought real tenacity to his game. Excellent at reading a game, a talent he later took into team management and his work as TG4 pundit, he maintained the highest of standards over several years. He won a second All-Ireland medal in 1985. Twice selected on the All-Stars, he was nominated six times.

10. J.J. 'Goggles' Doyle (Clare)

In 1984 (GAA centenary year) J.J. Doyle was chosen on a special selection drawn from players who hadn't won an All-Ireland title, a fitting tribute to a man whose exploits have stood the test of time. Stories of his brilliance from the mid-1920s to the late 1930s carried down through the decades. The high point of his career came in 1932 when Clare won the Munster title – however they lost the All-Ireland final to Kilkenny. His nickname was derived from the goggles he wore to protect his glasses.

⑤ RIGHT HALF-BACK

1. Tommy Walsh (Kilkenny)

One of the best hurlers in GAA history, Tommy Walsh had a phenomenal senior career that coincided with a glory period for Kilkenny. His aerial ability, even against much taller opponents, was a tribute to his timing and athleticism, which gave him an advantage wherever he played. He won nine All-Ireland senior titles and amassed nine successive All-Star awards between 2003 and 2011, five at right half-back, and one each at left corner-back, left half-back, midfield and left half-forward. That he won awards in so many positions highlights his adaptability.

2. Brian Whelahan (Offaly)

Brian Whelahan's most remarkable performance came, not as a defender, but as an attacker when he moved to full-forward in the 1998 All-Ireland final and led Offaly to victory over Kilkenny. He was later named as Hurler of the Year. However, it's as a half-back that his brilliance will always be recalled. He won All-Ireland titles in 1994, when he was also Hurler of the Year, and in 1998, as well as four All-Star awards and a place on the Team of the Millennium in 2000.

3. Joe Hennessy (Kilkenny)

A five-time All-Star winner in three positions (three at half-back, one each at midfield and corner-back) between 1978 and 1987, Joe Hennessy's versatility was invaluable for Kilkenny in an era when they won three All-Ireland titles in 1979, 1982 and 1983. Right half-back was his most natural position, enabling him to combine his sharp defensive skills with attacking instincts. He balanced them expertly – hence his ability to also excel at midfield and at right full-back where he finished his career.

4. Pete Finnerty (Galway)

Pete Finnerty typified a new breed of young, confident Galway hurlers who emerged in the mid-1980s when they embarked on the county's best run, which yielded successive All-Ireland titles in 1987 and 1988. Finnerty was equally effective in air or ground wars, which aligned with his powerful physique and fierce competitiveness to make him a very difficult opponent for even the best half-forwards. He won four successive All-Star awards between 1985 and 1988, and added a fifth in 1990.

5. Diarmaid Byrnes (Limerick)

The Limerick power surge, beginning in 2018, has taken them to unprecedented heights that few would have expected. It all came together under manager John Kiely, as a special group achieved true greatness. Diarmaid Byrnes can take his fair share of credit for the transformation, developing into an inspiring half-back, complete with all the essential ingredients required in the modern game. Indeed, he has added some of his own, including being one of the most accurate long-distance strikers – from frees and general play – in history.

6. Jimmy Finn (Tipperary)

Promoted to the Tipperary team in 1950, a year after he won an All-Ireland minor medal, Jimmy Finn went on to enjoy a great career that yielded three All-Ireland senior medals, one as captain in 1951. It was a special occasion as it secured Tipperary's first three-in-a-row since 1900. Finn won a third All-Ireland medal in 1958 and also featured regularly on Munster teams throughout the decade. He was chosen on the GAA's Team of the Century in 1984.

7. Tony Browne (Waterford)

When he captained Waterford to their first All-Ireland Under-21 title in 1992, he would surely have thought that senior success would follow. And it did in every form, except the most prized of all – a senior All-Ireland. Browne's extraordinary longevity took his Waterford career up to 2013 (aged forty), having been a model of consistency down through the years. He won All-Star awards in 1998, 2006 and 2007.

8. Séamus Cleere (Kilkenny)

Injury cut short a career in which a great deal had already been achieved by a player who was renowned for the style and class he brought to his craft. Séamus Cleere won two All-Ireland senior titles, the first as captain in 1963 and the second in 1967. The latter had a special significance, marking Kilkenny's first win over Tipperary in the final since 1922. He won the Hurler of the Year award in 1963.

9. Ger Loughnane (Clare)

The modern generation knows Ger Loughnane mainly for leading Clare, as manager, to All-Ireland successes in 1995 – their first since 1914 – and 1997, and for his outspoken views on hurling matters, but those who recall his playing days in a sixteen-year career remember him as a first-class defender. Clare were unable to make the championship breakthrough during his time (1970s and 1980s), losing no fewer than five Munster finals. However, they won successive National League titles in 1977 and 1978. He won All-Star awards in 1974 and 1977.

10. Tadhg O'Connor (Tipperary)

An All-Ireland senior medal winner in 1971, Tadhg O'Connor was later chosen on the All-Stars team in what was the inaugural year of the scheme. He would have thought much more glory lay ahead, and while he won two more All-Star awards in 1975 and 1979, Tipperary's championship decline was rapid and sustained.

Despite that, he remained a consistently effective presence throughout the 1970s and early 1980s.

6. CENTRE HALF-BACK

1. Ger Henderson (Kilkenny)
Learning the centre-back trade from his older brother Pat, Ger Henderson ticked all the requirement boxes for centre-backs of the time (1970s–1980s). Immovable under a high ball, good fielding skills and the strength to power clear when the ball had been secured topped a list of attributes that all came naturally to him. In addition, he was a fierce competitor. An All-Ireland senior medal winner in 1975 (sub), 1979, 1982 and 1983, he won five All-Star awards and was Hurler of the Year in 1979.

2. Seánie McMahon (Clare)
Would Clare's hurling history have taken a less favourable turn if Seánie McMahon hadn't shown such bravery when he defiantly ignored a collarbone injury to battle on in the 1995 Munster semi-final against Cork? He played a big part in their dramatic victory and went on to become one of the game's outstanding centre-backs in a career that yielded two All-Ireland titles, three All-Stars and seven nominations, plus a Hurler of the Year award in 1995.

3. John Keane (Waterford)
John Keane was chosen at centre-back on the Team of the Century (1984) and Team of the Millennium (2000), quite

an achievement given the standard of opposition. The Mount Sion club man played for Waterford from the mid-1930s, when he made his inter-county debut at the age of eighteen, to the early 1950s, winning an All-Ireland senior title in 1948. It was Waterford's greatest triumph during his career and, while they also had many disappointing days, his brilliance remained constant.

4. Pat Henderson (Kilkenny)

It was no surprise that Pat Henderson went on to become a successful manager as there was always something authoritative and measured about how he went about his business as a player. Allied to his strength and obsessive desire to be successful, it presented an intimidating barrier to opposition forwards in a career that yielded All-Ireland senior medals in 1967, 1969, 1972, 1974 and 1975, All-Stars in 1973 and 1974, and Hurler of the Year in 1974.

5. Tony Wall (Tipperary)

Hurler of the Year in 1958 – the inaugural year of the scheme – Tony Wall's career coincided with a golden age for Tipperary hurling, during which they won five All-Ireland senior titles between 1958 and 1965. He played a significant role in those achievements, anchoring a defence that was noted for its tight security. A regular on Munster teams too, winning five Railway Cup medals, he was chosen at number six on Tipperary's Team of the Millennium in 2000.

6. Ken McGrath (Waterford)

One of the most versatile players ever to emerge from Waterford, having played in all five outfield lines, Ken McGrath won All-Star awards at left half-forward in 2002, midfield in 2004 and centre half-back in 2007. His longest stint was at number six, a position where his father Pat had also excelled in the 1970s and 1980s. Ken's aerial ability, timing and touch were backed up by inspiring levels of energy and determination.

7. Mick Jacob (Wexford)

Blessed with the skills to be effective in most positions, Mick Jacob played in goal, defence and midfield in various grades for Wexford and also lined out in attack on occasions for his club, Oulart-The Ballagh. His early days with Wexford seniors were at midfield before he settled in at number six where he was a commanding presence. He played in three All-Ireland finals, losing each time to Cork in 1970, 1976 and 1977, but achieved individual honours as an All-Star in 1972, 1976 and 1977.

8. Ciarán Carey (Limerick)

A forward in his early senior days, Ciarán Carey later alternated between centre-back (All-Star, 1992 and 1996) and midfield (All-Star, 1994). Positions didn't really matter – he could slot in anywhere and produce accomplished performances, which was down to his natural talents and adaptability. His winning point, scored after a surging run, when Limerick beat Clare, then All-Ireland champions, in the 1996 Munster semi-final is regarded as one of the best scores in championship history.

9. Declan Hannon (Limerick)

There's an argument to be made that switching Hannon from attack to defence was one of the major catalysts in the launch – and subsequent consolidation – of Limerick's greatest era. He spent several seasons in attack where he did very well, before relocating to defence in 2017, the year before Limerick ended a forty-five-year wait for an All-Ireland title. Both as a centre-back and captain, Hannon's influence on Limerick hurling has been profound.

10. Tony Keady (Galway)

Promoted to the senior team in late 1984 as part of a new cohort of players introduced by manager Cyril Farrell at a time of panel transformation, Tony Keady built an outstanding career that saw him win two All-Ireland medals (1987 and 1988) and play in five finals. Strong under a high ball and fearless when the exchanges were at their most demanding, he also had exceptional skill and was an excellent long-range free-taker. He was Hurler of the Year in 1988, and won All-Star awards in 1986 and 1988.

LEFT HALF-BACK

1. J.J. Delaney (Kilkenny)

J.J. Delaney won seven All-Star awards – four at half-back and three at full-back – between 2003 and 2014, underlining his durability and adaptability. It all came so naturally to one of the most talented defenders in hurling history. Touch, timing and an innate ability to be in the right place at the right time were invaluable for Kilkenny during a period in which they dominated for so long. Hurler of the Year in 2003, he won nine All-Ireland senior medals.

2. Paddy Phelan (Kilkenny)

Paddy Phelan won his first All-Ireland senior medal in 1932 and added three more in 1933, 1935 and 1939, in what was a memorable decade for Kilkenny. Once described as a man who used his hurley like a magic wand, his high skill level was accompanied by an instinctive understanding of half-back demands. A long-time regular on Leinster Railway Cup teams, he was chosen on both the Team of the Century (1984) and Team of the Millennium (2000).

3. Pádraic Maher (Tipperary)

Pádraic Maher's first senior season was as a twenty-year-old full-back in 2009, but it was as a half-back, primarily on the left, that he built a huge reputation. By the time he announced his retirement in early 2022, he was recognised as one of the best half-backs in history. Strong and steady under a dropping ball and also gifted with a shrewd sense of positioning, he was at the heart of Tipperary's All-Ireland wins in 2010, 2016 and 2019. He won six All-Star awards.

4. Denis Coughlan (Cork)

An equally talented hurler and footballer – winning All-Ireland senior titles in both codes – Denis Coughlan achieved more in small-ball territory, helping Cork to a memorable All-Ireland three-in-a-row in 1976, 1977 and 1978. His contribution in 1977 earned him the Hurler of the Year award. A stylish performer, he was also wonderfully athletic, a combination that made him one of the most exciting players of his generation. He won four hurling All-Stars in 1972 (midfield), and 1976, 1977 and 1978 (left half-back).

5. Seán Óg Ó hAilpín (Cork)

Another from the Cork academy of top dual players, hurling served Seán Óg Ó hAilpín better in terms of titles and awards. By the end of his career in 2010, he had won three All-Ireland senior hurling titles in 1999, 2004 and 2005, the latter as captain. He won the Hurler of the Year award in 2004. An All-Star in 2003, 2004 and 2005, he was nominated eight times. He brought a great sense of flamboyance to his game, making him a big crowd favourite among Leeside fans.

6. Kyle Hayes (Limerick)

Very much a product of the modern game, where many players are interchangeable between defence and attack, Kyle Hayes has so much natural talent that designated positions aren't relevant. His reliability under a high ball, combined with his marauding runs into enemy territory, has been an inspiring sight for Limerick supporters since making his senior debut in 2017.

7. Anthony Daly (Clare)

A three-time All-Star, one each at right full-back (1994), right half-back (1998) and left half-back (1995), Anthony Daly brought a whole lot more than being a tight-marking defender to his game. He was also an inspirational leader as Clare emerged from the wilderness to win the 1995 All-Ireland title, adding a second two years later. Daly was captain on both occasions, leading by example in what was the best era in Clare history.

8. Iggy Clarke (Galway)

Injury kept Iggy Clarke out of the 1980 All-Ireland final, when Galway won the title for the first time in fifty-seven years, but he did so much for them, before and after, that he will always be remembered as one of the best half-backs. He was part of a crop of young talent that helped raised Galway's stature in the early 1970s, gradually building to a point where they were serious All-Ireland contenders from the middle of the decade. He won All-Star awards in 1975, 1978, 1979 and 1980.

9. Liam Dunne (Wexford)

Equally efficient all across the half-back line, Liam Dunne was a ferocious competitor both in the ground exchanges and in aerial combat, where he frequently out-smarted taller opponents. Like so many more of the Wexford team that won the 1996 All-Ireland title, he had endured lots of disappointment over previous seasons but never lost ambition or belief – something that was crucial in the 1996 change of fortunes. He was a three-time All-Star, in 1990, 1993 and 1996.

10. Tommy Doyle (Tipperary)

From the Thurles Sarsfields club, with whom he won seven Tipperary championships, Tommy Doyle played senior hurling for the county from 1937 to 1953. Such was his versatility that he won major honours as a defender and attacker. He was half-forward on the All-Ireland-winning teams of 1937 and 1945, and was half-back on the three-in-a-row teams of 1949, 1950 and 1951. During his long career he also won three National League titles and three Railway Cup medals.

8 & 9 MIDFIELD

1. Lory Meagher (Kilkenny)

Lory Meagher's exploits in the 1920s and 1930s made him a legendary figure throughout the land, though he was never comfortable in the limelight. But crossing the white line enabled him to cast aside all inhibitions and express himself as an extraordinary talent. A winner of three All-Ireland titles in 1932, 1933 and 1935, his performance as he captained Kilkenny to victory in the 1935 final against Limerick is recorded as one of the finest individual displays in hurling history.

2. Jack Lynch (Cork)

A man who went on to become a leading politician, rising to taoiseach (1966–1973 and 1977–1979), Jack Lynch first came to prominence as an equally proficient hurler and footballer in the 1940s. A member of the elite club reserved for All-Ireland winners in both codes, he won titles in six successive years, five in hurling (1941, 1942, 1943, 1944 and 1946) and one in football (1945). His stature – particularly as a hurler – has stood the test of time and he was selected on the Team of the Century (1984) and Team of the Millennium (2000).

3. John Fenton (Cork)

Regarded as one of the most stylish hurlers of his era, John Fenton was also among the best free-takers. An All-Ireland Under-21 medal winner in 1976, he had to wait until 1984 to win his first senior medal, when he had the honour of being captain when Cork beat Offaly in the GAA's centenary-year final. He was later named Hurler of the Year and was selected as an All-Star for five consecutive seasons (1983–1987).

4. Frank Cummins (Kilkenny)

In a career that spanned three decades, beginning in 1966 and continuing until 1984, Frank Cummins was an exceptional performer in a bountiful period for Kilkenny. Strong, forceful and oozing stamina, he imposed himself to great effect in the middle third of the pitch. A sub on the All-Ireland-winning team of 1967, he went on to win seven more medals as a member of the starting team. Hurler of the Year in 1983, he won All-Stars in 1971, 1972, 1982 and 1983.

5. John Connolly (Galway)

A member of one of the best-known hurling families, John Connolly was a key figure in the revival of Galway hurling in the 1970s. Given their long spell in the doldrums, it took quite a shift in mindset to force change – and he was very much part of that transition. Captain of the team that won the National League in 1975, he was equally influential when Galway won the All-Ireland title in 1980 with a team which also featured his younger brothers Michael and Joe (captain). John won All-Stars in 1971 and 1979.

6. Phil Grimes (Waterford)

Phil Grimes' midfield partnership with Séamus Power, also a multi-talented performer, was a major driving force for Waterford in the second half of the 1950s, a period in which they won one All-Ireland and two Munster senior titles. The 1959 season was the most memorable as they won the All-Ireland title, beating Kilkenny in a replayed final. Noted for his speed and stylish touches, Grimes was also very adaptable.

7. Liam 'Chunky' O'Brien (Kilkenny)

Known throughout Ireland by his nickname 'Chunky', Liam O'Brien was one of the most familiar figures on the Kilkenny team of the 1970s. He won the first three of his four All-Ireland medals as a midfielder in 1972, 1974 and 1975, and lined out at left half-forward on the successful team in 1979. He won four All-Star awards (three at midfield, one at left half-forward), was Hurler of the Year in 1975 and won an All-Ireland club title with James Stephens in 1976.

8. George O'Connor (Wexford)

An outstanding dual player whose passion never dimmed despite Wexford's lack of success for the greater part of his career, the ultimate prize eventually came George O'Connor's way when he won an All-Ireland senior hurling medal at the age of thirty-six in 1996. It was a fitting departure honour for a consistently effective performer, who was dubbed the 'Uncrowned King of Wexford' by team manager Liam Griffin. O'Connor won All-Stars in 1981 and 1988.

9. Michael Fennelly (Kilkenny)

Representing the third generation of the Fennelly hurling dynasty from Ballyhale, Michael surpassed the achievements of his grandfather Kevin, father Mick and six uncles when he collected eight All-Ireland senior titles between 2006 and 2015. Powered by huge stamina reserves, his driving runs into opposition territory were a regular source of scores in a career where, in addition to so much All-Ireland success, he also won three All-Star awards and a Hurler of the Year award in 2011.

10. Mick Roche (Tipperary)

Promoted to the Tipperary senior team in 1963 at a time when the squad was very strong, Mick Roche went on to win three All-Ireland titles in a career that lasted eleven years. Regarded in Tipperary as a hurling colossus and widely respected elsewhere, he was equally comfortable at midfield, where he won All-Ireland medals in 1964 and 1965, and centre-back, where he starred in 1971. He was an All-Star in the scheme's first year (1971).

11. Michael 'Brick' Walsh (Waterford)

Defence, midfield or attack ... they were all the same to a man whose versatility served Waterford so well for so long. Unfortunately for him, an All-Ireland senior title proved elusive, but it was about the only missing piece of the very large jigsaw he created. Winner of four All-Star awards in three different positions (two at centre-back in 2009 and 2010, one each at midfield in 2007 and left half-forward in 2017), he was nominated no fewer than ten times.

12. Timmy Ryan (Limerick)

Prior to the emergence of the county's current powerhouse squad, Timmy Ryan was one of a small band of Limerick hurlers to have won three All-Ireland senior titles. He achieved that notable triple in 1934 (as captain), 1936 and 1940. He also won five successive National League medals between 1934 and 1938 (two as captain). A prominent member of Munster teams for several seasons, he won five Railway Cup medals.

13. Gerald McCarthy (Cork)

Gerald McCarthy holds the distinction of having captained Cork seniors and Under-21s to All-Ireland success in 1966, before going on to win four more senior medals in 1970, 1976, 1977 and 1978. A superb stylist, he was a master at the overhead pull, a difficult skill largely absent from the modern game, where getting ball in hand is regarded as paramount. He won only one All-Star award (1975), a return that still puzzles many shrewd hurling followers who regard him as one of the all-time greats.

14. Tommy Dunne (Tipperary)

Captain and man of the match in the 2001 All-Ireland final win over Galway was Tommy Dunne's greatest day in a senior career that ran from 1993 to 2005. A classy performer, he always appeared to have that extra few seconds on the ball while also being expert at drifting into space to receive possession. There was a lovely rhythm to everything he did, making it all look quite effortless, which is the ultimate example of true craft. He was Hurler of the Year in 2001, and he won All-Stars in 1997, 1999 and 2001.

15. Joe Salmon (Galway)

A regular on the Galway team from 1949 to 1964, Joe Salmon played in three losing All-Ireland finals but in no way did that detract from his nationwide reputation as an immensely effective midfielder. He combined style and skill with a steely determination that made him a match for any opponent. In the GAA's centenary year (1984), he was chosen on a special selection comprised of players who had not won All-Ireland senior titles.

16. Tom Cashman (Cork)

Equally comfortable in the half-back line or midfield, Tom Cashman had a wonderful appreciation of the requirements for that general area and applied it expertly during a career in which he won four All-Ireland senior medals in 1977, 1978, 1984 and 1986, the latter as captain. He won three All-Star awards, two at midfield, one at half-back, and was nominated eight times between 1977 and 1986. He was chosen on the Cork Team of the Millennium in 2000.

17. Terence 'Sambo' McNaughton (Antrim)

Terence McNaughton's affable personality off the field, allied to the passion he displayed on match days, made him one of the most popular and admired players in the game. Selected wherever Antrim's need was greatest, he played in defence, midfield and attack during a long career where the high point came in 1989 when Antrim reached the All-Ireland final for the first time since 1943. One of only five Antrim hurlers to win All-Star awards, he was honoured at midfield in 1991.

18. Harry Gray (Laois & Dublin)

Harry Gray enjoyed a great career, initially with Laois and later with Dublin before returning to line out for his native county. The Rathdowney man was on the Laois team that lost to Kilkenny in the 1936 Leinster final, but by 1938 he was an influential member of the Dublin team that won the All-Ireland title. They lost All-Ireland finals to Cork in 1941 and 1943. Later in the decade, he returned to Laois, winning a Leinster title in 1949.

19. John 'Jobber' McGrath (Westmeath)

John McGrath started out as a goalkeeper before moving outfield where his all-round game enabled him to slot comfortably into a variety of positions. He was most effective around midfield in a senior career that extended from 1947 to the mid-1960s. He was a Railway Cup winner with Leinster in 1956 and in 1984 (GAA centenary year), he was chosen at midfield on a team drawn from players who hadn't won All-Ireland medals.

20. Pat Critchley (Laois)

Pat Critchley remains the only Laois hurler to have won an All-Star award, having been selected at midfield alongside John Fenton in 1985. It was the third successive year that he had been nominated during a period when Laois were going well, even if they couldn't quite make the big championship breakthrough. That certainly wasn't Critchley's fault as he was a consistently effective presence. The bigger the challenge, the more he thrived.

👕10 RIGHT HALF-FORWARD

1. Christy Ring (Cork)

From his senior inter-county debut, aged nineteen, in 1939 to his last game in 1963, Christy Ring set standards that made him a genuine contender to be regarded as the best of all time. Eighty-five years later, he remains in that category. Feted in song and story, the name Christy Ring will always be synonymous with excellence and a sense of magic. Winner of eight All-Ireland senior titles, four National League titles and no fewer than eighteen Railway Cups with Munster, he was an automatic choice on the Team of the Century (1984) and Team of the Millennium (2000).

2. T.J. Reid (Kilkenny)

For many players, decline begins in their early thirties, but not for T.J. Reid. He was thirty in 2017, by which time he had accumulated seven All-Ireland senior medals and numerous other titles and awards, including Hurler of the Year in 2015. Kilkenny's title flood – they had won eleven All-Irelands since 2000 – ebbed after that, but Reid has produced some of his best performances in subsequent years both with club (Ballyhale Shamrocks) and county.

3. Tony O'Sullivan (Cork)

Consistently accurate from frees and play, Tony O'Sullivan was one of the top scorers in the country throughout most of the 1980s and early 1990s. An All-Ireland minor winner in 1979, he added an Under-21 title in 1982. By then, he had graduated to senior status and was a high-profile presence when Cork won All-Ireland titles in 1984, 1986 and 1990. A five-time All Star (1982, 1986, 1988, 1990 and 1992), he was Hurler of the Year in 1990.

4. Michael Cleary (Tipperary)

In a senior championship career that ran for a decade, Michael Cleary was one of the most consistent score-getters from frees and play, shooting a total of 10–108. An All-Ireland senior winner in 1989 and 1991, he was chosen on All-Star teams in four successive years (1990–1993), winning two awards at right half-forward and two in the right corner. He was nominated eight times, a further indication of his high consistency levels.

5. Johnny Dooley (Offaly)

Johnny Dooley will be forever remembered for his game-changing goal from a free late in the 1994 All-Ireland final. It launched Offaly's astonishing comeback, which saw them recover from a five-point deficit after sixty-four minutes to beat Limerick by six points – but then, he had always had the knack of delivering crucial scores when most required. Alongside his brothers Joe and Billy, he added another senior title in 1998. Equally comfortable in attack or midfield, he won All-Star awards in 1994, 1995 and 2000.

6. Francis Loughnane (Tipperary)

Francis Loughnane's place in history was established early when he captained Tipperary to All-Ireland Under-21 glory in the inaugural year of the competition (1964). Seven years later, he won an All-Ireland club title with Roscrea in the inaugural year of that competition. By then, he was a regular with Tipperary and added an All-Ireland senior title in 1971. He won an All-Star award in the inaugural year of the scheme in 1971 and added two more over the next two years.

7. Ben O'Connor (Cork)

A sub on Cork's All-Ireland-winning Under-21 team in 1998, Ben O'Connor was one of the youngsters introduced to senior status in the summer of 1999 by manager Jimmy Barry-Murphy. It was a smart move. O'Connor grew quickly with the new challenge as Cork powered to All-Ireland glory. It marked the start of an outstanding career by a wonderfully skilful player, whose brother Jerry also made a huge contribution to Cork's All-Ireland wins in 2004 and 2005.

8. Jimmy Smyth (Clare)

A well-known administrator at GAA headquarters in Croke Park in later life, Jimmy Smyth enjoyed a long playing career with Clare. It began at the age of fourteen when he was selected for the minors and went on to play in the grade for five seasons before being promoted to the seniors. He scored 6–4 in a championship game against Limerick in 1953. Clare won no major titles during his time, but he enjoyed big success with Munster, winning Railway Cup titles in 1955, 1958, 1959, 1960, 1961 and 1963.

9. Martin Storey (Wexford)

When Martin Storey emerged as a senior in the mid-1980s, Wexford were ranked third in Leinster, behind Offaly and Kilkenny. They stayed there for the next decade. Storey never allowed the setbacks to detract from his ambitions and he played a massive role in the turnaround in 1996 when Wexford won the All-Ireland title. He captained the side, leading by example as they embarked on the great adventure which took them to the summit. He was a three-time All Star, in 1993, 1996 and 1998.

10. Gearóid Hegarty (Limerick)

When Limerick won the All-Ireland Under-21 title in 2015 – their first for thirteen years – it was clear that several of the team, including Gearóid Hegarty, had all the necessary attributes to make successful seniors. And so it proved. He was a half-back on the Under-21 team but it's as a half-forward that he has established himself as a star act at senior level. Big, strong and quick, he represents the ultimate nightmare for opposition markers.

CENTRE HALF-FORWARD

1. Henry Shefflin (Kilkenny)

King Henry! A genuine contender to be regarded as the best hurler of all time, Henry's achievement record is remarkable. Between 1999 and 2015, he won ten All-Ireland medals as well as multiple other titles, including a record-breaking eleven All-Stars and two Hurler of the Year awards. As a player he had it all – skill, determination, consistency, mental toughness, resilience and that special something extra that fused all the qualities together on days when they were most needed.

2. Mick Mackey (Limerick)

From a family steeped in Gaelic games, Mick Mackey was one of the most dominant and popular figures in hurling in the 1930s and 1940s. He made his senior debut in 1930 and enjoyed seventeen years at the highest level, winning All-Ireland titles in 1934, 1936 and 1940. He scored 5–3 of Limerick's 8–5 total in their win over Tipperary in the 1936 Munster final. His direct running style, backed up by sublime skill, terrorised even the best defences. He was chosen on both the Team of the Century (1984) and Team of the Millennium (2000).

3. Joe Cooney (Galway)

A quiet man off the field, Joe Cooney mesmerised crowds with his artistry in a career that yielded All-Ireland inter-county medals at minor, Under-21 and senior level, as well as All-Ireland club success with Sarsfields. Strong, quick and with a game-smart appreciation that outwitted most opponents, he gave fantastic service to club and county. Equally accurate from frees and play, he had a phenomenal strike rate. A five-time All-Star, he was Hurler of the Year in 1987.

4. Cian Lynch (Limerick)

Promoted to the senior ranks as a teenager in 2015, it was evident that a new star had emerged. Everything about Cian Lynch oozed class and as Limerick's fortunes changed dramatically for the better in 2018, when they won the All-Ireland title for the first time since 1973, he was a major creative force. Equally effective at midfield or centre-forward, his artistry brought an extra dimension to Limerick as they embarked on their greatest era.

5. Pat Delaney (Kilkenny)

An old-style, direct-running centre-forward, Pat Delaney also had an instinct for doing things differently. One of his specialities was the 'Delaney bounce', which involved tapping the sliotar off the ground while running at full pace. A very difficult skill to execute, it gave him a big advantage over opponents who found it virtually impossible to counteract. An All-Ireland winner in 1969, 1972, 1974 and 1975, and an All-Star in 1972 and 1973. His son P.J. was an All-Ireland winner in 1993.

6. Paddy Molloy (Offaly)

Long before Offaly hurling became fashionable or successful, Paddy Molloy was regarded as one of the most talented hurlers in the country. He played senior hurling from the early 1950s to the early 1970s and though he won no major honours with Offaly, he was a regular for Leinster in the Railway Cup for many years. His versatility was evident when he was left half-back on the successful 1965 Leinster team and right full-forward on the 1967 winning team.

7. Tom Cheasty (Waterford)

During a golden era for Waterford hurling in the late 1950s and early 1960s, Tom Cheasty earned a reputation as one of the great centre-forwards of his generation. A minor with Waterford at the age of sixteen in 1950, he was promoted to the senior ranks four years later and was a central figure in the All-Ireland triumph of 1959 when they beat Kilkenny in a replay. He also won three Munster championships and four Railway Cup medals.

8. Gary Kirby (Limerick)

Throughout the 1990s, Gary Kirby was one of the most consistent and prolific score-getters in the game, both from frees and play. An All-Star in 1991, 1994, 1995 and 1996 (three at centre-forward, one at full-forward), he was denied All-Ireland glory in 1994 and 1996 when Limerick lost finals to Offaly and Wexford respectively. He is a serious contender for a place on a team drawn from players who didn't win All-Ireland medals.

9. Mick Ryan (Tipperary)

On a Tipperary team that dominated hurling during the late 1940s and early 1950s, Mick Ryan was a powerhouse at centre half-forward. He won three consecutive All-Ireland titles in 1949, 1950 and 1951. Tipperary won the All-Ireland/National League double in 1949 and 1950, and Ryan collected further league honours in 1952, 1954, 1955 and 1957. A winner of five Railway Cup medals, he was selected on the Tipperary Team of the Millennium.

10. Martin Quigley (Wexford)

One of the best forwards whose career didn't deliver an All-Ireland senior title, Martin Quigley won a minor medal in 1968. He experienced disappointment in the 1970, 1976 and 1977 senior finals when Wexford lost all three to Cork. By then, he had established himself as a top-class forward who was comfortable in a number of positions. An All-Star winner in 1973, 1974, 1975 and 1976 in three different positions. He won a National League medal in 1973 and four Railway Cup medals in 1973, 1974, 1975 and 1977.

🎽12 LEFT HALF-FORWARD

1. D.J. Carey (Kilkenny)

D.J. Carey started out as a goalkeeper but it quickly became apparent that his real calling was on the more adventurous side. Blessed with the silkiest of skills, he delivered on his early potential, maturing into one of the best forwards in hurling history in a senior career that ran from 1991 to 2005. A five-time All-Ireland senior championship winner in 1992, 1993, 2000, 2002 and 2003, his top-of-the-range consistency also won him nine All-Stars between 1991 and 2002 and two Hurler of the Year awards.

2. Jim Langton (Kilkenny)

Promoted to the senior squad in 1938, Jim Langton made a quick impression and played a big part in Kilkenny's All-Ireland success a year later. He added a second All-Ireland title in 1947. He also featured in four finals that Kilkenny lost. It didn't damage the reputation of a player who was widely admired and respected throughout the hurling world. His enduring stature was underlined when he was chosen on the Team of the Century (1984) and Team of the Millennium (2000).

3. Jamesie O'Connor (Clare)

Hurler of the Year in 1997 after a spectacular season that he completed by shooting the winning point against Tipperary in the All-Ireland final, Jamesie O'Connor was one of the inspirations behind Clare's emergence from hurling's wilderness in the mid-1990s when they won two All-Ireland titles in three seasons.

Whether at midfield or attack, O'Connor's precise touch, speed and game-reading presented all sorts of problems for opposition. A four-time All-Star in 1995, 1997, 1998 and 2001, he was nominated seven times.

4. Richie Hogan (Kilkenny)

Richie Hogan's last appearance for Kilkenny was as a substitute in the 2023 All-Ireland final defeat by Limerick, bringing down the curtain on a fabulous career that yielded seven All-Ireland senior titles. Small in stature, his vast array of talents enabled him to match opponents of any size. It also widened his versatility range, taking him all over the attack and into midfield. A four-time All-Star, he was Hurler of the Year in 2014.

5. John Leahy (Tipperary)

A combination of skill, power and determination, reinforced by a fiercely competitive streak, made John Leahy highly effective in a variety of positions during a senior career that started as an eighteen-year-old in 1988. It was an exciting time for Tipperary, who went on to win two All-Ireland titles in 1989 and 1991. He made a big contribution to both successes and continued to be a central figure over the next decade. He was a three-time All-Star in 1991, 1994 and 1997.

6. Eoin Larkin (Kilkenny)

The All-Ireland-winning captain in 2012, Eoin Larkin was one of the most decorated players in hurling history when he retired from the inter-county game in 2016. In a senior career that began in 2005, he won eight All-Ireland medals, ten Leinster championship and six National League titles. He was the All-Star left half-forward in 2008 and 2009, and was also honoured as Hurler of the Year in 2008.

7. Liam Devaney (Tipperary)

Hurler of the Year in 1961, Liam Devaney had a hugely successful career that began at underage level in the early 1950s and continued until the late 1960s. He won consecutive All-Ireland minor titles in 1952 and 1953 and went on to contest eight All-Ireland senior finals in a variety of positions, winning five in 1958, 1961, 1962, 1964 and 1965, as well as eight National Leagues and three Railway Cups. Hugely versatile, he was equally effective at midfield or attack.

8. Eamon Grimes (Limerick)

Limerick's All-Ireland-winning captain in 1973 first came to attention as a gifted minor ten years earlier. Promoted to the Limerick senior team at the age of nineteen, Eamon Grimes played at both midfield and left half-forward in a career that, in addition to yielding an All-Ireland medal, saw him win All-Star awards in 1973 and 1975, and be named Hurler of the Year in 1973.

9. Lar Corbett (Tipperary)

How many players fulfil the great dream of delivering a special performance in an All-Ireland final? Corbett certainly did, scoring three goals from play in the 2010 final against Kilkenny. It was the high point of his career, but there were many other outstanding days too. In his debut season of 2001, he won a National League medal, a first Munster championship and the first of two All-Ireland medals.

His willingness to try for goals rather than take the safer point option added to the excitement around many of his performances. A three-time All-Star, he was Hurler of the Year in 2010.

10. Jackie Power (Limerick)

Twice an All-Ireland hurling winner, in 1936 and 1940 when he lined out in attack, Jackie Power was also an outstanding footballer. As a hurler, he was equally good in attack or defence and comfortable in a variety of positions. He won five consecutive National League medals between 1934 and 1938. His honours collection includes seven Railway Cup medals. With his club, Ahane, he won fifteen Limerick hurling titles and five football titles. His son Ger later won eight All-Ireland football medals with Kerry.

RIGHT FULL-FORWARD

1. Jimmy Doyle (Tipperary)

Just eighteen when he won the first of his six All-Ireland senior titles in 1958, Doyle initially played for his county at minor level as a goalkeeper in 1954. But it was as a prolific scoring forward that he began capturing headlines when winning three All-Ireland minor titles in succession from 1955 to 1957. One of the game's great stylists, he won his second senior title in 1961, was the winning captain in 1962, won a fourth title in 1964 – after which he was named Hurler of the Year – and was again a winning captain in 1965. He won his last championship as a playing substitute in 1971.

2. Eoin Kelly (Tipperary)

One of the most gifted forwards of his generation, Eoin Kelly played in goal for Tipperary minors before moving to attack where he went on to excel for many years. He made his senior debut in 2000 and became an All-Ireland winner a year later. He had to wait until 2010 for a second medal, by which stage he was recognised as one of the greats. His high-scoring feats helped him win six All-Star awards – a Tipperary record he shares with Nicky English and Pádraic Maher.

3. Aaron Gillane (Limerick)

From the hurling-mad village of Patrickswell, Aaron Gillane has enjoyed a spectacular run on one of the greatest hurling teams of all time. He made his first big breakthrough as top scorer on the Limerick Under-21 team that won the 2017 All-Ireland title. He made his senior championship debut in the same year and has since been one of the most prolific scorers in the game, regularly topping the scoring charts.

4. Charlie McCarthy (Cork)

What he lacked in size, Charlie McCarthy compensated for with skill and bravery. He won an All-Ireland minor title with Cork in 1964 and added an Under-21 honour two years later. By then, he was established on the senior team and won the first of five All-Ireland senior medals in 1966. A second was added in 1970 and he was an influential member of the team that completed consecutive All-Ireland wins in 1976, 1977 and 1978. He won All-Star awards in 1972, 1977 and 1978.

5. Eddie Brennan (Kilkenny)

In twelve seasons between 2000, when he made his senior debut in the National League, and early 2012 when he announced his retirement, Eddie Brennan enjoyed phenomenal success. Renowned as one of the deadliest finishers in the game, he had a particularly high goal rate and won eight All-Ireland championships, including four-in-a-row from 2006 to 2009. He won eleven Leinster titles, five National Leagues and was an All-Star four times.

6. Donie Nealon (Tipperary)

Well-known as a top administrator, having served as Munster Council secretary from 1977 to 2004, Donie Nealon had previously enjoyed a hugely successful playing career. First coming to attention in St Flannan's, Ennis, in the mid-1950s, he progressed to the Tipperary senior team in 1958. Between then and 1969, he won five All-Ireland senior medals in 1958, 1961, 1962, 1964 and 1965. A prolific forward, he played in a variety of positions, each with equal effectiveness. He was Hurler of the Year in 1962.

7. Pat Fox (Tipperary)

Pat Fox came to prominence as a midfielder on Tipperary's All-Ireland Under-21-winning team in 1979 and was corner-back on the winning teams at that grade in 1980 and 1981. A knee injury stalled his career but he battled back and, by 1987, was an outstanding corner-forward when Tipperary won the Munster title for the first time since 1971. He won two All-Ireland senior titles in 1989 and 1991, was Hurler of the Year in 1991 and was a three-time All-Star.

8. John Mullane (Waterford)

Although he has never won an All-Ireland title, John Mullane became one of the most recognisable figures in hurling between 2000 and 2012. During that time, he won four Munster championships (2002, 2004, 2007 and 2010). He won the first of five All-Star awards (a Waterford record) in 2003 at left half-forward and four in succession between 2009 and 2012, one at left full-forward and three in the right corner.

9. Paddy Kenny (Tipperary)

Paddy Kenny was selected at right corner-forward on the Tipperary Team of the Millennium, a status earned through a career where his talents were apparent from his teenage years when he featured on the Tipperary minor team for three successive years (1945–1947), one as captain. Promotion to the senior team followed and he added three consecutive All-Ireland senior titles (1949, 1950 and 1951), four National League and four Railway Cup titles to his collection.

10. Billy Fitzpatrick (Kilkenny)

One of the best finishers – from play and frees – of his or any era, Billy Fitzpatrick was destined for stardom from his secondary-school days. In 1972, he began his collection of All-Ireland honours with St Kieran's College and added a minor medal with Kilkenny a few months later. He won two Under-21 titles (1974 and 1975) and won the first of five senior medals in 1974. He was an All-Star in 1982 and 1983.

14 FULL-FORWARD

1. Nicky Rackard (Wexford)

How about this for scoring prowess: 6–4 v Dublin in the 1954 Leinster final; 7–7 v Antrim in the 1954 All-Ireland semi-final; 5–3 v Galway in the 1956 All-Ireland semi-final. Those three scoring feats – all completed in sixty-minute games – highlight how prolific Nicky Rackard was, but then he was a special talent. His career yielded All-Ireland titles in 1955 and 1956, and he was chosen on the GAA's Team of the Century in 1984.

2. Joe Canning (Galway)

Joe Canning played senior club for Portumna and minor for Galway at the age of fifteen in 2004, flagging the arrival of arguably the best hurler the county has produced. One of the most technically gifted players in hurling history, he electrified arenas all over the country in a career that yielded all the major team honours across the various grades, topped by All-Ireland success in 2017. He was also Hurler of the Year in 2017, and won five All-Star awards (he was nominated ten times).

3. Joe McKenna (Limerick)

An Offaly native, with whom he played at minor level, Joe McKenna moved to Limerick and established himself as one of the outstanding forwards of his era. Physically very powerful, he played in a variety of attacking positions, including left full-forward where he won an All-Ireland senior medal in 1973. However, it was at full-forward that he became best known, winning four successive All-Stars in 1978, 1979, 1980 and 1981, to add to ones he won at right half-forward (1974) and centre-half-forward (1975).

4. Ray Cummins (Cork)

One of the most successful dual players, Ray Cummins was an All-Star footballer and hurler in 1971. A year earlier, he had won the first of four All-Ireland senior hurling titles and was also part of the Cork football team that won the All-Ireland title in 1973. There was more to come from him in hurling as Cork won successive All-Irelands in 1976, 1977 and 1978. He won two football and three hurling All-Stars and was chosen on the hurling Team of the Millennium (2000).

5. Jimmy Barry-Murphy (Cork)

One of the greatest dual players in GAA history, Jimmy Barry-Murphy won an All-Ireland senior football title in 1973 and was an All-Star twice in that code. He chose to concentrate on hurling only in the early 1980s, by which stage he had accumulated three All-Ireland medals in 1976, 1977 and 1978. Two more followed in 1984 and 1986. A superb stylist, he also had a deep appreciation of the game, which transferred to his successful management career, including leading Cork to All-Ireland success in 1999.

6. Tony Doran (Wexford)

There was no more glorious sight for Wexford supporters than Tony Doran making a high catch and bursting in on the opposition goal. More often than not, a goal resulted. An All-Ireland minor (1963), Under-21 (1965) and senior (1968) winner, his career extended to

1984, by which time he had also accumulated seven Railway Cup medals, two National Leagues and an All-Star award in 1976. He was an All-Star nominee seven times.

7. Séamus Callanan (Tipperary)

From his championship debut in 2008 to his retirement in 2023, Séamus Callanan was one of the most consistent marksmen from frees and open play, with a special talent for goal-scoring. He won three All-Ireland medals, the first in 2010, the second as man of the match in the 2016 final after scoring 0–13 (0–9 from play) and a third as captain in 2019. A four-time All-Star, he was nominated for Hurler of the Year on four occasions and won the award in 2019.

8. Dan Shanahan (Waterford)

One of the great goal-scorers, 'Dan the Man' won four Munster championships but, unfortunately, an All-Ireland medal eluded him. Despite that, he enjoyed many special days when his powerful runs and accurate finishing helped bring Waterford Munster championships and National League glory in various years. His best year was in 2007 when he scored 8–12 from play in five championship games. He was later named Hurler of the Year, and was an All-Star in 2004, 2006 and 2007.

9. Kieran Purcell (Kilkenny)

Kieran Purcell was a goalkeeper in his early years, but it was as a powerful full-forward that he established himself on a team regarded as possibly the best Kilkenny had produced prior to the super outfits which won so much between 2000 and 2015. The team of the early 1970s, with Purcell a dynamic presence, won three of four All-Ireland titles (1972, 1974 and 1975) and might well have won the four-in-a-row if injury hadn't weakened them in 1973 when they lost to Limerick in the final. He won All-Star awards in 1973, 1974 and 1975.

10. Martin Comerford (Kilkenny)

Effective in most forward positions, Martin Comerford started his career at full-forward in 2002 at a time when Kilkenny were heading into their greatest era. By the time he retired in 2011, he had won six All-Ireland medals and three All-Star awards. A prolific marksman, one of his most important scores came late in the 2009 All-Ireland final when, after coming on as a sub against Tipperary, he scored Kilkenny's second goal that ensured victory and a fourth successive title.

👕 LEFT FULL-FORWARD

1. Eddie Keher (Kilkenny)

From the age of fifteen when he emerged as a minor star in 1956 to his retirement in 1976, Eddie Keher contributed so much to Kilkenny and hurling in general. But then he was as close as it comes to being the complete package. Six All-Ireland medals and five All-Star awards (won consecutively between 1971 and 1975), and a Hurler of the Year award in 1972 were among his many honours during his playing days and he was chosen on the Team of the Century (1984) and Team of the Millennium (2000).

2. Nicky English (Tipperary)

Nicky English was a star attraction in the 1980s and 1990s. Comfortable anywhere in attack, he won three All-Star awards at right half-forward in 1983, 1984 and 1985 at a time when Tipperary made little progress in the championship. Everything changed in 1987 when their fortunes took an upward swing with a Munster title success, followed in 1989 and 1991 by All-Ireland titles. English was a big driving force in the turnaround, as evidenced by him winning three more All-Stars in 1987, 1988 and 1989, and Hurler of the Year in 1989.

3. Eamonn Cregan (Limerick)

For nearly two decades, from 1964 until 1983, Eamonn Cregan was one of the most effective players in the game. An all-round athlete who could play in almost any position, he won a National League title in 1971 as a corner-forward, before switching to centre-back where he starred on the team that won the 1973 All-Ireland title. He later returned to attack where he continued to excel. He was a three-time All-Star at left corner-forward, in 1971, 1972 and 1980.

4. Liam Fennelly (Kilkenny)

Twice an All-Ireland-winning captain in 1983 and 1992, Liam Fennelly is from one of the most famous and successful hurling families in the country, with his brothers – Ger, Seán and Kevin – also featuring prominently for Kilkenny over many years. Liam was one of the best finishers of his era in a career where he won All-Ireland senior titles in 1982, 1983 and 1993. He was also a four-time All-Star in 1983, 1985, 1987 and 1992.

5. Michael 'Babs' Keating (Tipperary)

Christened 'Babs' at an early age to distinguish him from other family members, he was one of the most high-profile figures in hurling through the 1960s and 1970s. Wonderfully athletic (he was also an accomplished footballer with Tipperary and Munster), he won All-Ireland senior hurling medals in 1964, 1965 (as a sub) and 1971, a season in which he also became an All-Star in what was the scheme's first year. An intelligent game-reader, his post-playing days took him to the highest peaks as a manager, leading Tipperary to All-Ireland wins in 1989 and 1991.

6. Seánie O'Leary (Cork)

One of the most prolific goal-scorers of his or any era, Seánie O'Leary first came to prominence as an underage star, winning an All-Ireland minor title in 1969 and adding three Under-21 titles in 1970, 1971 and 1973. He was a star of the three-in-a-row All-Ireland-winning senior squad between 1976, 1977 and 1978 and added a fourth title in 1984. He was the All-Star left full-forward on three occasions in 1976, 1977 and 1984 and was nominated eight times.

7. Joe Deane (Cork)

Another in the long list of Cork players to represent the county in both hurling and football, Joe Deane carved out a reputation as a consistent score-getter from the mid-1990s to the late 2000s. An All-Ireland minor winner and twice an All-Ireland Under-21 winner, he won three senior titles in 1999, 2004 and 2005, and was an All-Star in 1999, 2000 and 2003.

8. Patrick Horgan (Cork)

On 15 May 2022, Patrick Horgan became the all-time leading scorer in championship hurling up to then when his four pointed frees against Waterford in Walsh Park gave him a total of 22–505 (571 points) in sixty-eight games. His consistent accuracy from frees and general play made him one of the most influential Cork players in a senior career that started in 2008. From the Glen Rovers club, Horgan has captained Cork at every level.

9. Paddy Barry (Cork)

Regarded as one of the greatest passers of the ball – his teamwork with Christy Ring was much heralded – Paddy Barry also had an eye for his own scores. He captained Cork to All-Ireland triumph in 1952 and they went on to complete the three-in-a-row with wins in 1953 and 1954. He continued to play until 1964 and won four Railway Cup medals with Munster. He was chosen on the Munster Team of the Millennium in 2000.

10. Noel Lane (Galway)

A prolific scorer, with a particular instinct for goals, in a senior career that lasted thirteen years, Noel Lane was an influential member of the team that brought the Liam MacCarthy Cup back to Galway for the first time in 1980, their first since 1923. He won two more All-Ireland medals in 1987 and 1988, coming on as a sub in both finals and scoring vitals goals. An All-Star in 1983 and 1984, he was nominated seven times.

3 DUAL JEWELS

Players with the natural talent to excel in hurling and football are forced to make a choice nowadays and I, for one, regret that. I believe it should be possible to accommodate them in both games.
Cork dual star Brian Murphy in an interview in an All-Star book *The Chosen Ones* **(2004)**

In the comfort of one of his favourite hostelries on Dublin's southside, preferably in Dún Laoghaire or the villages of Dalkey or Monkstown, Mick Holden would sometimes spend a winter's night in the company of family and friends, talking sport.

Hurling and Gaelic football, in that order, were the primary topics of conversation. But soccer and rugby got an airing from time to time. Golf was another sport for which time was allowed. And, to the surprise of some, cricket also found a place on the agenda.

If the football (Gaelic) fraternity were getting too loud or even cocky, or if conversation began to lag as the evening wore on, Mick had a surefire method of restoking the flames of debate.

'If a lad,' he would declare with as much solemnity as he could muster, 'can play hurling, he can play anything. But if a lad is good at any other sport or any variety of sports, it doesn't mean he would be any good at hurling.'

Verbal squabbles inevitably erupted. Mick would sit back, hand or pint glass lifted to hide a smile, and enjoy the discussion that followed.

Mick found fame and enjoyed success as an All-Ireland-winning footballer for Dublin in the 1980s, but he classified himself essentially as a hurler. He was one of the great dual players in Gaelic games, but football was no more than a pleasing distraction.

He loved playing hurling for Cuala, for Dublin and for Leinster. His rewards did not often take the form of silverware. It was enjoyment and camaraderie and the sheer joy of participating in what he believed was an art form that contented him.

There were some hurling successes and extraordinary achievements. He was just seventeen years old when he was selected as goalkeeper for the Dublin Under-21 team for the Leinster final in 1972. His older brothers Vinny and P.J. were also on the team that played Offaly.

By all accounts the youngest Holden was doing well in goal. 'Had played superbly in his chosen berth between the posts', was the verdict of the venerable Mitchel V. Cogley in the *Irish Independent*. But Dublin were trailing by five points with just three minutes remaining in the game and the selectors decided on drastic action.

The young goalkeeper was moved to midfield!

Central Council members in the mid-1880s.

Tipperary football team (Bohercrowe) that won the 1889 All-Ireland Senior Football Championship.

Dublin (Isle of the Sea) football team that won the 1901 All-Ireland Senior Football Championship.

Éamon de Valera throwing in the football to start the Wexford–Tipperary match in aid of the Irish Republican Prisoners Dependants Fund, Croke Park, 1919.

London-Irish Camogie team, winners of the 1921 McCarthy Shield.

Cork and Kilkenny contesting the 1931 All-Ireland hurling final.

Christy Ring (right) during the 1954 All-Ireland hurling final between Cork and Wexford.

Kilkenny and Tipperary parading before the 1937 All-Ireland hurling final in Fitzgerald Stadium, Killarney, as Croke Park was being redeveloped.

County Down became the first team from the Six Counties to win the 1960 All-Ireland senior football title.

The Master. Galway's Seán Purcell excelled both as a defender and attacker and was selected at centre half-forward on the football Team of the Millennium.

His Majesty. Kerry's Mick O'Connell soars above his opponents from Down in the 1968 All-Ireland final.

A genius in full flow, Matt Connor torments the Dublin defence during the 1980 Leinster football final.

Dermot Earley never had the honour of winning an All-Ireland senior title but in a two-decade long career with Roscommon, he attained legendary status as an outstanding footballer.

The Cork captain, via his birthplace in Kildare, Larry Tompkins lifts the Sam Maguire Cup in September 1990 as Cork recorded a unique double.

Determined and tenacious, Martin McHugh breaks the tackle of Dublin's Keith Barr and leads Donegal to the county's first All-Ireland senior football success in 1992.

Jack O'Shea and Mick O'Dwyer celebrate on the famous Hogan Stands steps after the 1986 All-Ireland final victory over Dublin.

Martin O'Connell played for Meath from 1984 to 1997, won three All-Ireland titles and was named at left half back on the football Team of the Millennium.

Seán O'Neill had the silky skills and tactical awareness that helped inspire Down to reach unprecedented heights during the 1960s.

He didn't collect many honours in a career that spanned the mid-1980s to 2001, but Wicklow's Kevin O'Brien was widely regarded as one of football's great forwards.

James McCarthy played in his first All-Ireland final for Dublin in 2011 against Kerry and embarked on a record-breaking career in which he collected every honour in the game.

The never-to-be-forgotten day when Kieran McGeeney became the first Armagh captain to lift the Sam Maguire Cup after their victory over Kerry, 22 September 2002.

One of Mayo's greatest footballers, despite not winning an All-Ireland senior title, Keith Higgins was also an accomplished hurler.

One of the most stylish hurlers in history, Eddie Keher won six All-Ireland titles and five consecutive All-Star awards during a hugely successful career with Kilkenny.

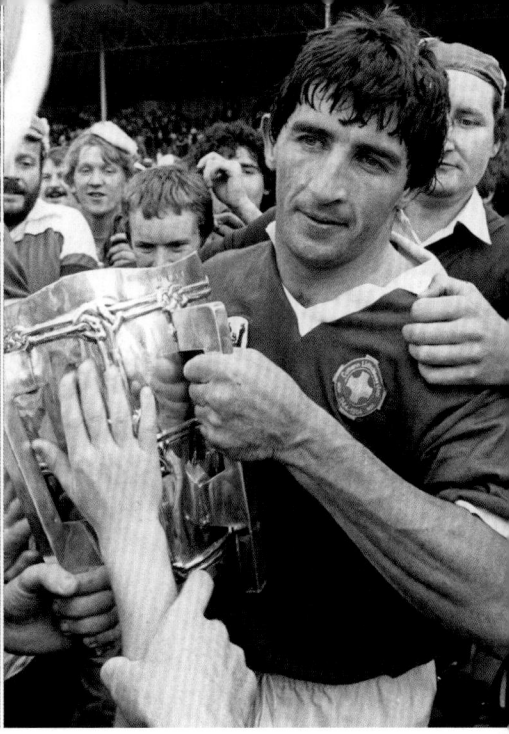

John Fenton carries the Liam McCarthy Cup through adoring fans at Semple Stadium in Thurles, after Cork defeated Offaly in the Centenary All-Ireland final, 1984.

Damien Martin was the first All-Star when he was named as goalkeeper on the first hurling selection in 1971, and was between the posts for Offaly when they won their first All-Ireland senior title ten years later.

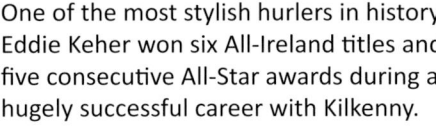

Limerick manager John Kiely and Kilkenny manager Brian Cody at the 2022 All-Ireland hurling senior final.

Tony Doran's hurling career with Wexford began in the mid-1960s and continued until 1984, during which time he won every honour in the game, including an All-Ireland medal in 1968.

Joe Cooney, seen here in action for Galway against Kilkenny in the 1987 All-Ireland final, the year he was named Hurler of the Year.

With his first touch, he scored Dublin's first goal. He won the puck-out and sent the ball back over the bar. Now just a point separated the teams.

A moment later, he was involved in the move that ended with his brother P.J. providing the final pass for Canice Hennebry to score the winning goal.

'Mick Holden was, of course, the Dublin hero, and in general usefulness through the hour, his brothers, P.J. and Vinnie, took high rating,' reported the man from the *Independent*.

Mick was back in goal for the All-Ireland final, but Galway proved too strong.

Three years later, in 1975, he was left half-back on the Dublin Under-21 football team that lost to Kerry in the All-Ireland final.

Mick won a Railway Cup hurling medal with Leinster in 1979 and was, by then, being pursued by Kevin Heffernan to commit to the Dublin senior footballers. He was full-back on the team that lost to Kerry in the All-Ireland final that year.

By the time Dublin returned to the All-Ireland final in the infamous encounter with Galway in 1983, Mick was established as a reliable right full-back. Despite having three men dismissed, Dublin's defiant dozen held out for a two-point victory. He won an inter-provincial football medal with Leinster in 1985 and toured Australia with the Ireland team for the International Rules series in 1986.

Mick died suddenly at the age of fifty-two in September 2007.

He was typical of most dual players in that his first love was hurling. Greg Blaney, Down's All-Ireland-winning footballer in 1991 and 1994, recalled that one of his favourite days as a player was when he played alongside his brother Michael on the Down team that won a rare Ulster senior hurling title in 1992.

The great Cork dual stars of the 1970s – Brian Murphy, Jimmy Barry-Murphy, Denis Coughlan and Ray Cummins amongst them – all chose hurling when the time came to concentrate on one game at inter-county level.

Liam Currams' career at inter-county level was a relatively short one – possibly due to wear and tear – so he never had to choose which Offaly team to play for. He just loved playing and brought wonderful athleticism to the Offaly hurlers when they won the county's first All-Ireland senior hurling title in 1981.

A year later, he had fully mastered the art of juggling top-class careers in both codes and brought that same level of athleticism to the footballers when they ended Kerry's five-in-a-row dreams.

Holden and Currams were the privileged ones. Other dual players soldiered with their counties for years in both codes for lesser rewards.

Pat Dunny, one of the finest footballers ever to play for Kildare and an All-Ireland Under-21 winner in 1965, was also an outstanding hurler. He won four Railway Cup medals with Leinster between 1971 and 1975, mixing comfortably with some of the legendary figures in the game.

Michael 'Babs' Keating won every honour possible with the Tipperary hurlers in a glittering career, but he will proudly point out that he also won a Railway Cup football medal for Munster in 1972, lining out alongside such legends as Mick O'Dwyer and Mick O'Connell.

Examples of dual service can be found all over the island. The names of Derry's Henry and Séamus Downey, Brian McGilligan, Kieran McKeever are etched in the football history of that county. They were stalwarts of the football team that brought the Sam Maguire Cup to the county for the first time in 1993, but they all gave years of service to the Derry hurlers. Kevin McCloy was the All-Star full-back and a National League winner with the footballers in 2008 and also won an Ulster senior hurling title in 2000.

Other players, like Carlow's Paddy Quirke, would not get the opportunity to play for All-Ireland prizes. But Quirke had a great career in both codes and won a Railway Cup hurling medal with Leinster in 1979, as a team-mate of Mick Holden. He travelled with All-Stars teams as a dual player, capable of slotting into the football or hurling team as required.

All of those great dual players watched in admiration in September 1990 when the only man to win All-Ireland senior medals in both codes in the same year in the history of the GAA took his special place of honour.

Teddy McCarthy always reckoned it was in the early days of summer 1979 – certainly before his fifteenth birthday on 1 July – when he first successfully manufactured an encounter with Jack Lynch.

There was a ritual amongst the youngsters around Glanmire in those days when the big state car was spotted arriving in the village on the outskirts of Cork city carrying the taoiseach on visits to old friends.

'I don't know if he was still the taoiseach at the time, but he was always the taoiseach to us,' McCarthy would later reflect.

Not only was Lynch a statesman and politician, he was a sporting hero – a hurler and footballer whose name was etched into the history of the GAA in Cork and nationally.

Word would spread quickly through the narrow streets and alleyways of Glanmire and Riverstown that Lynch was on his way. They knew his destination would be Michael McCarthy's home at the end of the terrace and that other heroes of the past would also be gathering.

Lynch had left Cork decades earlier to complete his legal studies in Dublin before embarking on the career that would make him one of the most recognisable figures in Irish history. But he had never forgotten his roots or the friends made while growing up in Cork. McCarthy, a hurley-maker for both Lynch and Christy Ring in their playing days, was one of those old friends. He was also a mentor to the young hurlers and footballers of Glanmire.

Teddy McCarthy had been reared in St Joseph's View on tales of the deeds of men like Lynch who had won five All-Ireland senior hurling championships with Cork between 1941 and 1946. In 1945, when Cork's hurling domination was briefly broken, Lynch was one of the dual stars who won an All-Ireland football medal.

And when Teddy's dream of attending North Monastery secondary school in the city was realised in 1978, with the intervention of influential family friends who convinced the school governors that academia could be nurtured in the young man, he was further entranced by the Lynch legend.

Around the school, photos were displayed of North Mon hurling teams that had won the Harty Cup, the Munster Colleges senior hurling championship. Lynch featured prominently as a member of the winning teams in 1934, 1935 and 1936. In the latter two years, North Mon also won the Munster Colleges football title with Lynch playing a starring role at midfield.

On that day in 1979, which McCarthy remembered with childlike enthusiasm as clear-skyed and warm, the word spread like wildfire that the taoiseach had arrived. Lynch, Michael McCarthy and another old friend, Bertie Murphy, sat around the stump of an old oak tree and engaged in fond reminiscence and chatter.

Teddy grabbed his hurley and ball from beside the front door of the family home and chased off down the street, belting the ball in front of him.

'When I got to the end of the terrace, I would make sure to hit the ball across the road towards the tree stump. I would go after it and hope that the men would notice me and that the great man might say something to me.

'Of course, they knew what I was at. I did it every time he came over a period of about ten years, so I wasn't very subtle about it. On this particular day, I went through my usual routine. However, when I went to retrieve the ball Michael stopped me from chasing away.

'"Hold it there, young Mac," he instructed. Then, he turned to the taoiseach and said, "Jack, this lad is going to be a good one." I ran off happier than I had ever been in my life.'

Teddy didn't just worship Lynch. He was in awe of Cork's dual heroes, like Jimmy Barry-Murphy, Ray Cummins, Denis Coughlan and Brian Murphy. They had won a football All-Ireland with Cork in 1973 and were stars of the hurling team that dominated the game in the mid-1970s, winning three Liam MacCarthy Cups in succession in 1976, 1977 and 1978.

And when he left North Mon, laden with honours, and embarked on a successful Under-21 career with Cork, McCarthy began to realise that he would get the chance to emulate the feats of those stars. That Barry-Murphy would be a team-mate when he won his first All-Ireland hurling title in 1986 was almost beyond comprehension.

In five incredible years between his debut in 1986 with the hurlers and the completion of the double in the 1990 All-Ireland championships, McCarthy not only matched his heroes. He did something that no one had done before – and something that no one is ever expected to repeat – he became the only man to win All-Ireland senior hurling and football titles in the same year.

After the hurling success of 1986, McCarthy played in five All-Ireland football finals, including a replay, over the next four seasons. Cork lost to Meath in 1987 and 1988 (replay) but won the title in 1989, beating Mayo.

He was busy with both the hurlers and footballers as the championships began in 1990. Denis Walsh was also a member of both panels. The team managers – Canon Michael O'Brien (hurling) and Billy Morgan (football) – enjoyed a good working relationship and devised a structured training programme for the two players to follow.

Canon O'Brien, popularly known amongst the hurlers as the 'Padre', agreed in late June that the two players would spend a weekend away with the footballers for some intensive training and to play two games. Mayo provided the opposition for the first of those games. There was no holding back. Players on both teams were eager to make an impression.

Teddy went for a trademark high catch. He leaped higher than everyone else and won the ball cleanly. As he landed, his right ankle crumpled. A five-week lay-off and a lot of mental anguish followed.

He missed the Munster final victories; he played a small part in the All-Ireland hurling semi-final but did not play in the football semi-final. He watched that football match from home and worried that his injury would prevent him from taking any further part in either campaign.

The doctors, the physios and – critically – the team managers kept faith and were patient. He was fit for the hurling final against Galway and the clamour began. He became the centre of attention, not something he was comfortable with, but he was fortunate. On trips abroad, to Australia and New York, he had become well known to the media personnel covering Gaelic games and was friendly with some. He engaged in the pre-match build-ups and was then left alone.

When the hurlers won the All-Ireland the hype intensified. Coach Morgan and his team-mates provided a protective cordon, as did his family. Meath, the old enemy, were again the opposition.

His good friend Colm O'Neill was dismissed in the first-half, but Cork responded to adversity. His midfield partner, Shea Fahy, played a blinder. As did Larry Tompkins. Teddy made a big contribution too. And when it was all over, he gave Fahy a huge hug and headed for the dressing room.

Years later, he recounted in his autobiography *Teddy Boy* what the next few minutes entailed.

I took more belts than I had throughout the entire championship. I felt none of them. Complete strangers hugged me. A few kissed me. At one stage, I thought I would be smothered. I wriggled free.

In the mayhem I tried to put my thoughts together. History had just been made and I was central to that. Cork had become the first county to win the All-Ireland senior football and hurling championships in the same season and I was the only player to feature on both teams.

My old pal Denis Walsh had played on the hurling team but had not been able to secure a starting place on the football team. He deserved enormous credit for his achievements, but the spotlight was focused on me because I played in both finals.

When it was all over and the supporters descended on the team, I felt a need to be alone. I don't think it was just for myself. I thought about the other players. I'd had my moment two weeks beforehand and I didn't want my presence to distract from what my team-mates had done.

These guys were my friends and they had soldiered hard over the years for everything they had achieved. And they had achieved a great deal, more than any other bunch of Cork footballers had ever achieved in history. They deserved their glory and I would not allow anything to affect that. I decided, there and then, to head for the dressing room.

The steward at the dressing-room gate was surprised to see me coming. 'Are you not going up for the presentation, Teddy?' he asked.

'I'll be back out in a minute,' I told him. I had no intention of coming back out, but I didn't expect the surprise that lay in store.

Expecting to be alone, I was momentarily taken aback when I noticed someone else in the dressing room. 'Who the hell—?' The thought ended abruptly.

One of my all-time heroes – Jack Lynch.

The former Taoiseach, the Cork GAA legend, stood there, pipe in mouth and a big smile lighting up his famous face.

'Congratulations, Teddy. What an achievement. You should be very proud of yourself.'

I was speechless. I think I said thanks.

The front page of the *Sunday Independent* on the morning of 18 March 1962 was heavily devoted to reportage of President Éamon de Valera's visit to the Vatican for an audience with Pope John XXIII on St Patrick's Day. The marriage break-up of Hollywood stars Tony Curtis and Janet Leigh also got a few lines on the bottom of the page!

But the main photograph adorning the broadsheet page, above the fold, was that of a handsome young man reclining with his arms behind his head and a tender smile on his face. The headline above the photo read: 'Two-game hero Foley goes to bed at nine.'

The 200-word report told the story of a unique achievement. It is one of the most celebrated examples of the feats of the dual player who excels in both hurling and football.

Des Foley, from a well-known north Dublin sporting family, who would later enter national politics, had just become the first –

and still only – player to win interprovincial medals in hurling and football on the same day when Leinster beat Munster and Ulster respectively in the Railway Cup finals at Croke Park.

That live television coverage of the second half of the hurling game and the entire football game was allowed for the first time added to the sense of occasion and national interest.

The *Sunday Independent* unnamed correspondent covered Foley's remarkable day:

> *This young man has every right to relax. You see him at the fireside of his home, Leafield, Kinsealy, Malahide. He is the amazing Des Foley, age twenty-one.*
>
> *When he woke up yesterday morning he had a severe cold – so bad that he ate scarcely any breakfast and an even smaller lunch. Then he went to Croke Park and played a big part in Leinster's win in the Railway Cup hurling final. When that game was over, he changed into another jersey and played a prominent part in Leinster's victory over Ulster in the Railway Cup football final.*
>
> *His name will go down in GAA annals as the first man to win two Railway Cup medals on the same day and on the day Telefís Éireann made history by telecasting their first live transmission from Croke Park. But that is not all. Today at Croke Park he plays football for Ireland against a Combined Universities side. Last night, Des Foley went to bed shortly after 9pm. Wouldn't you?*
>
> *FOOTNOTE: His mother, Mrs Elizabeth Foley, thinks television is wonderful. She watched the second half telecast*

of the Croke Park hurling game and the screening of all the football match in which her son played.

Quite what his brother Lar thought of this eulogy to his younger brother – two years separated them – was often the subject of banter amongst their team-mates at both the St Vincent's club, with the Dublin football and hurling teams and with the Leinster selections. Lar had played with the Leinster hurlers on St Patrick's Day alongside Des, but mention of his participation was restricted to the sports pages.

Like so many other young boys growing up in Ireland in the 1940s and 1950s it was natural to embrace both games played under the GAA banner. Both of the Foley brothers were very talented – Lar was physically imposing while Des was regarded as the more stylish. They didn't come from what might be described as a typical GAA background – their father Patrick played soccer for a number of clubs in Dublin, including Bohemians, and their brother Anthony played for both Dundalk and Bohemians.

Home was Kinsealy and the boys went to school in Fairview and came under the influence of the mentors at the St Vincent's GAA club. Their ascent to special status was swift. Both were members of the Dublin minor football team that won the 1956 All-Ireland championship. Lar was captain.

Two years later, Des was the All-Ireland-winning minor captain and Lar was right full-back on the Dublin senior team that also celebrated championship success in a rare All-Ireland double for the county.

In 1961, they lined out for the Dublin hurlers in the All-Ireland final, losing narrowly to Tipperary. And then they won an All-Ireland senior title together when the footballers beat Galway in 1963. Lar was full-back, while Des captained the team from midfield.

Des Foley's special status as one of the great dual players in the GAA's history was cemented on the national holiday in 1962. It was heralded by one of the leading GAA writers of the era, John D. Hickey, a native of Tipperary, in the pages of the *Irish Independent*.

> *St Patrick's Day 1962 will long be remembered as the day that Dublin and Leinster midfielder Des Foley mocked the might of Munster hurling and then, as if to set the seal on a magnificent day that saw him make GAA history, he played a vital part in rescuing the eastern province's footballers from seemingly imminent defeat against Ulster.*
>
> *The St Vincent's player turned in a tour-de-force in helping Leinster to defeat Munster, holders of the hurling trophy since 1957 and, although his part in forging victory over Ulster, to give his province their first Railway double since 1954 and fourth in all, was not as spectacular, he also earned much of the credit for that success.*
>
> *Tormented by his rampaging against Theo English in the hurling match, the Munster selectors sent a 'message' to Liam Devaney just before the interval to take on the Leinster colossus. A half-time huddle saw the men behind the southern team change their minds and, on the resumption, Terry Kelly*

was deputed to 'mark' the Dublin man. But, for all the move achieved, it might never have been made and Munster's last despairing effort – the transfer of Jimmy Smyth to midfield – was equally ineffective.

Foley's hurling activities, naturally, took a toll on his stamina and he had an inconspicuous first-half at midfield in the football match. The back-room boys wisely switched him to full-forward on the restart but when Leinster's midfield ills appeared likely to lay them low, Foley was recanted to the area after he had got his second wind, and his return, as I saw the game, meant all the difference between victory and defeat.

How fitting it was that the young Dublin man, who is still on the threshold of his career, should become the first player to win two Railway Cup medals on the same day.

Students at Fordham University in the Bronx, New York, especially those with specific interest in the sciences, will be familiar with the name William Spain.

Within the hallowed halls of learning at Fordham lies the William Spain Seismic Observatory, named in honour of a twenty-two-year-old physics student who died suddenly while attending the college in the early 1920s.

Since it opened in 1927, the observatory has been, according to *The New York Times*, 'an unlikely place to measure the earth's vibrations: inside a musty room 28 feet below the comings and goings of a borough of 1.3 million known for many things, but not tectonic activity. Yet over the years the William Spain Seismic

Observatory has become a respected, if little-known, registrar of the world's natural and unnatural trembling, including earthquakes, China's first atomic explosion in 1964 and the more local seismic occurrences, Grand Central-bound trains.'

The observatory was built as a memorial to the popular young student William Lavelle Spain and was funded by his father, also William, a prominent businessman in New York in the early decades of the twentieth century and the first man to win All-Ireland senior championship medals in Gaelic football and hurling.

William J. Spain, recorded in most historical texts relating to his sporting achievements as W.J. Spain, was a member of the Limerick team that won the first All-Ireland football title in 1887 (the final was played in 1888) and, two years later, was on the Dublin team that won the All-Ireland hurling championship.

Spain was born in the townland of Monafin in Kilruane, County Tipperary, in 1865. He moved to nearby Limerick in his late teens to serve his apprenticeship as a draper. The Commercials club was founded around the same time as the official formation of the GAA in 1884 and it attracted many players from the drapery business.

Some reports indicate that Spain had moved to Dublin to work in a major store prior to 1887, but he continued to line out for Commercials, who represented Limerick in the first All-Ireland championship. They beat the Louth representatives, Dundalk Young Irelanders, in the final played in what is now the Dublin suburb of Clonskeagh, on 29 April 1888.

Spain was one of the stars of the final, scoring the only goal of the game in Limerick's 1–4 to 0–3 victory. But the result could not be confirmed at the final whistle as Young Irelanders lodged an immediate objection and claimed Spain was not eligible to play for Commercials.

It was alleged that he had also played for Kickhams, the Dublin club, during 1887, something that was denied by Spain and Commercials officials. The matter came before the first meeting of the GAA's Central Council on the following day, Monday, 30 April, held at 15 Gloucester Street in Dublin.

Presiding over the meeting was the GAA's first president, Maurice Davin. The council decided 'on the evidence before it not to disqualify the player referred to'.

It was a decision and a match result that did not please the correspondent from the *Dundalk Democrat*. And he was not happy with the referee, Mr John Cullinane.

> *On two occasions, when there was a moral certainty of the Young Irelanders scoring, one of the Limerick men threw his arms round the neck of the Young Irelander running with the ball. For this violation of the rules, the referee gave a free kick, but this was not at all equivalent to the advantage which the Dundalk team would have had, were it not for the foul play of their opponents.*
>
> *As to the impartiality of the referee, his enthusiastic cheering when the Commercials scored a goal was, in itself, sufficient to deprive him of the confidence of the Young Irelanders.*

By 1889, Spain was certainly living in Dublin and was perfectly eligible to play hurling for Kickhams when they represented the county and beat Clare (represented by Tulla) in the final, 5–1 to 1–6. Spain scored three goals.

A year later, he moved to the United States. While building up a very successful business in the silk trade, he continued to play Gaelic games and is recorded as one of the players in a Gaelic football exhibition played at Madison Square Garden in December 1890.

Spain and his wife Mary had two children, a daughter Melissa and their son William, and lived at a prestigious Park Avenue address, number 311 according to some sources. They also had a home in Florida. The observatory in young William's name, according to *The New York Times*: 'Sits at the edge of a wide lawn in the center of campus, next to Freeman Hall, home of the department of physics. That Gothic stone building looks more like a country chapel than a seismic station.'

Announcing the donation to the college in its Sunday edition on 16 January 1927, the newspaper observed: 'The gift or Mr and Mrs Spain will make the Fordham Station the most important on the Atlantic Seaboard.'

There are no further records of Spain's involvement with the GAA in New York, though there are many references to his efforts to help Irish immigrants. Family members from Tipperary and Limerick followed him to New York and worked for his company.

His sister Nora married and settled in Limerick and was the

grandmother of Donogh O'Malley, who served as minster for health and minister for education during the 1960s.

In the early years of the GAA championships, there were a number of dual winners. Cork's population and the manner in which young men embraced both hurling and football ensured that the county provided the largest representation in this category.

Billy Mackessy was the first to achieve the feat. Later to become a successful businessman, who also enjoyed sporting success with his greyhounds, he won a hurling title in 1903 and a football title eight years later in 1911.

The Grace brothers from Tullaroan in Kilkenny were the most famous siblings in Ireland during the first two decades of the twentieth century. Between them, Pierce, Jack and Dick Grace won fifteen senior championship medals. Pierce won five of those, two in football with Dublin in 1906 and 1907 and three hurling championships with Kilkenny in 1911, 1912 and 1913.

Pierce left Kilkenny after finishing school to study medicine in Dublin. He joined his brother Jack, who worked in Dublin, at the Kickhams club. Jack was already established as a Dublin footballer of renown. He won All-Ireland titles in 1901 and 1902 and was a team-mate of Pierce in 1906 and 1907. Jack won a fifth medal with Dublin in 1909.

Pierce returned to Kilkenny to work in St Canice's Hospital and, with his younger brother Dick, played with Kilkenny's three-in-a-row-winning hurling team between 1911 and 1913. Dick also won another title in 1922, bringing the family haul to fifteen medals.

Paddy Mackey and Seán O'Kennedy were not just team-mates but housemates. Mackey, a native of Kilkenny, had moved to Wexford as a teenager for work and was given accommodation by the O'Kennedy family in New Ross. It is speculated that this was designed to persuade Mackey to declare for Wexford.

They won their first All-Ireland senior titles as hurlers in 1910. Together they won three football championships in 1915, 1916 and 1917, while Mackey went on to win another medal in 1918.

Dublin's Frank Burke was one of the more colourful characters of the era. Although born in Kildare, he was educated at St Enda's, a Dublin boarding school, where he first became influenced by Pádraig Pearse. He was politically active and was involved in the Easter Rising in 1916, after which he was interned in England before being released in December 1916.

Both as a student in UCD and later working as a teacher, Burke won All-Ireland hurling medals in 1917 and 1920 and was on the Dublin football team for their successes in 1921, 1922 and 1923.

He was also playing for Dublin against Tipperary on Bloody Sunday – 21 November 1920 – when Michael Hogan was shot by British armed forces.

Leonard McGrath was born to Irish parents in the Australian state of Queensland, but returned to Ireland after the family fell on hard times and he grew up in Galway. He wasn't just a sportsman, he was also a renowned actor and singer. And he was once banned from the GAA in the 1920s for playing rugby with UCG.

He played on the Galway hurling team that won the 1923 championship. Although small in height, he was renowned for his high fielding and won an All-Ireland football medal in 1925.

Gerard O'Kelly-Lynch is not a name that will be immediately familiar to hurling or football followers, outside Sligo at least.

But O'Kelly-Lynch is one of those extraordinarily talented sportsmen who combined careers as an inter-county hurler and footballer almost against the odds. For the record, Ger, as he is known to friends, has won a Lory Meagher Cup title and a Rackard Cup title with Sligo hurlers and it is in the winning of the former that his career can be put in perspective.

On 23 June 2018, Sligo played Lancashire in the Lory Meagher Cup final in Croke Park, throw-in at midday. O'Kelly-Lynch took his place at left full-forward as Sligo won the title by 4–15 to 2–20, snatching victory with a last-minute goal. His brother Tony was a second-half substitute.

Ger stayed around for the presentation, had some photos taken and then headed to the dressing room to collect his belongings.

He left Croke Park and made the three-hour, 210-kilometre journey to Markievicz Park in Sligo for an All-Ireland football qualifier game against Armagh, throw-in 6p.m. He didn't start but was called on as a blood substitute after fourteen minutes. He was reintroduced as a sub fourteen minutes into the second half and played to the end of the game, which Sligo lost.

One year later, almost to the day, his schedule was slightly less hectic. On Saturday, 22 June, he lined out at left half-forward for the hurlers in the Nicky Rackard Cup final and scored 2–1 as they beat Armagh 2–14 to 2–13. Tony played on the other wing. Then, the following day, Ger travelled to Tullamore to play in the All-Ireland football qualifier against Offaly, starting at left half-back and played for fifty-one minutes before being rested.

O'Kelly-Lynch is a shining example of the commitment and dedication displayed by dual players everywhere. But it is also becoming very rare and there are indications that the era of the dual player, at inter-county level at least, is coming to an end.

It hasn't happened overnight. The signs have been clear for a long time. Derry footballer Brendan Rogers tried to mix playing both games but found the demands eventually took their toll. Talking to Sky Sports in 2020, he explained his predicament.

> *It's very logistically hard. That [playing both games] was taking a mental toll. There was more than just going to training and recovering from training. There was so much more in the background of organising and ringing people, asking when can I train and when can I not train. Can I go to this game? Can I not? If I play a football game on the Saturday, do I have to get in a car and go over to the hurling game on the Sunday?*
>
> *When really you might need a break, and you don't know how tired you can be ... that mental strain while you're actually*

living your own life. I tore the sole of my foot. It took nearly ten months to get over that.

It took me so long to get over that. It was so difficult from game to game to say how I was going to be fine. Some weeks I'd be fine, and then on other weeks it would flare up on me and I'd be out. I was starting to think, is it the body telling me it's too much? There were other factors – time – but ultimately when the body is telling you no, you've got to listen.

Galway's Alan Kerins was one of the most high-profile dual players in the late 1990s and into the 2000s. A winner of an All-Ireland senior football title in 2001, he also lined out in the hurling final that year but was unable to add to the minor and Under-21 medals he had won earlier in his career.

By 2005, he had chosen to play hurling only and was on the team that reached the All-Ireland final, losing to Cork. A year earlier, Conor Hayes, the Galway hurling manager and former All-Ireland-winning captain, expressed his concerns in an interview with the *Irish Examiner* about the difficulties facing dual players in the modern era.

If a dual player is to give full commitment to both teams nowadays, he's going to be training six nights a week, playing at least one game a week if not two. It's not on anymore, not for an amateur player trying to hold down a full-time job.

The demands are totally different, incompatible even, with football requiring extreme physical fitness while hurling demands a lot more time on skills. It's a crazy schedule now for anyone, probably the best you could hope for is that a fella concentrates on one, does all his training in that code, then just plays his games with the others and if he's good enough, he holds his place.

Alan [Kerins] is a superb athlete and he tried to keep both going at the very top level, but he ended up probably costing himself in the football.

Kerins continued playing hurling and football at club level and won All-Ireland club titles in both grades with different clubs – football in 2006 with Salthill-Knocknacarra and hurling in 2011 with Clarinbridge.

In his autobiography, Teddy McCarthy expressed his concerns about the future for the dual player.

I fear for the future of the dual player. I hope I'm wrong, but all the signs are that he is an endangered species.

When they introduced the back-door system to the championship, they sounded the death knell for the dual player. And now that the back-door system applies at club level, I predict that the dual player will be extinct in our lifetime.

I know I wouldn't have lasted as long as I did, had there been a qualifier system in the championship when I played. I wonder if I would have got my opportunity to win my unique place in the history of the GAA. By 1990, I would have a lot of mileage completed. I was suffering injuries with the schedule I had. Imagine the demands if there had been qualifiers to contend with. It would have been impossible.

Dual Jewels

I fear for the dual player and that is a crying shame. Everyone who loves Gaelic games loves to see the best players playing and that is not possible any more. More and more they are being forced to make choices because they simply cannot fit in all the games.

Forget about my own career and 1990. Wouldn't it have been a terrible pity if the public had not been able to see Jimmy Barry-Murphy and Ray Cummins playing football? I was only a kid when Jimmy played in 1973, but he inspired another generation with the way he played the game.

We seem to be forever trying to increase the number of games our players are playing. It is almost at an unsustainable level now for players sticking to one code only. It is impossible for a player to try and combine the two.

The list of dual players in the past is endless. I wonder will there be a list in the future at all.

4 OUR GREATEST DAYS
COUNTY BY COUNTY

I can't think of a better position or a better place to be in right now anywhere in the world than where I stand.
Peter Canavan in his victory speech on the Hogan Stand after captaining Tyrone to their first All-Ireland senior football triumph in 2003.

Golden days – those days that are just so much better than others – remain the lifeblood of any sport.

The recollections below emanate from various sources – first-time success, a return to glory after a long absence, an accumulation of triumphs over a certain period or even a one-off, when the spotlight beams down on a county and a warm glow unifies the community in a unique way.

Since the first playing of the All-Ireland football and hurling championships in 1887 and the introduction of the National Leagues in 1925, all thirty-two counties, plus teams in

Britain and America, have at some stage basked in the glory of achievement.

It is not just the superpowers in the two codes that have had reason to celebrate. The range and grandeur of their triumphs may be greater than the rest, but it's all relative. Lower-ranked counties may be light on titles, but they have all had days that meant so much to them.

Population imbalances and various other factors – including tradition, competition from other sports and even a rivalry between football and hurling within a county – are also important factors in establishing the success pyramid. Despite all that, every county has its special times. For example, neither Fermanagh nor Wicklow have ever won a provincial senior football title, but the supporters will still identify days when they were bursting with pride.

Pinpointing the greatest day is easier in some counties than others. Among the highly successful, it's a matter of choosing the standout occasion from an extensive range of options. At the lower end of the achievement scale, the choices are more limited, but no less interesting.

It's a question of identifying the day when a team, often against the odds, made the whole county feel really good about itself.

Like all other debates on all-time rankings, there will be differences of opinion as to the best day for any county, but that merely adds to the intrigue. We offer our choices for all thirty-two counties, plus London and New York. We have given first what we regard as the best overall day for each county, which varies between football and hurling depending on which is the stronger.

ANTRIM

Hurling

6 August 1989, All-Ireland semi-final, Croke Park

Antrim 4–15 Offaly 1–15

Over the previous three years, Antrim had lost semi-finals to Tipperary, Kilkenny and Cork by an average of seven points – close enough to give them continued hope, but not sufficient to unduly worry the opposition. The Leinster and Munster champions would have felt that they could always find a way of quelling an Antrim rebellion, however spirited it might be.

So, when Offaly led Antrim by four points at half-time in the 1989 semi-final, they appeared to be poised for a routine win, possibly even by a sizeable margin. But it didn't happen. In one of the most extraordinary performances ever witnessed in Croke Park, Antrim – for whom Aidan McCarry scored 2–4 and Olcan McFetridge 2–3 – overpowered the Leinster champions in a second half they won by 3–9 to 0–5.

There was a lot more than sheer determination to their game. Offaly had far greater big-day experience than Antrim, but Jim Nelson's side overcame that handicap and played at such a high tempo that they looked like a team who were convinced something different was about to unfold.

The reward was a stunning victory, and Antrim's first qualification for the All-Ireland final since 1943. The 1989 semi-final win is still recalled in Antrim as their greatest hurling achievement, a victory for a special brand of resilience from a county that would have felt it didn't always get the respect it deserved from hurling strongholds elsewhere. They did that day as the Offaly team displayed sportsmanship at its best by lining up to applaud them off the pitch afterwards.

The atmosphere in Antrim in the four weeks between the semi-final and final was something never previously experienced in the county. It was as if everyone had been lifted high on a tidal wave of emotion and remained determined to savour every precious moment.

Massive media coverage accompanied Antrim's preparations for the final, as every angle of the romantic story of how the underdogs finally had their day was explored in minute detail. It was the ultimate promotional asset for a county that had spent so long trying to make an impact.

Unfortunately for Antrim, that was as good as it got. A far more experienced Tipperary team were too strong in the final, winning by 4–24 to 3–9.

Antrim were very disappointed with their performance, but then the build-up and the All-Ireland final occasion may have got to them, which was perfectly understandable. Still, nothing could take away from the memories they created in the semi-final.

Antrim N. Patterson; G. O'Kane, T. Donnelly, D. Donnelly; J. McNaughton, D. McKinley, L. McKeegan; P. McKillen, D. McMullan; B. Donnelly, A. McCarry, O. McFetridge; D. Armstrong, C. Barr, T. McNaughton
Sub D. McNaughton for McMullan

Football

14 September 1969, All-Ireland Under-21 final, Croke Park

Antrim 1–8 Roscommon 0–10

In the 140-year history of the GAA, only one Antrim county team has won an All-Ireland football title, the honour resting with the Under-21s in 1969, a year in which they displayed remarkable survival skills in no less than four of their six games.

It was a tense time in the Six Counties with the outbreak of the Troubles, a development that the Antrim players still believe brought them together in a special bond as they pursued the big prize.

They were certainly a united group, a quality that enabled them to work their way through the closest of encounters – including a one-point win over Derry (the 1968 All-Ireland winners), a two-point win over Down in the Ulster final, and one-point wins over Cork and Roscommon respectively in the All-Ireland semi-final and final.

In a rather strange scheduling arrangement, Antrim had to travel to the Cork Athletic Grounds to play Cork in the semi-final, a journey undertaken by plane. It was the first time many of the team had ever flown, but it didn't prove a distraction as they nudged to a one-point – 3–7 to 1–12 – win over a highly rated Cork team that included Ray Cummins, Dinny Long, Ned Kirby and Jimmy Barrett, all of whom went on to win All-Ireland senior medals in 1973.

Roscommon, captained by Dermot Earley, awaited Antrim in the final and, once again, they edged to victory by the slimmest of margins in a game where Andy McCallin, who became their first

All-Star in 1971, scored 1–5. As the first Antrim team to win an All-Ireland football title, it ensured them a special place in the county's affections, one that has lasted to this day.

Antrim R. McIlroy; D. Burns, S. Killough, M. McGranaghan; J. Mullan, B. Millar, M. Culbert; L. Boyle, T Dunlop; A. Hamill, G. McCann, G. Nellis; A. McCallin, G. Dillon, D.J. McBrogan **Sub** G. Pollock for Culbert

ARMAGH

Football

22 September 2002, All-Ireland final, Croke Park

Armagh 1–12 Kerry 0–14

Three minutes into stoppage time, referee John Bannon blows the final whistle. Armagh are All-Ireland champions for the first time, having beaten Kerry by the narrowest of margins. Manager Joe Kernan feels a strange sensation welling inside him.

'Deliverance day had arrived. For a few seconds, I felt as if I was on my own, surrounded by a serene ocean of relief but, of course, it didn't last long. Suddenly, the hordes arrived in an orange torrent to begin the celebrations that would go on for months,' he wrote in his autobiography *Without a Shadow of a Doubt.*

In those very same moments, Armagh people in Croke Park, back home and in many places across the globe were having their own special thoughts as they absorbed the emotion and the significance of what had unfolded. Their county had finally joined an elite club.

Not only that, they had done so by the toughest possible means, beating Tyrone, reigning National League champions, in a replay, Fermanagh, Donegal, Sligo (replay), Dublin and Kerry.

Beating the latter two by a point each was especially satisfying. 'They were the big two in All-Ireland terms. There could be no question now about our right to be All-Ireland champions,' Kernan wrote.

Not that anybody would have disputed it. Armagh had been a slow burn but had finally reached boiling point. After a lengthy slump in the 1990s – they had won only two championship games in five seasons (1994–1998) – the relaunch began under joint-managers Brian McAlinden and Brian Canavan in 1999 when they won the Ulster title for the first time in seventeen years. They were captained by current GAA president Jarlath Burns.

They lost that All-Ireland semi-final to Meath, a fate that befell them again in 2000, this time against Kerry in a replay. Tyrone beat them in the 2001 Ulster championship in what was the first year of the All-Ireland qualifiers. They reached Round 3, losing to Galway by a point.

It was all very frustrating for Armagh, who watched three teams – Meath, Kerry and Galway – who beat them in 1999, 2000 and 2001 all go on to win the title. Still, other positive developments were feeding into a growing sense that the great day would come eventually.

Crossmaglen Rangers, with Kernan as manager, had won All-Ireland club titles in 1997, 1999 and 2000 and when a county vacancy arose at the end of the 2001 championship, Kernan was the obvious successor to McAlinden and Canavan. A year later, Armagh were All-Ireland champions after what was only the county's third appearance in the final.

The nature of Armagh's win over Kerry in 2002 underlined just how much their mentality had evolved and hardened after the disappointments of previous seasons. Having had Oisín McConville's penalty saved, they were four points behind at half-time. History shows that not many teams win an All-Ireland final if they're that much behind at the interval, but Armagh ignored the past and wrote their own script.

They restricted Kerry to three points in the second half and made the decisive break when McConville scored the game's only goal at the three-quarter-stage. Its impact was immense, sending a jolt of confidence through the entire team. This was new territory for them, but they negotiated it expertly and held Kerry at bay in a thrilling finish.

Captain Kieran McGeeney was later chosen as Footballer of the Year, while he and five others won All-Star awards. A year later, they had a chance to win successive titles, but lost the final to Tyrone by three points on a day that crowned the Red Hand's greatest year.

Armagh B. Tierney; E. McNulty, J. McNulty, F. Bellew; A. O'Rourke, K. McGeeney, A. McCann; J. Toal, P. McGrane; P. McKeever, J. McEntee, O. McConville; S. McDonnell, R. Clarke, D. Marsden
Subs B. O'Hagan for J. McEntee, T. McEntee for McKeever

Hurling

3 July 2010, Nicky Rackard Cup final, Croke Park
Armagh 3–15 London 3–14

There's something extra special about a first-time success, especially when it's achieved in such dramatic circumstances as Armagh's Nicky Rackard Cup win in 2010. They had experienced the disappointment of a two-point defeat by Roscommon in the 2007 final, but, three years later, it was all so different as they edged past London. They led by seven points in the first half before being pegged back by half-time. It was close all the way through the second half and into injury time when Paul Breen, who finished on 2–4, scored the winning point.

Winning a competition that had been introduced five years earlier was a significant achievement for Armagh and, a year later, they reached the Ulster final for the first time since 1946 when they beat Down in the semi-final. Unfortunately for them, Antrim were too good in the final, and they lost by eight points.

Armagh J. Burke; B. Mallon, P. Gaffney, F. McMullan; B. McCormack, E. McDonnell, N. Curry; P. McArdle, B. Green; R. Gaffney, J. Corvan, K. McKernan; P. McCormack, G. Enright, P. Green
Subs C. Carvill for McArdle, M. Lennon for McKernan

CARLOW

Football

30 July 1944, Leinster final, Athy

Carlow 2–6 Dublin 1–6

2024 is the eightieth anniversary of Carlow's best football achievement. At the start of the 1940s, Carlow was one of only two counties in Leinster, alongside Longford, who had never contested a provincial senior football final. Their briefest flirtation with success was at junior level where they had been Leinster champions in 1933.

But, in 1941, a new and ambitious group of players was assembled and began to show promise. They reached the Leinster final for the first time later that year, losing by eleven points to Dublin.

A year later, the margin between the two teams was reduced to just two points. And when Dublin went on to win the All-Ireland title that year, there was a growing belief within Carlow – and especially among the squad – that they had the capacity and ability to make the big breakthrough.

Disappointment followed in 1943 when they lost by two points to Laois in the Leinster semi-final. But, by then, the team had become seriously competitive and were quietly confident about their prospects at the start of 1944. A victory over Kildare, after a replay, was followed by successes against Laois and Wexford, which qualified them for another final against familiar opposition, Dublin.

The final, fixed for Athy, created an unprecedented fervour in the county. *The Nationalist* and *Leinster Times* provided a colourful depiction of match day.

'From an early hour, the trek to Athy from Carlow began. Supporters from the southern end of the county poured into Carlow, where they heard Mass before finishing their journey to Athy. The number that left the capital town must have been a record, as on the road we saw people of all classes and creeds in the apparently never ending stream of cyclists, and horse-drawn vehicles. For seats in the latter as much as one pound was cheerfully paid. In the motley crowd, we noticed a cheerful party on a bay bogey and another lot in an ancient-covered car.'

An estimated 15,000 people crammed into the ground, situated on the edge of Athy town. The Carlow supporters might have despaired during the first half as Dublin sauntered into a 0–5 to 0–1 lead, Carlow's only score coming in the tenth minute from corner-forward Jimmy Rea.

Gradually, the tide turned. Carlow's midfielders Luke Kelly and Jim Morris began to dominate the area and goals from Rea and John Doyle levelled the game with ten minutes remaining. Doyle's accuracy from play and frees gave them the advantage and they held out for what remains Carlow's only senior provincial title.

'The opinion was expressed by many competent judges that it was the fastest and best Leinster final played for many a long year. As one old player remarked, it was played at the same speed as a first-class hurling match,' was the verdict of *The Nationalist*.

Carlow lost by two points to Kerry in the All-Ireland semi-final and have not reached a Leinster final since.

Carlow J. Quinlan; J. Lawler, J. Archbold, P. Farrell; P. Whelan, B. O'Rourke, E. Joyce; L. Kelly, J. Morris; J. Moore, M. Byrne, W. Hosey; P. Sullivan, J. Doyle, J. Rea
Sub J. Darcy for Joyce

Hurling

1 July 2018, Joe McDonagh Cup final, Croke Park
Carlow 2–26 Westmeath 1–24

Carlow, Ireland's second-smallest county, is an enigma. Despite having to choose from a vastly smaller pool of players compared to some of its neighbours, it continues to field competitive teams in both football and hurling. And its proudest day in hurling was surely in July 2018 when they became the first winners of the Joe McDonagh Cup.

Not only did it make them the Tier 2 champions, it also earned them promotion to the top level. And they did it in style with an emphatic victory over Westmeath.

It was Carlow's third major success in two years. In 2017, they had captured the Christy Ring Cup to qualify for the inaugural Joe McDonagh Cup competition. And, in the spring of 2018, they won the National Hurling League Division 2A title, a victory that set them up for the Joe McDonagh Cup campaign.

Coached by former Tipperary All-Ireland winner and All-Star Colm Bonnar, they won four of their five group games, beating Kerry, Meath, Laois and Westmeath. Their only loss was to Antrim, but they qualified for the final against Westmeath in a game where goals from Chris Nolan and James Doyle, allied to a ten-point contribution from Denis Murphy, secured the title.

Carlow B. Tracey; A. Corcoran, P. Doyle, M. Doyle; K. McDonald, R. Coady, D. English; J. Kavanagh, D. Byrne; J.M. Nolan, P. Coady, E. Byrne; J. Doyle, D. Murphy, C. Nolan
Subs R. Smithers for D. Byrne, S. Murphy for E. Byrne, R. Kelly for Kavanagh, J. Murphy for P. Coady, T. Joyce for C. Nolan

CAVAN

Football

26 September 1948 All-Ireland final, Croke Park
Cavan 4–5 Mayo 4–4

Nineteen of the thirty-two counties have won the All-Ireland senior football titles but, of those, only twelve have completed the two-in-a-row. That underlines just how difficult it is and illustrates why the 1948 win has to be classed as Cavan's greatest day.

Ulster titles came easily to Cavan, long before and long after the successive All-Ireland wins of 1947 and 1948. By 1945, they had won twenty-eight provincial titles and added another ten between then and 1969, after which a lengthy drought set in, the next not coming until 1997.

Dominating Ulster for so long was rewarding for Cavan, but it also came with a sense of frustration that they weren't winning more All-Ireland titles. By the mid-1940s, they had only won two (1933 and 1935).

That's why the 1947–1952 era is still so fondly recalled in Cavan. The 1947 All-Ireland win over Kerry had the unique aspect of being played in the Polo Grounds in New York to mark the centenary of the Great Famine. For obvious reasons, it attracted far more attention than usual and as Cavan won, their profile soared all over the country.

They retained the Ulster title without being really stretched in 1948, beating Down, Monaghan and Antrim. But what happened from there on was quite astonishing.

Paired with Louth in the All-Ireland semi-final, Cavan led by 1–10 to 0–1 at half-time and seemed set for the easiest of advances to the final. However, everything changed dramatically in a second half that Louth won by 4–1 to 0–4. They cut the deficit to a point late on, but Cavan countered with two points to win by 1–14 to 4–2.

'The closing half hour of this game will go down in GAA history as one of the most exciting ever witnessed,' reported the *Irish Press*.

The final against Mayo followed a near-identical pattern, with Cavan controlling the first half to such a degree that they led by 3–2 to 0–0 at half-time. They extended the advantage to twelve points early in the second half before the game veered in a completely different direction.

Cavan centre half-back and inspirational captain John Joe O'Reilly was forced off with an injury and his loss quickly became apparent. Their defensive security weakened, enabling Mayo to build up a powerful momentum that yielded four goals. The sides were level late on before Cavan full-forward Peter Donohue pointed a free to give them a 4–5 to 4–4 win.

Remarkably, Cavan had won an All-Ireland semi-final and final, despite conceding four goals in each game.

There was an unusual development off the field too on All-Ireland final day. A crowd of 74,645 were inside Croke Park but it was estimated that at least another 20,000 were locked outside. It all added to the drama of a final that, for the first time, produced eight goals. It has happened only once since then, when Dublin beat Armagh (5–12 to 3–6) in 1977.

Having secured the two-in-a-row in 1948, Cavan fancied their chances of adding another title a year later, especially when they retained the Ulster title with wins over Tyrone, Antrim and Armagh and eliminated Cork in the All-Ireland semi-final. However, that was as good as it got as they lost the final to Meath by four points.

Cavan D. Benson; W. Doonan, B. O'Reilly, P. Smith; P.J. Duke, J.J. O'Reilly, S. Deignan; P. Brady, V. Sherlock; T. Tighe, M. Higgins, J.J. Cassidy; J. Stafford, P. Donohoe, E. Carolan
Sub O.R. McGovern for J.J. O'Reilly

Hurling
1 April 2023 National League Division 3B final, Abbottstown
Cavan 0–17 Leitrim 0–16

Success in the lowest division of the National League may not appear very important in the stronger counties but it mattered greatly to those who drive hurling with such passion in Cavan. Six years after returning to the National League, following an eleven-year absence, they hit a big target by winning Division 3B and earning promotion to 3A. In a group with Longford, Leitrim, Lancashire and Warwickshire, Cavan won three of their four games, qualifying directly for the final. Their only defeat came against Warwickshire.

Leitrim were their opponents in a fiercely contested final, the outcome of which was in doubt right until the end. Ultimately, it was Cavan's day, edging home by 0–17 to 0–16.

Writing in the *Anglo Celt*, Paul Fitzpatrick summed up the county's improved fortunes succinctly. 'At one time, hurling in Cavan ranked somewhere between a rumour and a running joke, but such talk has been banished.'

Cavan D. Sheridan; S. Briody, D. Crudden, L. Óg Cooke; J. Barry, C. Sheanon, M. Hynes; D. Mulligan, N. Kenny; T. Leonard, C. Maher, C. Sheanon; S. Keating, D. Carney, C. Gargan
Subs R. Delaney for Keating, A. Sheridan for Gargan, M. Moffett for Carney, P. McCabe for Cooke, E. Shalvey for Leonard

CLARE

Hurling
3 September 1995, All-Ireland final, Croke Park
Clare 1–13 Offaly 2–8

In late 1994, a cloud of despair weighed heavily over Clare hurling. Outgoing manager Len Gaynor described that year's Munster hurling final defeat to Limerick – 0–25 to 2–10 – as 'one of the most disappointing days I have encountered in sport'. The *Clare Champion* reflected the sombre mood.

'Last Sunday's failure to neighbours Limerick will rank as one of Clare's greatest blows', was the verdict of journalist Séamus Hayes.

They had also lost the Munster final to Tipperary in 1993 and there was a sense that they would always be the 'nearly' county. That background contributed greatly to the joy of witnessing the dispersal of the clouds through the heady days of 1995, beginning with a major breakthrough when Clare won their first Munster senior hurling title since 1932.

Ger Loughnane, the new manager, had not only introduced a demanding physical training regime, he also added a mental toughness to his squad that helped them through difficult tests against Cork and Limerick in Munster, followed by Galway in the All-Ireland semi-final. Offaly awaited in the final.

This was an Offaly team full of experience and, for long periods, the reigning All-Ireland champions looked as if they would retain their title. Nineteen minutes into the second half, Johnny Pilkington scored Offaly's second goal to give them a 2–7 to 0–10 lead. Clare might have wilted in previous years, but not this time. Instead, they dug deep into their resilience reserves and were richly rewarded.

With four minutes of normal time remaining, team captain Anthony Daly drove a long-range free towards goal. Offaly goalkeeper David Hughes batted down the ball and Clare substitute Eamon Taaffe reacted quickest to score a vital goal. Clare led by a point and while Offaly equalised, the Banner men sensed that something special was happening. They were right. Two points from Daly (65) and Jamesie O'Connor (free) steered them to a splendid victory and a first All-Ireland win for eighty-one years. The celebrations that followed – not just for days but months – were the stuff of legend.

Clare were certainly no one-hit wonders. Defeated by Limerick in a classic Munster semi-final in 1996, they returned to the summit in 1997, beating Kerry, Cork and Tipperary (1–18 to 0–18) in Munster and Kilkenny in the All-Ireland semi-final. Tipperary awaited them again in the final and this time it was even closer than their Munster final clash, with a single point – 0–20 to 2–13 – separating them. Indeed, it took a stunning save by Davy Fitzgerald from a John Leahy shot to rescue Clare in the final minute of a cracking contest.

Clare D. Fitzgerald; M. O'Halloran, B. Lohan, F. Lohan; L. Doyle, S. McMahon, A. Daly; J. O'Connor, O. Baker; F. Tuohy, P.J. O'Connell, F. Hegarty; S. McNamara, C. Clancy, G. O'Loughlin **Subs** E. Taaffe for McNamara, C. Lyons for Clancy, A. Neville for Taaffe

Football
19 July 1992, Munster final, Gaelic Grounds
Clare 2–10 Kerry 0–12
Two apparently unrelated events during 1990 came together in an unlikely combination to pave the way for one of the seismic results in the history of the All-Ireland football championship two years later.

The first was the appointment of Mayo man John Maughan as Clare football coach. And then, prompted by passionate Clare football official Noel Walsh, the Munster Council agreed to scrap the seeding system for the Munster championship, which had previously bestowed an advantage on Kerry and Cork by keeping them on opposite sides of the draw. Instead, an open draw would apply.

Maughan guided Clare to the All-Ireland B title in 1991, but their victory over Longford in the final went largely unnoticed except in Banner-land. By April 1992, however, there were interesting stirrings within the Clare football community. Clare topped Division 2A of the National League and were heralded for the quality of their display in the quarter-final defeat by Meath, who were then one of the game's major forces.

Yet, those signs of progress did not prepare even the most optimistic supporters for what followed. Just over 24,000 people went through the Gaelic Grounds stiles for the Munster final. Many were there to see Kerry stars, such as Jack O'Shea, Séamus Moynihan and Maurice Fitzgerald, and to check how close Clare could come to a team with genuine All-Ireland ambitions.

They left hours later reciting the names of new heroes, the Claremen who had produced one of football's big shock results.

Mainly through the enterprising efforts of Fitzgerald, Kerry led by 0–7 to 0–6 at half-time. Despite being led, Clare felt there was more to come from them if they stuck to the game plan. Colm Clancy scored their first goal in the forty-eighth minute and, ten minutes later, the Kerry defence was again under pressure. This time it was Martin Daly who took advantage, adding the second goal to give Clare a five-point lead.

Kerry reduced the deficit to three points and, in previous times, Clare might have faded. Not anymore. They dug deep in the closing minutes to hold out for a famous victory that secured a first Munster title for seventy-five years.

Clare's run ended at the All-Ireland semi-final, when Dublin proved too strong, winning by 3–14 to 2–12, but nothing could detract from what had been achieved that summer.

Clare J. Hanrahan; S. Clancy, G. Kelly. C. O'Mahoney; F. Griffin, J. Rouine, C. O'Neill; T. Morrissey, A. Moloney; N. Roche, F. McInerney, G. Killeen; P. Conway, C. Clancy, M. Flynn **Sub** M. Daly for O'Neill

CORK

Hurling

3 September 1978, All-Ireland final, Croke Park
Cork 1–15 Kilkenny 2–8

Why classify the day in 1978 when Cork secured an All-Ireland three-in-a-row ahead of the 1944 final when they completed a four-timer? The answer rests in a comparison of the finals. Cork's 1944 win was achieved with the easiest of victories over Dublin (2–13 to 1–2), leaving a sense of anticlimax.

A year earlier, Cork had won the final with a 5–16 to 0–4 defeat of Antrim. It suggests that, outside Munster, the standard was pretty mediocre. Indeed, Munster counties took all but one All-Ireland title between 1940 and 1954, the exception being 1947 when Kilkenny won.

It was different in the 1970s when there were more genuine All-Ireland contenders, including Galway, who had re-emerged as a powerful force mid-decade. Kilkenny had won three of four All-Irelands between 1972 and 1975; Wexford were a serious outfit too. Clare were also enjoying a fruitful period, winning successive National League titles in 1977 and 1978 and, in another era, they might well have ended their All-Ireland famine, but they lost both Munster finals to Cork.

All-Ireland final wins over Wexford in 1976 and 1977, and a successful Munster campaign in 1978 set up the Rebels for a shot at the three-in-a-row. Kilkenny, who had beaten Cork in the 1972 final, awaited them and were fuelled by a fierce determination to stop their great rivals winning the treble.

Unlike the 1972 final, which Kilkenny won by 3–24 to 5–11, the 1978 final is not recalled as a classic contest. It was, in fact, more a war of attrition, with Cork showing a steely side to their character when it was most needed. Their defence was especially impressive – it needed to be when Kilkenny powered up the momentum after falling five points behind coming up to the hour mark.

A Billy Fitzpatrick goal brought Kilkenny back into strong contention, but the Cork defence – anchored by full-back Martin O'Doherty and centre-back John Crowley – held firm. No classic, but a case of very well done by Cork. They had completed the three-in-a-row the hard way, with selector Christy Ring offering an accurate assessment of how they did it.

'People are saying it was a bad game of hurling but it was the right type of hurling to beat Kilkenny. On other occasions,

Cork have played brilliantly against Kilkenny but lost. Today, the lads played the game the way they were instructed and did it triumphantly.'

Cork retained the Munster title in 1979, but their four-in-a-row bid ended with a four-point defeat to Galway in the All-Ireland semi-final.

Cork M. Coleman; B. Murphy, M. O'Doherty, J. Horgan; D. McCurtain, J. Crowley, D. Coughlan; T. Cashman, P. Moylan; J. Barry-Murphy, G. McCarthy, T. Crowley; C. McCarthy, R. Cummins, S. O'Leary
Subs J. Allen for Cashman, E. O'Donoghue for O'Leary

Football

16 September 1990, All-Ireland football final, Croke Park
Cork 0–11 Meath 0–9

Pressure comes in many forms, external and internal. It is a natural element of any major sporting occasion and something for which coaches will have prepared their teams as a unit and as individuals.

For the Cork footballers of 1990, however, pressure also came in a form rarely experienced. Not only was their All-Ireland title on the line, not only were they facing their nemesis, Meath, who had beaten them in the 1987 and 1988 All-Ireland finals, they were also trying to create history.

Within their powers lay the claim to the most unique prize in Gaelic Games history – the All-Ireland double of one county winning All-Ireland hurling and football titles in the same year.

Within their squad were two players seeking to do what no one had ever done. Teddy McCarthy stood on the brink of personal history as the only player to win both titles on the field of play in the same year. Denis Walsh had been a member of the hurling team that had won the title a few weeks earlier and though he was also on the football panel, he did not play in the final.

When the hurlers won the title, the intriguing question dominating sport was whether the footballers would complete the historic double.

They had qualified impressively through Munster and the All-Ireland semi-final (beating Roscommon), reaching their fifth final (including a replay) since 1987.

It was always going to be a pressurised occasion for them, and it zoomed higher after half an hour when full-forward Colm O'Neill was dismissed following a clash with Meath's full-back Mick Lyons.

Inspired by Kildare-born Shea Fahy and New York-born Danny Culloty in the middle of the field, Cork rose to the occasion in splendid style. Just two points separated the sides at the end, but it was enough to steer Billy Morgan's men into a special place in history.

Cork J. Kerins; T. Nation, S. O'Brien, N. Cahalane; M. Slocum, C. Counihan, B. Coffey; S. Fahy, D. Culloty; D. Barry, L. Tompkins, T. McCarthy; P. McGrath, C. O'Neill, M. McCarthy
Subs J. O'Driscoll for M. McCarthy, P. Hayes for Barry, J. Cleary for McGrath

DERRY

Football

19 September 1993, All-Ireland final, Croke Park

Derry 1–14 Cork 2–8

Eamonn Coleman wasn't impressed with media commentators. Not on this particular day anyway. Most of them had predicted a Down win in the 1993 Ulster quarter-final and now as he stood outside the Derry dressing room in Páirc Esler in Newry after watching his team run out the easiest of winners, the manager was in mischievous mood. 'Do youse boys know anything about football – all tipping Down. I told youse we were as good as any team in the country,' he declared to the assembled media.

Down, All-Ireland champions in 1991 and 1994, had been ripped apart, losing 3–11 to 0–9.

'That was probably the worst Down performance in my period as team manager,' said puzzled Down manager, Pete McGrath.

Four months later, Derry were All-Ireland champions for the first time, having also beaten Monaghan, Donegal (1992 All-Ireland champions), Dublin and Cork. They didn't concede a single goal in their first four games and while Cork scored two in the final, Derry had the required firepower to beat them.

The tale of how Derry built their way, step-by-step, to become first-time champions is one of single-minded vision and an utter refusal to accept that because something hadn't been done before, it couldn't be done at all.

Unlucky against Down in the 1991 Ulster semi-final, and unable to exploit an extra man in the second half of the 1992 final against Donegal, they saw their conquerors in both seasons go on to win the All-Ireland title.

Frustrating times, but there was an upside as they harnessed the lessons from those tough experiences and turned them into something powerful and positive. Winning the National League title for the first time in forty-five years in 1992 gave them a taste of what was possible.

The misery of the 1991 and 1992 championship defeats was fed into the mix too as they embarked on the glorious run in 1993. Some All-Ireland campaigns are less demanding than others, but nobody could ever say Derry in 1993 was in the easier category. Having survived a fierce battle with Donegal in a Clones mudbath on Ulster final day, Dublin awaited in the All-Ireland semi-final.

That semi-final really was the day Derry proved beyond doubt there was something different about them. Trailing 0–9 to 0–4 at half-time, they worked their way back with systematic intent. Previous Derry teams might have buckled, but not this one. Johnny McGurk's spectacular late point won the day, taking Derry into the final for the first time since 1958.

The final against Cork again underlined just how far Derry had advanced. Their resolve was stretched to the limit. Leading by three points at half-time, they trailed by a point in the forty-fifth minute after John O'Driscoll scored Cork's second goal.

Incredibly, that was Cork's final score. Derry added four points, each greeted with thunderous roars as their supporters shared in the joy of the county's greatest day.

Derry's huge achievement in becoming the seventeenth county to win the football title was further acknowledged later in the year when captain Henry Downey was named Footballer of the Year and also selected on the All-Stars team, along with Tony Scullion, Johnny McGurk, Gary Coleman, Anthony Tohill, Brian McGilligan and Enda Gormley. In one season, their All-Star haul equalled their combined total for the previous twenty-two years.

Derry D. McCusker; K. McKeever, T. Scullion, F. McCusker; J. McGurk, H. Downey, G. Coleman; B. McGilligan, A. Tohill; D. Heaney, D. Barton, D. Cassidy; J. Brolly, S. Downey, E. Gormley
Subs D. McNicholl for Cassidy, E. Burns for S Downey

Hurling

9 July 2000, Ulster final, Casement Park
Derry 4–8 Antrim 0–19

A ninety-two-year wait for an Ulster senior hurling title ended in the most dramatic circumstances as Derry staged a late flourish that wiped out a four-point deficit. Oliver Collins' pointed free in the seventieth minute was the winning score on a day when fortunes fluctuated wildly.

Derry led by eight points at half-time before Antrim took control and appeared to be on their way to a third successive title. Cue Derry's defiant response, which finally delivered the title for the first time since 1908 when they had beaten Cavan in the final.

Their 2000 success was based on steady progress over the previous two years when they had reached the Ulster final, only to lose to

Antrim. Despise those setbacks, they continued on an upward trend and were rewarded in millennium year. They acquitted themselves well in the All-Ireland quarter-final, running Offaly, who later reached the final, to six points. Despite that defeat, the season was a splendid success for a Derry squad that went on to retain the Ulster title in 2001.

Derry K. Stevenson; C. McGurk, C. Murray, N. Mullan; B. Ward, C. McEldowney, D. Cassidy; O. Collins, M. Conway; K. McCloy, K. McKeever, R. McCloskey; Gary Biggs, M. Collins, J. O'Dwyer **Sub** Gregory Biggs for Conway

DONEGAL

Football
20 September 1992, All-Ireland final, Croke Park
Donegal 0–18 Dublin 0–14

On the first Sunday in April 1992, Donegal led Dublin by four points after sixty-eight minutes in the National League quarter-final in Breffni Park. Such was their dominance that they should have been further ahead, but at least they had done enough to book a semi-final place. Or so it seemed.

By the time referee Paddy Russell blew the final whistle a few minutes later, it was Dublin who were celebrating, having pulled off a dramatic rescue. Goals by Paul Clarke and Vinny Murphy left Donegal shattered. It had happened again – a game they should have won had been lost.

It wasn't the first time they had been caught – a reality colourfully encapsulated by 'The Follower' in his column in the *Donegal Democrat*. 'On Sunday last, we saw exposed every pimple, boil, ulcer and wart in Donegal's football fabric. Looking back, I saw the old faults, the old failings, the traditional inability to bury our footballing dead after the massacre,' he wrote.

Few Donegal supporters would have argued with his assessment. Would their day ever arrive or would they always come up short? Five months later, the Sam Maguire Cup was on its way to Donegal for the first time. So, what changed?

The second half of the Ulster final is a good starting point. Level at half-time with Derry, the reigning National League champions, but reduced to fourteen players after John Cunningham's dismissal and facing the wind in the second half, Donegal appeared to be in serious trouble.

Manager Brian McEniff, probably the most influential football person in the county's history, still regards that second-half performance as arguably the best produced by a Donegal team. Given their history, and with the odds stacked against them, they might have been expected to wilt but instead they soared to a new level. It yielded a two-point win, while also filling the squad's confidence tanks to overflowing.

The new-found belief would be required again in the All-Ireland final (they had beaten Mayo in a poor-quality semi-final) when Dublin started with an impressive swagger. However, Dublin missed a penalty (Charlie Redmond shot wide) and, gradually, Donegal got their own game working. By half-time, they were three points ahead and six clear at the three-quarter mark.

Over the next ten minutes, their nerve was seriously tested as Dublin cut the deficit to three points and, with the memory of the league quarter-final still fresh in Donegal minds, the pressure grew. Were they ready for it this time?

Little enough had changed in personnel since the defeat by Dublin in April, but the mentality was completely different. Self-belief was underpinned by an obsessive desire to walk where no other Donegal players ever had. It was a victory and a breakthrough for sheer persistence.

Long-serving players like Martin McHugh, who was later chosen as Footballer of the Year, never lost faith in what they could achieve – nor did McEniff, whose life had been dedicated to exploring new territory ever since he had led Donegal to their first Ulster title as player-manager in 1972. Twenty years later, he got his ultimate wish.

Donegal G. Walsh; B. McGowan, M. Gallagher, N. Hegarty; D. Reid, M. Gavigan, J.J. Doherty; A. Molloy, B. Murray; J. McHugh, M. McHugh, J. McMullan; D. Bonner, T. Boyle, M. Boyle
Sub B. Cunningham for Murray

Hurling

4 June 2011, Lory Meagher Cup final, Croke Park
Donegal 2–12 Tyrone 0–17

Between 2001 and 2010, Donegal lost five hurling finals, going down to Roscommon and Mayo respectively in the 2001 and 2003 All-Ireland junior finals, to Derry in the 2006 Nicky Rackard Cup, and to Tyrone and Longford respectively in the 2009 and 2010 Lory Meagher Cup deciders.

Any wonder they thought the gods were against them?

Still, they battled on and when they reached the 2011 Lory Meagher Cup final against Tyrone, there was a growing feeling in the camp that things had to come right one day. Management, led by Andrew Wallace, enlisted the help of Clare All-Ireland-winning captain Anthony Daly, inviting him to work with the squad the week before the game.

Daly told the Donegal players of the psychological barrier Clare had had to overcome in the 1990s and how anything was possible if they believed in themselves – that it would have to come from within themselves.

The following weekend, that's exactly what happened.

The final was tight and tense throughout, the sort of game Donegal might have lost in previous years but this time they weren't taking no for an answer. Trailing by two points in the closing minutes, Ciarán Matthewson took his total for the day to 2–3 with the match-winning goal. Two years later, Donegal won the higher-grade Nicky Rackard Cup but, for sheer emotion alone, nothing could compare with that special feeling after finally winning a national title in Croke Park in 2011.

Donegal P. O'Brien; S. O'Connor, C. Breathnach, A. McDermott; J. Donnelly, C. Dowds, J. Boyle; S. McVeigh, P. Sheridan; E. Organ, S. Boyle, C. Matthewson; M. McCann, E. McDermott, N. Campbell
Subs P. Hannigan for Organ, L. Henderson for McCann, M. McGee for S. Boyle

DOWN

Football

25 September 1960, All-Ireland final, Croke Park
Down 2–10 Kerry 0–8

Pádraig Puirséal's account in *The Irish Press* of the explosion of sound that reverberated around Croke Park at the final whistle brilliantly captured the essence of the historic occasion as Down became the first team from the Six Counties to win the All-Ireland senior football crown.

'The roar, which formally announced what had been obvious for ten minutes before – Down's first senior All-Ireland triumph – must have gone sweeping north across Fingal, the cradle-land of Gaelic football, and through the Gap of the North to echo and re-echo among the Mournes from Slieve Gullion to Slieve Donard before carrying the tidings of a famous victory across Strangford Lough to Portaferry and then away to Donaghadee in the far Ards of Down.'

There were many other descriptive flourishes splashed across other newspapers too, as writers attempted to catch the mood of a highly emotional occasion. Not only had Down created history, they had done it with a comprehensive victory over Gaelic football's aristocratic Kingdom. It was as close to a perfect sporting day as they could have hoped for, the culmination of a carefully constructed project that had steered them to a first Ulster title in 1959.

They lost the subsequent All-Ireland semi-final to Galway, but gained valuable experience, which added greatly to their armoury as they headed into the 1960 campaign. They beat Antrim, Monaghan and Cavan to retain the Ulster title, before eliminating Offaly in a replayed All-Ireland semi-final.

Down brought a new dimension to the game around that time. Their players were better looked after than most of their counterparts in other counties. They worked harder at raising fitness levels to new heights, factoring it into a gameplan that combined physical power with tactical flexibility. There was method and purpose in everything they did – on and off the pitch. They were on a mission and weren't going to be denied. They even looked different – their black shorts contrasting starkly with the white worn by their opponents.

Down had never previously played Kerry in the championship, which may have been an advantage in the 1960 final. They had no hang-ups going in against the defending champions and, having edged two points ahead by half-time, goals by James McCartan and Paddy Doherty (penalty) sent them on their way to a triumph watched by a crowd of 87,768, a record up to then.

It was beaten a year later when 90,556 saw Down complete the two-in-a-row with a one-point win over Offaly in the final. Truly, a special time in Down GAA history.

Down E. McKay; G. Lavery, L. Murphy, P. Rice; K. Mussen, D. McCartan, K. O'Neill; J. Lennon, J. Carey; S. O'Neill, J. McCartan, P. Doherty; T. Hadden, P. O'Hagan, B. Morgan
Sub K. Denvir for Lennon

Hurling

21 March 1993, National Hurling League, Nowlan Park
Down 1–12 Kilkenny 1–11

It might appear an unlikely choice for the greatest day in a county that has won an All-Ireland junior title, Ulster senior titles and the Christy Ring Cup, but context is everything and, in this case, it had a very special significance.

Down, who won the Ulster title for the first time in fifty-one years in 1992, were in Division 1 of the National Hurling League in a group with Tipperary, Kilkenny, Limerick, Offaly and Antrim. This was high-powered territory, and they acquitted themselves well in their first four games, beating Offaly and Antrim and losing narrowly to Limerick and Tipperary.

They headed for Nowlan Park for the final group game, knowing that a win over the reigning All-Ireland champions would earn them a league quarter-final place for the first time. Still, it was asking a lot to expect them to beat the mighty Kilkenny, featuring twelve of the team that had played in the All-Ireland final win over Cork just six months earlier.

When Kilkenny opened up a four-point lead in the first half, it looked as though Down's dreams of achieving something special were about to be crushed. The players thought otherwise, digging deep into their reserves of determination and resilience to stage a splendid second-half show that delivered the sweetest of victories. Chris Mageean scored the winning point.

Not only did victory guarantee them a place in the quarter-final and another season in Division 1, it had immediate repercussions for Kilkenny, who were relegated. Down lost the quarter-final to

Cork, but the day they beat the All-Ireland champions on their own ground will always be treasured in the county.

Down N. Keith; K. Coulter, G. Coulter, P. Branniff; M. Mallon, P. McMullan, D. Woods; D. Hughes, D. O'Prey; G. McGrattan, C. Mageean, N. Sands; M. Blaney, M. Bailie, L. McMullan
Subs P. Dorrian for L. McMullan, J. McCarthy for Bailie

DUBLIN

Football
15 September 2019, All-Ireland football final replay, Croke Park
Dublin 1–18, Kerry 0–15

It was entirely fitting that Dublin's bid for a place in history – their attempt to do what Kerry had twice previously failed to manage – should pit the two old, great rivals against one another. And it was even more fitting that it took a second engagement before the argument was settled and the Dubs became the first team to win five successive All-Ireland senior football championships.

As monumental as the breakthrough achieved by Kevin Heffernan's mighty army of 1974 was – or the six-in-a-row success of 2020, for that matter – the 2019 win elevated this Dublin team to a new status, a place where no other team since the launch of the championships in 1884 had occupied. They climbed higher in 2020, but 2019 was the record-breaking year. That will never change. It was also their seventh All-Ireland success in nine seasons, their sixth under the management of Jim Gavin.

Only Wexford in 1919 and Kerry in 1933 and 1982 – when Offaly's Séamus Darby denied them in the closing minutes – had previously put themselves in a position to win five-in-a-row.

Croke Park, on an autumn Saturday evening in 2019, was a seething cauldron. The drawn game two weeks previously had merely whetted appetites. Dublin played much of the second half with fourteen men after the dismissal of Johnny Cooper. Dean Rock kicked ten points but none as crucial as the one from play in the fourth minute of added time that levelled scores at 1–16 apiece.

The replay lived up to the hype. At the beginning of the second half, Eoin Murchan, a late call-up to the Dublin team that was made public just before the game, scored one of the great championship goals. Powering forward from his wing-back position, he galloped straight in on the Kerry goal before driving the ball to the net. It was an inspiring strike that would prove crucial.

Kerry reduced the deficit to one point after forty-five minutes, but they never got closer. In the final half hour, including added time, Dublin's systematic control was impressive and they outscored Kerry by 0–7 to 0–2.

It was the culmination of an extraordinary run under manager Jim Gavin, who had taken over at the start of the 2013 season. By the end of 2019, Dublin had won six All-Ireland titles, having lost only one (v Donegal in the 2014 All-Ireland semi-final) of forty-seven championship games between 2013 and 2019.

In the *Sunday Independent*, journalist Sean McGoldrick was prophetic in his comments about those stats. 'These are astonishing figures which will probably never be broken, unless by Dublin themselves. Goalkeeper Stephen Cluxton has now skippered Dublin to six Sam Maguire successes, another record which is unlikely to be broken, apart from by Cluxton himself.'

It was indicative of Dublin's strength on the day that eight players – Con O'Callaghan, Ciarán Kilkenny, Paul Mannion, Eoin Murchan, Dean Rock, David Byrne, James McCarthy and Niall Scully – contributed to their scoreline. Kerry had just four scorers – David Clifford, Seán O'Shea, Paul Geaney and Adrian Spillane.

Dublin went on to break further records in 2020, but the five-in-a-row success will always have the most special of places in the county's sporting consciousness.

Dublin S. Cluxton; D. Byrne, M. Fitzsimons J. Cooper; E. Murchan, J. Small, J. McCaffrey; B. Fenton, J. McCarthy; N. Scully, C. Kilkenny, B. Howard; P. Mannion, C. O'Callaghan, D. Rock
Subs D. Connolly for McCaffrey, P. McMahon for Murchan, C. Costello for Scully, K. McManamon for Mannion, M.D. Macauley for Howard

Hurling

4 September 1938, All-Ireland hurling final, Croke Park
Dublin 2–5 Waterford 1–6
The new Cusack Stand, with a 5,000 capacity and opened just a month previously, was a source of fascination for the 37,129 spectators.

To add to the connections that would become historic, it was the first All-Ireland final from which the voice of a youthful Michael O'Hehir would broadcast details of the day. O'Hehir's family background was in Clare, but he was born in Glasnevin in Dublin. And in a long and distinguished career as a broadcaster and journalist, the 1938 final was the only All-Ireland senior hurling success for Dublin that he called.

Mick Daniels, Dublin's captain in 1938, was playing in his third final. A native of Carrick-on-Suir who had moved to Dublin in the late 1920s, he was a substitute on the team that lost the 1930 final to Tipperary and started in the defeat to Limerick in 1934.

Midfielders Daniels and Harry Gray dominated the early stages of the 1938 final, helping Dublin to an interval lead of 2–3 to 1–3. A dour second half yielded only five points in a 3–2 split to Waterford for whom John Keane, one of the best centre half-backs ever to play the game, was outstanding. However, the Dublin defence held out, ensuring a sixth All-Ireland title for the county.

Dublin C. Forde; T. Teehan, M. Butler, C. McMahon; M. Gill, P. Farrell, J. Byrne; M. Daniels, H. Gray; R. Ryan, M. McDonald, P. Doody; M. Brophy, M. Flynn, W. Loughnane
Sub J. Gilmartin for Daniels

FERMANAGH

Football

22 August 2004, All-Ireland semi-final, Croke Park

Fermanagh 0–9 Mayo 0–9

The background: Fermanagh had never previously reached an All-Ireland senior semi-final. They had never won an Ulster title and hadn't been in the provincial final since 1982. They had been relegated from Division 1 of the National Football League in April 2004, after winning only one of seven games.

They had lost to Tyrone in the Ulster quarter-final in early June and their All-Ireland qualifier journey looked likely to be short. They were due to play Tipperary in the first round but got a walkover when Tipperary players opted out of the game in a protest over club-fixture scheduling.

The turnaround: the drawn All-Ireland semi-final will always be recalled as a magical occasion in Fermanagh, the day they came so close to hitting a target that had seemed well beyond their range a few months earlier. It was made possible by an amazing transformation in their performances over the previous seven weeks.

It began in a second-round qualifier when they beat Meath by a point after extra-time. Many saw it as a fluke result, but Fermanagh were even more impressive when they beat Cork by six points in Round 3. The drama continued in Round 4 when they beat Donegal by a point in extra-time. This was new and exciting territory.

Armagh, the 2002 All-Ireland winners and reigning Ulster

champions, awaited Fermanagh in the All-Ireland quarter-final. Surely, that's where the fairytale would end. Not so. Fermanagh had built a powerful momentum and, with their confidence rising all the time, they were ready for any challenge. Not even a team as experienced as Armagh could wear them down. For the third time in four games, Fermanagh won by a point and were in the All-Ireland semi-final, despite not scoring a goal in five games. Significantly though, they had only conceded three goals, thanks to a well-structured defence.

The semi-final: Mayo, who had beaten New York, Galway, Roscommon and Tyrone, awaited Fermanagh, and while the Connacht champions had beaten them in the National League the previous February, the margin had been only two points. It was close enough to convince the Fermanagh players and their manager, Charlie Mulgrew, that they had a real chance.

An unseasonably cold and blustery afternoon in Dublin did its best to spoil the atmosphere but that was never going to be allowed to happen. It was as if Fermanagh had emptied for the day, with the entire population congregated in Croke Park to share in an occasion nobody thought remotely likely two months earlier.

A crowd of 64,518 witnessed the lowest-scoring semi-final – 0–9 each – for twenty-three years but it scarcely mattered as the novelty aspect alone guaranteed nationwide interest. Fermanagh had enough chances to continue their amazing run, but weren't quite clinical enough on the big moments.

A pointed free by Stephen Maguire late on earned them a draw and a second chance to become the most unlikely All-Ireland finalists.

Unfortunately for Fermanagh, it wasn't to be. They were equally defiant in the replay six days later but, again, missed several good chances and lost by two points – 0–13 to 1–8. The dream was over, but the memories linger to this day.

The aftermath: Fermanagh had two players – Barry Owens and Marty McGrath – selected on the All-Stars team. The heights of 2004 weren't replicated in 2005 when they were beaten by Armagh in the Ulster preliminary round and by Down in the first round of the All-Ireland qualifiers.

Fermanagh N. Tinney; N. Bogue, B. Owens, R. McCluskey; R. Johnston, S. McDermott, P. Sherry; M. McGrath, L. McBarron; E. Maguire, J. Sherry, M. Little; C. O'Reilly, S. Maguire, C. Bradley
Subs T. Brewster for Little, H. Brady for P. Sherry, M. Murphy for J. Sherry

Hurling

6 June 2015, Lory Meagher Cup final, Croke Park
Fermanagh 3–16 Sligo 1–17

Fermanagh knew all about the pain of defeat in the Lory Meagher Cup, having been narrowly beaten in both the 2012 (extra-time v Tyrone) and 2014 (Longford) finals. Those setbacks tested the squad's resolve, and they responded positively in 2015.

They beat Warwickshire, Lancashire and Leitrim in the group section but suffered a heavy defeat against Sligo. It loaded on the pressure in the final and when they trailed by nine points in the first half, another big-day disappointment seemed likely. All changed quite quickly as Fermanagh asserted themselves and went on to take the title for the first time.

Perseverance had paid off as they enjoyed that special feeling that comes from winning a final in Croke Park.

Fermanagh M. Curry; D. Teague, E. Mahon, K. Kehoe; M. Slevin, B. Duffy, J. Duffy; D. Teague, J.P. McGarry; D. McGarry, A. Breslin, S. Corrigan; B. MacLaughlin, C. Corrigan
Subs F. Barron for Mahon, D. Curran for D. Teague

GALWAY

Football

25 September 1966, All-Ireland final, Croke Park
Galway 1–10 Meath 0–7

For reasons that weren't apparent, most of the tipsters in the national newspapers predicted a Meath win in 1966. That was despite the fact that Galway hadn't lost a championship game since the 1963 All-Ireland final against Dublin and, in the interim, had beaten Kerry (twice), Mayo (twice), Sligo (twice), Meath, Down, Cork and Roscommon.

They had beaten Meath in the 1964 semi-final and their bid to join Kerry, Dublin and Wexford as All-Ireland three-in-a-row winners depended on them mastering the Royals again in 1966. At face value, Galway should have been favourites, but Meath were so impressive when they beat Down by ten points in the semi-final that they convinced many observers that they were the real deal.

'Never have I found myself so rapt in admiration of a football match and it was all because of the sheer brilliance of the Meath men, whose classical performance after the change of ends must rank with anything ever seen,' wrote John D. Hickey in the *Irish Independent*. High praise indeed.

In contrast, Galway had come very close to being dethroned by Mayo in the Connacht final before squeezing through by a point, and might well have lost the All-Ireland semi-final to Cork only for a series of excellent saves by goalkeeper Johnny Geraghty.

It raised suspicions that the Galway players were past their best, and ready to be picked off by an improving Meath team. The reality was far different. In fact, Galway produced arguably the best performance of their three-in-a-row run, dismantling Meath's resistance surprisingly easily. A goal by Mattie McDonagh, who was on his way to becoming the only Connacht man to win four All-Ireland medals, set them on their way and the result was never in doubt when they led by 1–6 to 0–1 at half-time.

Meath rallied in the second half, which they won by 0–6 to 0–4, but had left themselves with far too much to do against a team whose defensive solidity was exceptional – they had conceded only one goal (v Cork in 1966) in three All-Ireland semi-finals and three finals.

Securing three successive All-Ireland titles ensured the Galway team a place in history as one of the greatest sides and raised hopes of a four-timer. However, that ambition was wrecked by Mayo in ruthless fashion as they ended the Tribesmen's run with a thumping victory in the 1967 Connacht semi-final. Galway had to wait until 1998 for their next All-Ireland win.

Galway J. Geraghty; E. Colleran, N. Tierney, J.B. McDermott; C. McDonagh, S. Meade, M. Newell; P. Donnellan, J. Duggan; C. Dunne, M. McDonagh, S. Leydon; L. Sammon, S. Cleary, J. Keenan
Sub J. Donnellan for Meade

Hurling

7 September 1980, All-Ireland final, Croke Park
Galway 2–15 Limerick 3–9

The Galway team from the second half of the 1980s entered the record books as the first from the county to win two successive All-Ireland senior titles, so it could be argued that the day they beat Tipperary in 1988 was the county's greatest hurling day. However, that would be to ignore the very special final eight years earlier.

The 1980 success was more than just an All-Ireland win. It was a release from fifty-seven years of championship disappointment, with the 1960s a particularly miserable period when their eleven-year venture into the Munster championship yielded just one win.

Despite that, progress was being made at underage level and when Galway won the 1972 All-Ireland Under-21 title, hopes grew that better times were ahead. And so it proved. A National League title was secured in 1975 and while All-Ireland success was slow to follow, it finally arrived in 1980.

Coached by Cyril Farrell, who had the unusual distinction of being in charge of a senior team at the age of thirty, Galway finally made the breakthrough, beating Offaly in the All-Ireland semi-final by two points and Limerick in the final by three points. Galway raced into a 2–1 to 0–0 lead early on, but Limerick fought back and looked at one stage as if they might complete the recovery – but Galway held on in a tense finish.

The final hasn't gone down in history as one of the most memorable matches, but the aftermath certainly has. The rousing speech by Galway captain Joe Connolly after receiving the Liam MacCarthy Cup, followed by Joe McDonagh's booming rendition of 'The West's Awake' from the Hogan Stand presentation area united Galway people at home and abroad in an emotional bond that was palpable. Without an All-Ireland win since 1923 – they had lost nine finals between 1924 and 1979 – the clouds had lifted. Galway were back among the elite at the start of a decade that went on to produce lots more riches across all grades.

Galway M. Conneely; C. Hayes, N. McInerney, J. Cooney; S. Linnane, S. Silke, S. Coen; M. Connolly, S. Mahon; F. Burke, Joe Connolly, P.J. Molloy; B. Forde, John Connolly, N. Lane
Subs F. Gantley for M. Connolly, J. Ryan for Molloy

KERRY

Football

24 September 1978, All-Ireland final, Croke Park
Kerry 5–11, Dublin 0–9
On the last Sunday of January 1978, Kerry football coach Mick O'Dwyer faced what amounted to a vote of confidence. Following defeat by Dublin in the 1977 All-Ireland semi-final, Gerald McKenna, the county chairman, and the Kerry selectors put

O'Dwyer through a lengthy period of questioning that had been fiery and intense, and was the main item for discussion at the Kerry Convention in Killarney.

It was a bruising time, during which O'Dwyer himself, in an interview with the *Kerryman* newspaper, indicated that he might not be willing to continue in the role. If McKenna had been ousted as chairman, O'Dwyer might not have had a choice, as he readily admitted. Had that happened, who knows how history would have unfolded?

O'Dwyer survived, comfortably enough in the end, as did McKenna. However, three of O'Dwyer's selectors failed to survive a vote for retention, and two of his most vocal critics, Liam Higgins and Joe Keohane, were among the replacements. That was a clear message to O'Dwyer – win or bust in 1978.

The experience made O'Dwyer even more determined than he had been when he was first appointed in autumn 1974. His regime, already renowned as almost brutal, became tougher. Not only was he determined to re-establish Kerry dominance over Dublin, he wanted to prove to his detractors that they had judged 1977 all wrong.

He made squad changes too, among them the promotion of Eoin Liston, a big, strapping forward from Beale, who was soon to become known as 'Bomber'.

Kerry smashed the challenge of Waterford in the 1978 Munster semi-final and had seven points to spare over Cork in the final. Roscommon were next in line in the All-Ireland semi-final but were swept aside – 3–11 to 0–8. O'Dwyer got what he wanted – another crack at the Dubs.

The final didn't go smoothly for Kerry early on. Dublin led 0–6 to 0–1 after twenty minutes before a John Egan goal brought some respite for Kerry. They were still a point behind late in the first half when a history-changing moment descended on Croke Park.

Referee Séamus Aldridge awarded a free to Kerry after Dublin goalkeeper Paddy Cullen was penalised for a late tackle on Ger Power. Mikey Sheehy quickly placed the ball and chipped it into the net as a despairing Cullen raced back to his line. Despite Dublin's protestations, the goal was allowed to stand, and Kerry led by 2–3 to 0–7 at half-time. The second half was a rout. Kerry scored 3–8, Liston getting in for a hat-trick of goals. Dublin replied with a mere two points. The Kingdom had returned to power for what was the start of their golden years.

By 1981, Kerry had won four titles in a row. They added three more in 1984, 1985 and 1986, by which time they had won eight in twelve seasons.

Kerry C. Nelligan; J. Deenihan. J. O'Keeffe, M. Spillane; P. Ó Sé, T. Kennelly, P. Lynch; J. O'Shea, S. Walsh; G. Power, D. Moran, P. Spillane; M. Sheehy, E. Liston, J. Egan
Sub P. O'Mahoney for Deenihan

Hurling

23 May 1993, Munster quarter-final, Walsh Park
Kerry 4–13 Waterford 3–13
Traffic between north Kerry and Waterford city was no busier than usual on a late-May Sunday morning in 1993. Not even all the die-hard hurling followers from north Kerry were making the long

journey for what looked like a hopeless cause. By mid-afternoon those who had stayed at home were excitedly, and somewhat bemusedly, listening to their radios. And those in the estimated attendance of 4,000 in Walsh Park were bearing witness to that rarest of sights – Kerry winning a Munster hurling championship game.

Kerry's coach, the former Wexford and Cork hurler John Meyler, had been bullish about their chances. No one listened. Less than a minute into the game, Kerry were a goal down, the gifted youngster Paul Flynn giving Waterford the advantage. A second Flynn goal after twenty minutes further stunned Kerry, but their response was impressive. In the next five minutes, Brendan O'Sullivan and D.J. Leahy breached the Waterford defence to give Kerry a 2–8 to 2–7 half-time lead.

The drama was only beginning. Another Flynn goal in the forty-first minute gave Waterford a six-point lead – 3–11 to 2–8. But Kerry would not relent. A kicked goal by Joe Walsh helped cut the deficit. They were level at 3–13 each when Leahy seemed to mishit a free. The ball, however, deflected off a Waterford defender and ended up in the net. It secured a famous victory, described by the manager, John Meyler as 'the performance of a lifetime'.

It was certainly one of the biggest shocks the hurling championship had seen for many years. It gave Kerry hurling an immediate boost, and it also sounded a warning to Tipperary. They presented a much higher level of opposition in the semi-final that Kerry couldn't match, and they lost by 4–21 to 2–09.

Kerry J.P. Hickey; S. O'Shea, M. Casey, S. McIntyre; B. O'Mahony, S. Sheehan. M. McKivergan; M. O'Shea, N. Roche; T. O'Connell; C. Walsh, B. O'Sullivan; T. Maunsell, J. Walsh, D.J. Leahy
Subs L. O'Connor for O'Connell, D. O'Sullivan for O'Mahony

KILDARE

Football

30 September 1928, All-Ireland final, Croke Park
Kildare 2–6 Cavan 2–5

During Kildare's Golden Age – the years between 1919 and 1932 when their footballers were trading lucratively amongst football's elite – there were numerous highlights. But nothing that went before or after could have matched the drama of the 1928 season that began before a ball had been kicked in the championship and lasted all the way to the All-Ireland final.

As defending champions, having beaten Kerry in the 1927 final, Kildare were basking in the glory of success. In early 1928, they were invited to visit New York before their championship defence began. Fundraising events were launched and they proved to be a distraction. Despite that, Kildare reached the league final, scheduled for 29 April in Croke Park.

On the eve of the final, and just a week before their departure date, Kildare were informed that permission for the trip had been revoked by the GAA's Central Council. It was reported that fractured relationships between the GAA in Dublin and their American counterparts were the cause of the unexpected development.

Disappointed and distracted by the news, which they received in their Dublin hotel on the morning of the league final, Kildare's performance was undoubtedly affected and they lost to Kerry.

However, by the time the championship started, they had regrouped and were fiercely determined to retain the All-Ireland crown.

The most sensational result of the summer was Kerry's defeat by Tipperary in Munster. With their great rivals out of the way, Kildare's path was certainly more smooth. Cork proved no match for Kildare in the All-Ireland semi-final, losing by 3–7 to 0–2. Cavan, the other finalists, sprung a few surprises before the game.

Kildare had selected Peter Pringle to replace the injured Joe Curtis for the final. Before the teams arrived on the pitch, a delegation of Cavan officials called to the Kildare dressing room. They claimed to have photographic evidence that Pringle had played illegally in Laois during the summer.

There were some reports that Pringle's misdemeanour also involved attending a dance run by a hockey club, which would have been contrary to Rule 27, the GAA Ban. Kildare could not take a risk. Curtis, his broken ribs heavily bandaged, was back on the team.

Cavan raced into an early three-point lead, but Kildare fought back and a Paul Doyle goal helped them to a two-point lead at half-time. Cavan regained the lead in the second half, but Kildare countered with a controversial goal, scored by Paddy O'Loughlin. Cavan protested that he had thrown the ball into the net, a view shared by newspaper reporters, but the goal was allowed to stand.

It was a crucial score and while Cavan maintained the pressure all the way to the end, Kildare won by a point.

Kildare were two-in-a-row champions – joining Dublin, Kerry and Wexford in that achievement.

Kildare captain Bill 'Squires' Gannon became the first player to lift the new All-Ireland senior football championship trophy, the Sam Maguire Cup. Their three-in-a-row bid in 1929 took them all the way to the final, where they lost to Kerry.

Kildare M. Walsh; M. Buckley, T.M. Goff, G. Fitzpatrick; F. Malone, J. Higgins, J. Hayes; J. Loughlin, B. Gannon; J. Curtis, P. Martin, P. Doyle; B. Mangan, P. Loughlin, T. Keogh
Sub D. Ryan for J. Loughlin

Hurling

23 June 1974, All-Ireland B final, Croke Park
Kildare 1–26 Antrim 3–13

Pat Dunny was just seventeen years old when he lined out as Kildare's goalkeeper in the first All-Ireland junior hurling championship final against London in New Eltham in September 1962. Twelve years and a lot of hurling and football adventures later, Dunny was full-back on the Kildare side that won the first All-Ireland senior B hurling championship, when they beat Antrim in Croke Park.

Antrim, the pundits' favourites, had been overwhelmed by the speed of Kildare's start. The Lilywhites scored an unanswered eight points before Eddie Donnelly registered Antrim's first score. Kildare's top scorer was Jackie Walsh with 0–10 as they powered to a comfortable win.

They lost the All-Ireland quarter-final by six points to a rapidly emerging Galway team, a very credible performance and there was more to follow. In the 1976 Leinster championship, Kildare beat Dublin in the opening round and faced Wexford in the semi-final. Few fancied them to match Wexford, but they acquitted themselves well, testing Wexford all the way before losing by four points. Wexford went on to reach the All-Ireland final, losing by four points to Cork.

Kildare won three more B titles before the competition was discontinued.

Kildare J. Curran; R. Cullen, P. Dunny, M. O'Brien; M. Moore, A. Carew, M. Duane; B. Burke, J. O'Connell; J. Walsh, T. Carew, J. O'Leary; N. Walshe, J. Wall, M. Deely.

KILKENNY

Hurling

6 September 2009, All-Ireland final, Croke Park
Kilkenny 2–22 Tipperary 0–23

Brendan Cummins imploring referee Diarmuid Kirwan to look at the big screen ... Henry Shefflin walking calmly towards the twenty-metre line ... Kilkenny supporters on the edge of their seats ... TV viewers at home and abroad enthralled by the unfolding drama in Croke Park.

With seven minutes remaining in the 2009 All-Ireland final, there was a high probability that Kilkenny's attempt to become the first team to win the four-in-a-row since Cork (1941–1944) depended on what happened next. They had been awarded a penalty after Richie Power was adjudged to have been fouled in the square.

Tipperary protested the decision, contending that Power was outside the square at the point of contact – hence Cummins' plea to the referee to check on the big screen – but Kirwan had made up his mind. Besides, the rules didn't allow a TV check. Despite being down to fourteen players from the three-quarter mark after Benny Dunne's dismissal, Tipperary were leading by two points and were showing no signs that the numerical disadvantage was a major problem.

Kilkenny needed a goal and Shefflin delivered, whipping his shot to the net with ferocious power. 'There isn't a guy on earth you'd want more than Henry Shefflin in that situation,' wrote manager Brian Cody in his autobiography.

Having nudged in front, Kilkenny's confidence soared and they struck again shortly afterwards when Martin Comerford scored their second goal. It proved too much for Tipperary, whose brilliant effort wasn't quite enough.

The 2009 final is regarded as one of the best in history, a fascinating physical and mental battle, during which there was never any more than one score between the teams until Comerford's goal took Kilkenny's lead out to four points.

Kilkenny led 0–13 to 0–11 at half-time, but Tipperary had the edge in the first twenty-five minutes of the second half, a period in which they out-scored Kilkenny by 0–9 to 0–4. Indeed, were it not for Kilkenny goalkeeper P.J. Ryan, Tipperary would have been further ahead. He made a series of outstanding saves, which had a huge influence on the outcome. Later in the year, he was selected on the All-Stars team, the first Kilkenny goalkeeper to land the honour since Michael Walsh in 1993. Ryan's colleague Tommy Walsh won Hurler of the Year and the team won six All-Star awards.

The 2009 final was a fitting spectacle to mark a historic occasion and completed a decade in which Kilkenny had won seven of the ten All-Ireland championships. They also won five National League titles.

Between 2000 and 2009, they played forty-four championship games, winning thirty-nine, drawing one and losing four. Their only defeats were against Galway in the 2001 and 2005 All-Ireland semi-finals, against Wexford in the 2004 Leinster semi-final, and against Cork in that year's All-Ireland final.

It was an extraordinary success level that left them favourites to complete the five-in-a-row in 2010. They did reach the final but, this time, Tipperary found their measure and won by eight points. It was quite a turnaround from the previous year, but didn't herald a major power-shift as Kilkenny came back to win the 2011, 2012, 2014 and 2015 titles.

The 2000–2015 period really was an extraordinary time for Kilkenny, an era when they set new standards. They had many special occasions, but none can quite compare with the 2009 All-Ireland final, the day they took the county into new territory.

Kilkenny P.J. Ryan; M. Kavanagh, J.J. Delaney, J. Tyrrell; T. Walsh, B. Hogan, J. Tennyson; D. Lyng, M. Rice; E. Brennan, E. Larkin, R. Power; R. Hogan, H. Shefflin, A. Fogarty

Subs T.J. Reid for Fogarty, M. Fennelly for Lyng, M. Comerford for R. Hogan

Football

22 October 1911, Leinster final, Jones' Road (Croke Park)
Kilkenny 2–4 Meath 1–1

There was controversy aplenty on a day when Kilkenny lost and won the Leinster final in the space of a few hours. Having arrived well past the scheduled throw-in time, they discovered that Meath had been awarded the game by the Leinster Council. Negotiations followed, after which Meath, who alleged that Kilkenny had a reputation for turning up late, agreed to play under protest, rather than accept a walkover.

'This was very generous on the part of the Meath players, considering that they were hardly in a position to do themselves justice after their long vigil in the cold and rain,' reported the *Meath Chronicle*.

Meath scored an early goal, but Kilkenny asserted themselves from there on in and ran out six-point winners, taking the Leinster title for the third and last time. They lost the All-Ireland semi-final to Antrim. Games were seventeen-a-side at the time, having been reduced from twenty-one in 1892. Teams were further reduced to fifteen in 1913.

Kilkenny R. Holohan, P. Dalton, W. Dalton, R. Dalton, J. Doyle, J. Dwyer, W. Dwyer; J. Donovan, J. Coady, R. Purcell, W. Hoynes, J. Fitzgerald, P. Power, W. Saunders, T. Brennan, T. Buller, M. Hughes

LAOIS

Football

20 July 2003, Leinster final, Croke Park

Laois 2–13 Kildare 1–13

Why choose this match rather than their other Leinster title wins in 1889, 1936, 1937, 1938 and 1946, or indeed their National League wins in 1926 and 1986? It's all about context and the impact the 2003 win had on Laois people at home and abroad.

Without a Leinster title win for fifty-seven years, and having lost eight finals in the interim, there was something magical about the 2003 success. Thousands of people crammed into Portlaoise on the Sunday night to share in the joy that had been released by the win in Croke Park earlier in the day.

'It's easy to speak of the fifty-seven-year gap since the last Leinster title, but it's much more difficult to endure it. That's why Sunday's result was more than just a game, more than just sport. It was history being made in front of 61,786 in Croke Park. It was the ending of a famine, the lifting of a curse, the banishing of a monkey from the back,' wrote Gearoid Keegan in the *Leinster Express*.

The atmosphere around the county was in marked contrast to a year earlier when Laois exited the All-Ireland championship after an embarrassing 1–15 to 0–7 defeat by Meath in a qualifier tie in Portlaoise. They had earlier lost to Kildare in the Leinster semi-final. It was a dispiriting time for Laois. Having won successive All-Ireland minor titles in 1996 and 1997, hopes were high of a quick advance at senior level. It didn't happen. By the end of 2002, there was little optimism that better days were imminent.

Then, in a sensational managerial swoop, Laois intercepted Mick O'Dwyer on his way home from Kildare. He had signed off after the Lilywhites' exit from the championship, and Laois saw it as an opportunity. Could Micko do for them what he did for Kildare, who he steered to Leinster titles in 1998 and 2000? Laois officials persuaded him to have a go.

He had attended the Laois–Meath game some weeks earlier and didn't like what he had seen from the home team.

'Some of them were hiding, hoping that the ball wouldn't come their way. You spot the signs very quickly when players are doing that,' he wrote in his autography *Blessed and Obsessed*.

Still, he believed in the county's potential and set about harnessing it. The rate of improvement over a short period was remarkable. By the following May, Laois were in the National League final after finishing top of their group and beating All-Ireland champions Armagh in the semi-final.

They lost the final to Tyrone, but it was obvious that they were going to be a real force in the Leinster championship. Wins over Wexford and Offaly (replay) set up a semi-final clash with Dublin, who Laois hadn't beaten in the championship since 1981. That was about to end – Laois won by two points. Powered by a momentum that wasn't going to be denied, they headed for the final against Kildare. They were tested to the limit, but had the answers this time, scoring three late points that ensured victory and launched the county into celebratory orbit. All-Ireland glory became the new target, but that ended at the quarter-final stage when Laois lost to Armagh by two points.

Laois F. Byron; J. Higgins, C. Byrne, A. Fennelly; D. Rooney, T. Kelly, K. Fitzpatrick; P. Clancy, N. Garvan; R. Munnelly, M. Lawlor, G. Kavanagh; B. McDonald, I. Fitzgerald, D. Delaney **Subs** C. Parkinson for Delaney, B. Brennan for Kavanagh, D. Miller for Lawlor, S. Kelly for Munnelly

Hurling

17 July 1949, Leinster final, Nowlan Park
Laois 3–8 Kilkenny 3–6

The 1915 All-Ireland final, in which Laois beat Cork, is their most significant win in purely achievement terms but the 1949 team were operating in a much more competitive environment, as underlined in the Leinster championship that also featured Kilkenny and Dublin, respective All-Ireland champions and runners-up in 1947 and 1948. Laois beat both. By the time Laois reached the Leinster final, they had scored a total of 13–11 against Offaly and Dublin. Beating Dublin was a real achievement and left Laois in a very positive mindset ahead of the final.

Kilkenny had home advantage in Nowlan Park but it didn't bother Laois who dominated the first half, opening up a ten-point lead. Kilkenny, as expected, launched a powerful comeback in the second half, cutting the lead to two points in the closing minutes, but Laois held out to win the provincial title for the first time in thirty-four years.

They saw off Galway in the All-Ireland semi-final – 4–6 to 3–5 – but lost the final by seventeen points to an outstanding Tipperary team in what was that county's first year of an All-Ireland three-in-a-row.

Laois T. Fitzpatrick; L. White, J. Bergin, P. McCormack; J. Murray, T. Byrne, P. Ruschitzko; W. Bohane, J. Styles; P. Hogan, P. O'Brien, W. Dargan; P. Lalor, H. Gray, P. Kelly
Sub F. Moloney for O'Brien

LEITRIM

Football

24 July 1994, Connacht final, Dr Hyde Park, Roscommon
Leitrim 0–12 Mayo 2–4

In a quarter of a century hosting major football occasions, national and provincial, Dr Douglas Hyde Park on the Athlone Road in Roscommon had never witnessed anything like the outpouring of emotion from thousands of Leitrim supporters on the evening of 24 July 1994.

As Leitrim captain Declan Darcy – the Dublin-born son of a proud Leitrim man – lifted the Nestor Cup with the aid of ninety-five-year-old Tom Gannon to celebrate Leitrim's second Connacht senior football title, tears of joy flowed. Gannon had been the last man to captain Leitrim to provincial success back in 1927.

Watching from the periphery, attempting to remain anonymous but ultimately not succeeding, was the mastermind of the triumph.

John O'Mahony, who had brought his native Mayo to the brink of All-Ireland success five years earlier, had now plotted his adopted county's path to glory at the expense of his native place.

O'Mahony was appointed Leitrim team manager in late 1992. The county had been enjoying, by their own standards, considerable improvement in status under the previous manager P.J. Carroll. They won the All-Ireland B Championship in 1990 and won the Connacht Under-21 crown for only the second time in 1991.

Leitrim claimed a notable scalp in 1993, beating Galway in the Connacht championship for the first time in forty-four years. Interestingly, five of the Galway players would feature on the team that won the All-Ireland final, with O'Mahony at the helm, five years later.

Roscommon beat Leitrim by two points in the 1993 Connacht semi-final but there were clear signs that O'Mahony's philosophy and meticulous attention to detail were getting through to the players and that, given time, further improvement would emerge.

The draw for the 1994 championship could not have been more demanding. Leitrim would have to beat the province's 'Big Three' – Roscommon, Galway and Mayo in that order – if they were to claim a rare provincial title. Even within the county borders, there was little optimism that the dream of Connacht glory would be realised.

A one-point win against Roscommon sowed the first seeds of hope. They drew with Galway in Carrick-on-Shannon, travelled to Tuam for the replay and won by a point – 0–11 to 0–10. Pádraig Kenny's winning score ensured Leitrim's place in the provincial final for the first time since 1967.

The roar that greeted the team's arrival on the field in Hyde Park for the final was an indication of the passion generated among Leitrim people. Many had travelled from abroad for the big occasion. Not even the concession of a goal in the first minute quelled the enthusiasm of the supporters or, more significantly, the players. Mayo did not score again in the first half as Leitrim dominated and led by 0–6 to 1–0 at the break.

They were the better team for much of the second half too, extending their lead to eight points before a Kevin O'Neill goal reignited Mayo's effort. It tested Leitrim's resolve and, this time, they were ready, holding out for a superb win which electrified the county. They were Connacht champions for the first time in sixty-seven years.

Writing in the *Irish Press*, Seán McGoldrick, a proud Leitrim man, brilliantly captured what it meant. 'For Mayo, it was just another Connacht final. But for Leitrim, generations of emotional turmoil were crammed into seventy minutes of football. This success will do more for Leitrim's self-confidence than the one million political promises they have heard over the past sixty years. Never did Larry Cunningham, with the rendition of 'Lovely Leitrim' sound so sweet as it did last night,' he wrote.

Dublin proved too strong in the All-Ireland semi-final, although Leitrim proved themselves worthy of a place in the last four. Still, it was a year that will never be forgotten in the county.

Leitrim M. McHugh; J. Honeyman, S. Quinn, F. Reynolds; N. Moran, D. Darcy, G. Flanagan; M. Quinn, P. Donohue; P. Kieran, G. Dugdale, A. Rooney; C. McGlynn, P. Kenny, L. Conlon
Subs J. Ward for Dugdale, B. Breen for Conlon

Hurling

22 June 2019, Lory Meagher Cup final, Croke Park

Leitrim 2–23 Lancashire 2–22

Three minutes of added time had been played. Lancashire led by three points and Leitrim's hopes of capturing a first national hurling title seemed to have been shattered once again. It called for something special, and it came in the form of a James Clancy goal that sent the game into extra-time.

'Once the game went to extra-time, Leitrim were in the driving seat as their energy and deeper resources told. Yet, even then, Lancashire had some bad misses and closed a five-point gap down to just one when the final whistle sounded,' wrote John Connolly in the *Leitrim Observer* under a piece headed 'LEITRIM DRAMA KINGS'.

'Am I dreaming?' asked team captain Declan Molloy on the steps of the Hogan Stand as he prepared to accept the trophy. He wasn't. The dream was real.

Leitrim D. Molloy; P. Earley, D. McGovern, N. McLoughlin; E. Moreton, J. Glancy, F. Earley; L. Moreton, K. McDermott; A. Byrne, C. Moreton, B. Murray; G. O'Hagan, C. Cunniffe, C. O'Donovan

Subs S. Goldrick for Byrne, D. Ryan for Earley, Z. Moradi for McDermott, K. McGrath for McLoughlin, K. McDermott for Earley

LIMERICK

Hurling

23 July 2023, All-Ireland final, Croke Park
Limerick 0–30 Kilkenny 2–15

They lingered and mingled in a joyous green movement of players, management, families and supporters, all longing for that summer Sunday evening in Croke Park to last indefinitely.

Limerick hurling had reached its highest peak and was basking in the sheer glory of it all. The disappointing years – all forty-five of them, when they went from 1973 to 2018 without winning an All-Ireland title – became a distant memory, replaced by a sense of elation and pride after being crowned champions for a fourth successive year and for a fifth time in six seasons.

Only Cork (1941–1944) and Kilkenny (2006–2009) had previously completed the four-in-a-row, underlining the enormous challenge involved in trying to stay at the top for so long.

When Kilkenny led the 2023 final by five points in the forty-second minute, it looked like Limerick would be the latest county to discover that the hurling gods are very selective in who they allow through the four-in-a-row door.

What happened from there on was quite remarkable and proved that the Limerick squad were well-qualified to take their place among the all-time greats.

From that point, they out-scored Kilkenny by 0–19 to 0–5, growing in confidence and efficiency as they took their total to 0–30.

A year earlier, they had beaten Kilkenny by two points, having had sixteen and eleven points to spare against Waterford and

Cork respectively in the 2020 and 2021 finals. It left Limerick with an average winning margin of 9.8 points in the four finals, an extraordinary level of superiority.

They performance in the final twenty-eight minutes of the 2023 final was as good as ever seen in a final. Their point-scoring from all distances and angles was quite mesmerising.

'They got scores from out the field, outrageous scores, fantastic scores. Sometimes, there is nothing you can do about it,' said Kilkenny manager, Derek Lyng in a post-match interview.

It was an honest admission, a concession to greatness from a man who had played a significant role as a player in Kilkenny's four-in-a-row success in 2006 to 2009.

For Limerick, it was a day that will never be forgotten. Despite being without inspirational captain, Declan Hannon – ruled out by injury – they worked their way calmly and systematically through the puzzle set for them by Kilkenny.

'It was a phenomenal second half, there's no two ways about it,' said Limerick manager John Kiely. And nobody could possibly disagree.

Limerick's bid to become the first county to win five successive All-Ireland titles ended in the 2024 semi-final when they lost by two points to Cork.

Limerick N. Quaid; M. Casey, D. Morrissey, B. Nash; D. Byrnes, W. O'Donoghue, K. Hayes; D. O'Donovan, C. Lynch; G. Hegarty, D. Reidy, T. Morrissey; A. Gillane, S. Flanagan, P. Casey
Subs C. O'Neill for T. Morrissey, G. Mulcahy for Flanagan, C. Boylan for Hegarty, B. Murphy for O'Donovan, A. Costello for M. Casey

Football

11 July 2004, Munster final, Gaelic Grounds

Limerick 1–10 Kerry 1–10

In spring 2000, Limerick football emerged from the shadows. A talented Under-21 team won the Munster championship and it took an exceptional Tyrone team to thwart them in the All-Ireland final.

And it was that underage team that provided the inspiration and much of the talent for a rare courtship that might have led to a senior-championship romance. That it was not properly consummated in no way detracts from the achievements of the seniors during 2004 when they came within moments of a famous victory against Kerry.

A year previously, Limerick had lost to Kerry by five points in the Munster final. They gave a good performance for much of the way, suggesting there was more to come when they were more experienced.

After an encouraging league campaign in 2004, Limerick reached the semi-final by topping Division 1B, ahead of Galway. They lost to Kerry by two points in the semi-final but brought their form into the championship and qualified for the Munster final and another outing with Kerry in the Gaelic Grounds.

The bookmakers offered odds of 7/2 against Limerick. It looked exceptional value for long periods. John Quane, Muiris Gavin, goal-scorer Stephen Lavin and John Galvin led the way as Limerick took the fight to Kerry. They should have been more than three points ahead after an enterprising first half.

Kerry clawed their way back in a tight, tense second-half, eventually drawing level. Limerick had a few chances late on, but were denied by Darragh Ó Sé's high fielding on his own goal line that prevented at least one, and possibly two, points. On a day of very tight margins, that was crucial.

'We gifted them a goal and a point in the first half,' lamented manager Liam Kearns. 'That was hugely disappointing because this is a game we should have won. That is the bottom line.'

Limerick journeyed to Fitzgerald Stadium, Killarney a week later. They led by 1–6 to 0–2 after twenty minutes and the dream remained alive. It didn't last, however, and in the end they lost by four points – 2–9 to 3–10. It really was a season of what might have been. But that special day when they came so close to winning Munster for the first time in 108 years provided lots of memories.

Limerick S. O'Donnell; M. O'Riordan, J. McCarthy, T. Stack; C. Mullane, S. Lucey, S. Lavin; J. Stokes, J. Quane; S. Kelly, M. Gavin, M. O'Brien; C. Fitzgerald, J. Galvin, E. Keating
Subs J. Murphy for Gavin, D. Reidy for Lavin

LONDON

Football
30 June 2013, Connacht semi-final replay, Dr Hyde Park
London 2–11 Leitrim 1–13

Between 1975, when they first entered the Connacht championship, and 2012, London played thirty-eight games, winning only one (against Leitrim in 1977). Between 26 May 2013 and 23 June 2013, they played three games – and they won two and drew one.

The second victory, achieved against Leitrim in a replay, provided them with a special prize – qualification for the Connacht final for the first time. Magical times for London.

Their quarter-final win – 1–12 to 0–14 – over Sligo in Ruislip stunned the GAA world, but was generally regarded as a one-off. Leitrim had home advantage for the semi-final in Carrick-on-Shannon and, since they had beaten London by five points a year earlier, they were fancied for a repeat win.

London were not impressed with their 'outsiders' tag and turned in a defiant performance that earned them a draw. It sent their confidence soaring for the replay in Roscommon a week later and when they led by 2–10 to 0–2 at half-time, after completely dominating the first half, a place in the final seemed certain.

They achieved it, but not without enduring a scary second half in which Leitrim shook off their first-half lethargy and launched a major rescue bid. They came tantalisingly close to succeeding, but London, who scored only one point in the second half, held on for the narrowest of wins.

The margin was irrelevant. They had reached a peak never previously explored by a London team. Next stop was Castlebar and a clash with Mayo, beaten All-Ireland finalists a year earlier.

The build-up to the Connacht final was different to anything that had gone before, and the London players and supporters were determined to enjoy it. Judging by the atmosphere in Castlebar on the weekend of the game, the visiting fans certainly embraced the occasion.

Coping with the step-up was a major challenge for the team and with Mayo powering forward from the start, the gulf in class became obvious. Mayo won by sixteen points but not even a big defeat could dampen London spirits.

And they weren't finished yet. Defeat in the Connacht final left them in Round 4 of the All-Ireland qualifiers, where they were paired with Cavan in Croke Park.

Despite it being only six days after losing to Mayo, London were strong and composed in the first half, stretching Cavan all the way. It was level at half-time and close throughout the third quarter until London's energy levels dropped, enabling Cavan to pull away for a nine-point win.

London's best championship season was over, but the memories lived on, especially that emotional Connacht semi-final win over Leitrim. Later in the year, their high-scoring forward Lorcan Mulvey, a native of Cavan, became the first London player to win an All-Star nomination.

London D. Traynor; P. Butler, S. Curran, D. McGreevy; S. Hannon, S. Mulligan, T. Gaughan; P. Geraghty, C. Doyle; D. Dunleavy, G. Crowley, C. McCallion; C. Magee, L. Mulvey, E. O'Neill
Subs E. McConville for Hannon, S. Kelly for McCallion, B. Mitchell for Dunleavy, C. Daly for Doyle, B. Collins for Magee

Hurling

29 July 1973, All-Ireland quarter-final, Ballinasloe
London 4–7 Galway 3–5

The start was everything for London, who stunned the home side by racing into a 3–2 to 0–0 lead after sixteen minutes. The Galway defence had been ripped apart and while they settled into the game from there on – conceding only 1–5 – the damage was done. London were on their way to the semi-final.

Featuring six of the team that had won the All-Ireland Under-21 title in 1972, Galway felt they had the right balance between newcomers and experienced players, but they were never allowed to settle into a progressive rhythm. Ironically, no fewer than six of the London side were Galway men, including the entire full-forward line of Lennie Burke, Frank Canning and Martin Linnane.

The report in the *Connacht Tribune* the following week suggested that the result showed 'that some of Galway's best hurlers are no longer in the county'.

It really was a splendid day for London, who headed for Ennis the following Sunday to take on Limerick in the semi-final. They found the Munster champions a much different proposition and were beaten by eleven points. Limerick went on to win the final.

The defeat by London was a sobering experience for Galway, but it didn't disrupt their progress and, two years later, they reached the All-Ireland final after beating Munster champions Cork in the semi-final. They lost to Kilkenny in the final but the graph remained on an upward trajectory and, five years later, they won the All-Ireland title for the first time in fifty-seven years.

London E. Walsh (Kilkenny); W. Twomey (Cork), G. Rea (Limerick), J. Barrett (Tipperary); P. Cronin (Kerry), M. Connolly (Galway), D. Lawlor (Wexford); L. Corless (Galway), R. Cashin (Waterford); P. O'Neill (Tipperary), T. Connolly (Galway), B. Barry (Offaly); L. Burke (Galway), F. Canning (Galway), M. Linnane (Galway)
Sub D. McCarthy (Cork) for Corless

LONGFORD

Football

21 July 1968, Leinster final, Croke Park

Longford 3–9 Laois 1–4

When Longford edged out Galway by a point in the 1966 National League 'home' final and later went on to take the title outright for the first time by beating New York over two legs, it completed their best year up to that point.

Beating Galway was especially memorable as the Tribesmen had won successive All-Ireland titles in 1964 and 1965. That Longford were not only good enough to stretch them but to actually win underlined the quality of their squad. That Galway team is regarded as one of the best in GAA history but, in front of a crowd of 45,317 in Croke Park, Longford had their measure, winning 0–9 to 0–8 in a tense, exciting encounter. It was no fluke – Longford fully deserved their victory.

It raised hopes in the county that a big championship breakthrough was imminent but, for some reason, it took two years to come to fruition. In 1966, they lost to Louth by six points in the Leinster first round, two weeks after beating Galway and, a year later, they lost the semi-final to Offaly.

It prompted questions over whether Longford's big chance had passed, but they answered emphatically in 1968 when they beat Dublin, Meath and Laois to win the Leinster title for the first time. The win over Meath was especially significant as the Royals were reigning All-Ireland champions and were well fancied to make a strong bid for two-in-a-row. However, reputation mattered little to Longford, who took control from the start and were full value for their five-point win.

In many ways, that was their defining performance of the year, and it left them in the unusual position of being favourites in a Leinster final. Fears that the Longford players wouldn't live up to the billing against Laois didn't last long. Ahead from the sixth minute, they never looked like losing control in a game where Seán Donnelly (2–1) and Jimmy Hanniffy (1–1) were top scorers as Longford powered to an eleven-point win.

They were in no way flattered by the size of the margin on a day of huge emotion for players and supporters. Sixty-six years after playing in the championship for the first time, Longford were Leinster champions. It remains their only senior title.

The *Longford Leader* had no doubt about where that group of players stood in the county's history.

'They made a historic breakthrough when winning the National League title in 1966 and now they have created another record. There can be no doubt that this is the greatest team ever to represent Longford.'

The extent of the goodwill towards a squad that had taken Longford to unprecedented heights was underlined the following Sunday when the county board were given permission to hold collections near churches to help defray training costs. The Longford public responded enthusiastically, happy to make their contribution towards the drive for even greater glory.

Longford were paired with Kerry in the All-Ireland semi-final and had their supporters ready for take-off to a magical orbit when they led by a point with eight minutes remaining. However, a Mick O'Connell–Johnny Culloty-inspired Kerry finished strongly and won by two points. It was disappointing for Longford, but nothing could take away from the undeniable fact that they had provided the county with its greatest championship season.

Longford J. Heneghan; S. Flynn, L. Gillen, P. Barden; B. Barden, J. Donlon, J.P. O'Reilly; J. Flynn, T. Mulvihill; V. Daly, J. Hanniffy, J. Devine; S. Murray, M. Hopkins, S. Donnelly
Subs M. Reilly for Murray, P. Burke for J. Flynn

Hurling

3 July 2010, Lory Meagher Cup final, Croke Park
Longford 1–20 Donegal 1–12

Introduced in 2009, the Lory Meagher Cup provided Longford with a historic day in the competition's second year, when they won the title with an eight-point win over Donegal in the final.

Seven teams – Longford, South Down, Leitrim, Donegal, Cavan, Fermanagh and Warwickshire – competed and though Longford lost to Donegal by four points in the first round, they recovered and won their next three games. Donegal had come through to reach the final and, this time, the outcome was very different.

Longford led by five points at half-time but were put under severe pressure when Donegal cut the deficit to a point early in the second half. Longford's response was quick and effective, and they powered to a great victory.

Longford P. Cullen; B. Stakem, S. Browne, C. Finucane; C. Egan, S. Hannon, R. Donnellan; M. Coyle, E. Donnellan; S. Stakelum, N. Casey, D. Tanner; G. Ghee, J. O'Brien, J. Newman
Subs F. Daly for Stakelum, J. Minnock for Casey, B. Stakelum for Newman, S. Lynam for R. Donnellan

LOUTH

Football
22 September 1957, All-Ireland final, Croke Park
Louth 1–9 Cork 1–7

Louth won All-Ireland titles in 1910 and 1912, but neither of those successes could compare with what happened in 1957. The first two triumphs came at a time when there were not many counties competing in the All-Ireland series – in 1912, just seventeen counties were involved.

In 1910, Louth were crowned All-Ireland champions without even playing the final after Kerry refused to travel to Dublin because of a dispute with the Great Southern Railway Company over travel arrangements. Louth accepted the walkover, much to the annoyance of Kerry, who felt they should have been supported in their attempt to get a refixture.

Two years later, Louth, represented by the Tredaghs club, won the title by more straightforward means, beating Antrim in the final.

It was thirty-eight years before Louth reached another final, losing to Mayo in 1950. They won a Leinster title in 1953, but then went three years without getting past the provincial quarter-finals.

Indeed, spirits were very low after the three-point defeat by Kildare in the 1956 Leinster quarter-final in Navan, with the *Dundalk Democrat* in no mood for sugarcoating what they deemed a very poor performance.

'To fall at the first fence was a disheartening experience but the pill was made all the more bitter because long before the final whistle, quite a number of the red-jerseyed players seemed to accept defeat as inevitable. The fighting spirit which characterised displays of 'Wee County' teams in the last decade or so was conspicuous by its absence. Truth to tell, we were mediocre.'

It was against that rather gloomy background that Louth set out on the 1957 championship trail. Few expected them to make any impression even after they beat Carlow by eleven points in the Leinster first round. Clearly, the camp had a different mindset, and they beat Wexford (six points), Kildare (eleven points), Dublin (five points) and Tyrone (six points) to reach the All-Ireland final.

It was an impressive march, during which they scored 11–48 while conceding just 2–36. Whatever the origin of the vast improvement, it was clear that this was an altogether different approach to what had gone before.

Their opponents in the final were Cork, whom they had never previously played in the championship. Adding to the interest was the smallest versus biggest county angle, much emphasised in newspaper coverage.

Cork went into the game as overwhelming favourites, with almost all the tipsters in the national newspapers predicting that the experience gained when losing to Galway in the 1956 final would hand them a decisive advantage.

It didn't. Cork led by two points at half-time and were ahead by the same margin after fifty-five minutes. However, Louth were far from finished and a goal by Seán Cunningham gave them a precious lead, which they retained to the end.

Captain Dermot O'Brien became the first – and only – Louth man to receive the Sam Maguire trophy (it was first presented in 1928) after a win that was made all the sweeter for players and supporters by the underdogs tag that had accompanied them into the game.

Indeed, it was mentioned several times in homecoming speeches the following night, when speakers asserted that sections of the national media had disrespected Louth. It all added to the sense that the previous Sunday was indeed Louth's greatest day.

Beating Dublin (the beaten 1955 All-Ireland finalists), Tyrone (Ulster champions in 1956 and 1957) and Cork (Munster champions in 1956 and 1957) underlined the extent of Louth's improvement. The manner in which they dealt with Cork was especially impressive.

'The men who scorn the odds against them; the footballers who simply refuse to be beaten,' was Pádraig Puirséal's description in the *Irish Press*.

Louth S. Óg Flood; O. Reilly, T. Conlon, J. Meehan; P. Coleman, P. Smith, S. White; K. Beahan, D. O'Neill; S. O'Donnell, D. O'Brien, F. Lynch; S. Cunningham, J. McDonnell, J. Roe

Hurling

4 June 2016, Lory Meagher Cup final, Croke Park
Louth 4–15 Sligo 4–11

On a league table of extraordinary comebacks, Louth's revival in the 2016 Lory Meagher Cup final is very close to the top.

They trailed by twelve points in the first half and by eleven at half-time. They were much-improved in the second half but still faced a five-point deficit with three minutes remaining. Then, in an amazing finish, Louth hit three goals, earning them a spectacular win.

The gods had finally smiled on them after four defeats in Nicky Rackard Cup finals in 2005, 2008, 2011 and 2012.

Louth J. Connolly; C. Matthews, B. Minogue, M. Wallace; M. Lyons, R. Maher, A. McCrave; D. O'Hanrahan, S. Callan; G. Smith, N. Stanley, D. Kettle; D. Murphy, L. Dwan, P. Lynch
Subs N. Cafferkey for Matthews, A. Mackin for Smith, S. Connelly for O'Hanrahan

MAYO

Football

23 September 1951, All-Ireland final, Croke Park
Mayo 2–8 Meath 0–9

In early November 1947, five members of the Mayo football team – Seán Flanagan, Pádraic Carney, Liam Hastings, Tom Langan and Eamon Mongey – penned a letter to the Mayo County Board expressing serious concerns about the future prospects for football in the county.

They had drawn a league game with Kerry in Tralee, but so chaotic was the organisation of the team that the county secretary Finn Mongey (a brother of one of the signatories) and one of the car drivers had been called on to don the colours and make up the numbers.

'We feel the time has come when something must be done before football disappears completely in Mayo – unwept, unhonoured and unsung,' was the uncompromising message from the players' missive.

It was a provocative gesture and a bold one. It worked.

Four years later, in September 1951, Mayo clinched their second successive All-Ireland senior football title and the county's third in championship history.

From the issuing of the letter and subsequent reorganisation of their structures, Mayo went on to win the Connacht championship in 1948 (losing the All-Ireland final to Cavan by one point) and 1949. They won their third consecutive provincial title in 1950 and went on to win the All-Ireland title, beating Louth by 2–5 to 1–6.

Flanagan, their captain and natural leader, was determined that they would successfully defend the title a year later. And after retaining the Connacht title, they defeated Kerry in the All-Ireland semi-final in a replay, with full-back Paddy Prendergast giving what is still regarded as one of the greatest performances by a player in the position. Meath awaited in the final.

Though the scoreline suggests a close game, the general consensus was that Mayo were deserving winners. Tom Langan and Joe

Gilvarry scored two first-half goals and Pádraic Carney dominated around the centre of the field.

Journalist John D. Hickey in the *Irish Independent* wrote that 'had their [Mayo's] margin been three times five points at the final whistle it would have been no false guide as to the measure of their superiority'.

'Seldom has Mayo played such brilliant football,' wrote the match reporter identified only as 'M O'C' in the *Connaught Telegraph*. 'They out-manoeuvred the Meath men, fielded higher and kicked longer, while the Meath backs were flustered and bewildered by the varying tactics employed by the Mayo forwards, whose rapier-like thrusts – all beautifully executed movements – were a treat to watch. It was a tough, hard-fought game, tackling was keen and heavy, hard knocks were given and taken and both teams seemed to revel in this hard, rugged type of football as they stood shoulder to shoulder and fought tooth and nail for each ball.'

Mayo S. Wynne; J. Forde, P. Prendergast, S. Flanagan; J. Staunton, H. Dixon, P. Quinn; E. Mongey, J. McAndrew; P. Irwin, P. Carney, S. Mulderrig; M. Flanagan, T. Langan, J. Gilvarry
Sub L. Hastings for Dixon

Hurling

5 June 2016, Nicky Rackard Cup final, Croke Park
Mayo 2–16 Armagh 1–15

Amidst seemingly never-ending days of disappointment for Mayo in Croke Park, a rare beacon of light shone on the red and green in June 2016. And it was the less glamourous hurling team, rather than the footballers, that basked in the joy of winning a national title after they captured the Nicky Rackard Cup for the first time.

Just a year earlier, they had suffered the heartbreak of losing their status in the higher grade Christy Ring Cup, after losing a play-off to Roscommon. But they recovered quickly and displayed massive resolve to qualify for the Rackard final and win a first national hurling title for the county since the All-Ireland-winning junior team of 1981.

For dual-player Keith Higgins – one of Mayo's all-time greats – the final provided the opportunity to gain some compensation for the growing number of footballing setbacks endured by the county in Croke Park. He played a huge part in ensuring that Mayo hurlers realised their dream.

But even Higgins had to bow to the masterclass brought to Croke Park by Kevin Feeney, who scored 1–9 over the seventy-plus minutes, 1–3 from play.

'What a difference a year makes. Last summer, Mayo hurling was in its darkest place in years after defeat to Roscommon in a relegation play-off robbed them of their long-held Christy Ring status. On Saturday, that same team – with a handful of notable additions – stood jubilant in Croke Park as Nicky Rackard champions,' wrote Mark Higgins in the *Western People*.

Mayo D. O'Brien; B. Hunt, G. McManus, E. Collins; C. Freeman, K. Higgins, A. Lyons; D. Kenny, C. Charlton; J. McManus, K. Feeney, S. Regan; S. Boland, P. O'Flynn, D. McTigue
Subs P. Connell for Lyons, F. Boland for McTigue, C. Scahill for O'Flynn, K. McDermott for Hunt, G. Nolan for Boland

MEATH

Football
9 October 1988, All-Ireland final replay, Croke Park
Meath 0–13 Cork 0–12

It has never been suggested – nor will it be – that this game be added to the All-Ireland final classics contender list. Dour, dogged and attritional, there were times when it crossed the line into spiteful territory.

As an advertisement for Gaelic football, it failed on many fronts, yet it will always be recalled in Meath as arguably the best day in their football history. That's certainly the case in achievement terms as it was the first time they had retained the All-Ireland title.

Their All-Ireland winners of 1949, 1954 and 1967 failed in the two-in-a-row bids – in fact none of them survived the Leinster championship stage. It was all very different in 1988 when Meath won the entire set of available prizes – National League, Leinster and All-Ireland.

They had close calls in the National League, where they beat Dublin in a replayed final and, again, in the All-Ireland final where only a point separated them from Cork after 140 minutes. A pointed free by Brian Stafford late in the first game earned Meath a replay on a day when they weren't nearly as efficient as they had been a year earlier when they beat Cork by six points in the final. They were fortunate to get a second chance in 1988 as Cork had been the better team but, as that Meath team showed so often, their survival instinct was immense.

The replay was three weeks later, which gave a long time for soul-searching in both camps. Indeed, it may have been responsible for a build-up of tension that erupted in the replay. Meath felt they hadn't come close to reaching their usual standards in the drawn game, even allowing themselves to be bullied. They vowed it would be different next time. 'We said we were going to be a more aggressive team and Cork had overheard us. There's no doubt about that. Nevertheless, it was important to tell them personally in the first few minutes of the game,' wrote Liam Hayes in his autobiography *Out of Our Skins*.

Seven minutes into the game, Meath were reduced to fourteen men when Gerry McEntee was sent off for a foul on Niall Cahalane. Facing more than an hour with a numerical disadvantage was quite a challenge, but their response was so driven that Cork couldn't exploit the extra man.

In terms of defiance, the performance was probably the best produced by a Meath team. It wasn't that Cork played badly, but Meath were so obsessed that nothing was going to stop them. It was especially evident in the first half hour of the second half, which they won 0–8 to 0–3. Cork rallied and scored three late points, but Meath's sheer tenacity saw them through. They had achieved a famous victory, one that was made all the sweeter by what they perceived as a grudging response nationally to their success. They didn't care – Sam Maguire was back in Royal territory for another year.

Meath M. McQuillan; R. O'Malley, M. Lyons, T. Ferguson; C. Coyle, L. Harnan, M. O'Connell; L. Hayes, G. McEntee; D. Beggy, J. Cassells, P.J. Gillic; C. O'Rourke, B. Stafford, B. Flynn **Sub** M. McCabe for Gillic

Hurling

25 June 2016, Christy Ring Cup final replay, Croke Park
Meath 4–21 Antrim 5–17, after extra-time

Huge relief, sheer joy, total satisfaction. A whole range of emotions coalesced to make the replay of the 2016 Christy Ring Cup final a very special day for Meath hurling. They thought they had won it three weeks earlier when the official score recorded them as one-point winners – 2–18 to 1–20. They were presented with the trophy and began the celebrations, only to discover that they had been awarded a point in error.

It prompted the GAA to order a refixture. Building back up for a final they thought they had won was mentally challenging for Meath and when they trailed Antrim by eight points at half-time, it appeared that events of the previous weeks had taken their toll.

It called for a real resolve and Meath delivered in spectacular style. They led by three points in stoppage time, but Antrim struck for a last-minute goal to send the game to extra-time. It really was beginning to look as if the gods were conspiring against Meath, but they held their nerve and won by a point.

The manner of the victory, coupled with the dramatic events of previous weeks, made it a truly memorable day for Meath.

Meath S. McGann; S. Geraghty, R. Sherlock, D. Donoghue; S. Brennan, K. Keoghan, S. Whitty; S. Heavey, S. Morris, J. Keena; D. Healy, A. Gannon; G. McGowan, N. Heffernan, J. Toher
Subs S. Clynch for Brennan, S. Quigley for S. Heavey, M. O'Grady for J. Keena, J. Keena for O'Grady, S. Heavey for Heffernan

MONAGHAN

Football

7 April 1985, National Football League final, Croke Park
Monaghan 1–11 Armagh 0–9

Was this a better achievement than when Monaghan drew with Kerry, arguably the greatest team of all-time, in the 1985 All-Ireland semi-final? Better than the 1930 All-Ireland semi-final win over Kildare? Better than the 1979 Ulster title win, Monaghan's first since 1938?

It's all a matter of opinion. What's a matter of fact is that Monaghan's National League success in 1985 gave them a senior national title for the first time, strengthening the argument about why it can be classified as their greatest day. That they followed up by winning the Ulster title and coming so close to beating Kerry in the All-Ireland semi-final later in the year only strengthens that case.

The groundwork had been laid a year earlier when they were promoted from Division 3, before reaching the final of the Centenary Cup, an open-draw competition that was added to the calendar to mark the GAA's 100th anniversary. Featuring all thirty-two counties, it was run on a straight knockout basis.

Monaghan beat Limerick, Mayo, Offaly and Derry to reach the final, where they lost to Meath by two points. Despite that disappointment, there were clear signs that they were re-emerging as an ambitious force under Seán McCague, who had also guided them in their successful 1979 Ulster championship run.

Monaghan topped the Division 2 table in the 1984–1985 season, winning four, drawing two and losing one in a group that also included Dublin, Donegal, Mayo, Roscommon, Offaly and Louth.

Quarter-final and semi-final wins overs Kildare and Tyrone in a replay earned them a place in the league final for the first time. Armagh, who had finished second in Division 1, were their opponents for a contest that was never going to be a thing of joy for purists.

The weather decided to add its own mischief, dropping icy-cold rain on Croke Park. The game was always going to be a war of attrition and while many fancied a more experienced Armagh side to be better equipped for the challenge, it didn't work out like that.

Luck deserted Armagh, who had also lost the 1983 league final to Down. Just before half-time, they had a penalty awarded against them in unusual circumstances. Full-back Thomas Cassidy made a fine catch just to the left of his square and as he turned inside the line in an attempt to find an escape from his markers, he was adjudged to have overcarried by referee John Gough.

Eamonn McEneaney slotted the penalty to the net to give Monaghan an advantage they held all the way to the finish, winning by 1–9 to 0–7. The scenes afterwards were reminiscent of All-Ireland final day, as Monaghan players and supporters celebrated with all the enthusiasm associated with a big breakthrough.

'Scenes reminiscent of Down's historic All-Ireland victory twenty-five years ago greeted Monaghan's hard-fought and richly deserved success in Croke Park yesterday. The absolute delight on the faces of the Monaghan supporters told its own story,' wrote Tom O'Riordan in the *Irish Independent*.

The win sent Monaghan's confidence levels soaring and, after winning the Ulster title, they came very close to beating Kerry in the All-Ireland semi-final. Kerry had won six of the previous ten All-Ireland finals (and would go on to win the next two) but on this particular day, Monaghan matched them all the way, forcing a draw through a long-range pointed free by McEneaney. They lost the replay by five points.

It was disappointing as they felt they should have won the first day, but it was still an excellent year, with the league success ensuring the squad of a special place in Monaghan history.

Monaghan P. Linden; E. Sherry, G. McCarville, F. Caulfield; G. Hoey, C. Murray, B. Murray; H. Clerkin, D. Byrne; D. Flanagan, E. McEneaney, B. Murray; R. McCarron, E. Murphy, E. Hughes

Hurling

3 June 2023, Lory Meagher Cup final, Croke Park
Monaghan 3–22 Lancashire 3–20

At last – a national hurling title for Monaghan! The thrill of success was enhanced by the manner of victory, surviving a hard-fought struggle. They led by a point at half-time but Lancashire opened up a three-point lead early in the second half.

It presented Monaghan with a real challenge, and they responded impressively. Two goals from Niall Garland, who finished on 2–3, and the continued accuracy of Niall Arthur (0–10, 0–4 from play) helped Monaghan to a historic victory.

Monaghan H. Byrne; J. Guinan, P. Finnegan, C. McHugh; C. Flynn, K. Crawley, D. Hughes; C. Merrick, A. Kenny; N. Arthur, N. Garland, S. Lambe; T. Hughes, C. Gernon, E. Flynn **Subs** F. Rafter for Gernon, P. Malone for Lambe, C. McNally for Kenny, C. Guinan for Merrick

NEW YORK

Football

21 May 1967, National Football League final, second leg, Gaelic Park
New York 4–3 Galway 0–10

1967 was the third time New York won the National League title, but it was by far the most satisfying. They had beaten Cavan and Dublin respectively in the 1950 and 1964 finals, but both were one-off games, whereas the 1967 final was played over two legs on successive Sundays.

Unlike Cavan and Dublin, neither of whom were All-Ireland champions when they lost to New York, Galway were the undisputed number one when they travelled to New York in May 1967. In fact, they were triple All-Ireland winners, having swept all before them in the 1964, 1965 and 1966 championships.

The only big-league setback came in the 1966 'home' final when they lost to Longford, who went on to beat New York over the two-legged final in Croke Park. Galway put the defeat by Longford behind them to clinch the All-Ireland three-in-a-row in September 1966 and added the National League 'home' title to their haul when they beat Dublin in April 1967.

Galway's successes maintained their rating as one of the best teams of all time and offered no sign whatsoever of the imminent decline. Granted, they had found New York to be difficult opposition in the 1965 league final, losing the first leg by a point, but improved dramatically in the second leg, which they won by eight points.

Two years later, New York won both legs by five points – 3–5 to 1–6 and 4–3 to 0–10 – to take the title on an aggregate score of 7–8 to 1–16. New York winning was a major surprise, even more so the margin of victory, but the biggest shock of all centred on their goal tally.

In ten games with Kerry (three), Meath (two), New York (two), and Cork, Down and Longford (one each) in All-Ireland semi-finals, finals and National League ('home' and outright finals) in 1964, 1965, 1966 and 1967, Galway had conceded only two goals.

It was defensive security at its strongest, the basis for the most successful run in the county's history. Now, in the space of a week, their reputation as security experts had evaporated after New York took them for seven goals in two games. Offaly-born Tom Furlong scored four goals – two in either game – Pat Cummins grabbed two in the second game and Jimmy Halpin hit one in the drawn game.

Galway's defensive collapse was a big talking point back in Ireland as their rivals eyed the possibilities ahead of the championship. Mayo were first in line to check if Galway's trans-Atlantic flop was a temporary setback or a sign of serious decline, and were delighted to discover the latter to be the case.

Five weeks after returning from New York, Galway lost the Connacht semi-final to Mayo by 3–13 to 1–8 in Pearse Stadium.

Indeed, were it not for some excellent saves by goalkeeper Johnny Geraghty, they would have been beaten by a lot more. It would be another thirty-one years before Galway next won the All-Ireland title.

As for New York GAA, those two Sundays in May 1967 will always be recalled with immense pride. Deservedly so.

New York W. Nolan (Offaly); P. Maguire (Kildare), P. Nolan (Offaly), K. Finn (Louth); D. Finn (Louth), S. Nugent (Kildare), S. Kenna (Roscommon); J. Foley (Kerry), B. Tumulty (Wicklow); P. Cummins (Kildare), M. Moynihan (Kerry), P. Caulfield (Offaly); J. Halpin (Meath), B. O'Donnell (New York), T. Furlong (Offaly) **Subs** T. Brady (Cavan) for Halpin, T. Feighery (New York) for Caulfield

Hurling

26 September 1965, National Hurling League final, second leg, Gaelic Park

New York 3–9 Tipperary 2–9

On 5 September 1965, Tipperary beat Wexford by twelve points in the All-Ireland final, securing their second two-in-a-row of the decade. There was little time for celebrations as they headed to New York eleven days later to prepare for the first leg of the National League final, which they won by 4–10 to 2–11.

New York led by two points with ten minutes remaining, but a strong Tipperary finish gave them a five-point win.

A week later, New York got their victory and while it wasn't quite enough to take the league title, it still made for a wonderful occasion in front of 8,000 spectators in Gaelic Park.

Tipperary led by two points at half-time, but a spirited New York effort was rewarded with a three-point win, leaving them just two short – 6–19 to 5–20 – on aggregate. Despite that disappointment, they had the satisfaction of having beaten the All-Ireland champions just three weeks after their big triumph in Croke Park.

New York K. Croke (Galway), S. Custy (Clare), J. Maher (Galway), M. Morrissey (Wexford); P. Hennessy (Waterford), P. Dowling (Cork), J. Murphy (Tipperary); B. Hennessy (Kerry), P. Donohue (Galway); M. Curtin (Galway), P. Kirby (Clare), D. Long (Waterford); J. Donohue (Offaly), J. Naughton (Clare) P. Egan (Galway)
Subs W. Carey (Tipperary) for P. Donohue, J Kelly (Galway) for Carey

OFFALY

Football
26 September 1971, All-Ireland football final, Croke Park
Offaly 1–14 Galway 2–8
There is an argument, put forward by some of the chief protagonists of the period, that Offaly's most momentous triumph in their football history was achieved in the 1972 All-Ireland final replay, when they beat Kerry to secure a remarkable two-in-a-row. There are also those who claim that the dramatic win over Kerry a decade later brought Offaly's best day.

As alluring as those successes undoubtedly were, the big question is whether they would have happened at all without the breakthrough year of 1971. Its historical value, crowned by the win over Galway in the All-Ireland final, instilled a powerful self-belief among the Offaly players and public and provided them with a platform from which to build towards new targets.

Offaly's emergence into football's elite was one of the special stories of the 1960s, a decade full of sporting romance mainly involving Down, Galway, Meath, Dublin, Kerry and Longford.

By reaching the All-Ireland finals of 1961 and 1969, Offaly had defied both tradition and population. Unfortunately for them, they lost both games, first to Down and then to Kerry, and great players must have feared that rare opportunities had been squandered.

They had lost their Leinster title in a dramatic final against Meath in 1970 and had faced what must have looked like an arduous climb back. But, during 1971, they blitzed Leinster, completed by beating Kildare by fourteen points in the final, and then Cork by five in the All-Ireland semi-final.

Could they complete the great adventure in the final?

In a game affected by heavy rain, there were times when some of their old insecurities returned. Galway dominated for long periods and would regret a series of missed opportunities – they led by 1-6 to 0-4 at half-time after kicking no fewer than twelve wides. As the rain poured down in the second half, it was Offaly that adapted, gradually growing in confidence and efficiency.

John Smith's introduction strengthened Offaly's case and they gradually whittled down Galway's lead. The sides were level after sixty minutes (finals were eighty minutes long at that time) before Murt Connor's goal, followed by a Galway goal from Séamus Leyden set the scene for a frantic finish. Offaly fared better, kicking three points without reply, to secure a memorable victory.

Veteran GAA correspondent Pádraig Puirséal described the aftermath in the *Irish Press*: 'What this success meant to the vast throng of Offaly followers was amply demonstrated after the final whistle, when be-flagged supporters, almost delirious with joy, ignored the monsoon-like rain and thronged in such thousands to mob their heroes that a strong force of gardaí was hard pressed to shepherd the exhausted but delighted players on to the Hogan Stand rostrum for the presentation of the trophy.'

The Sam Maguire Cup was on its way to Tullamore for the first time.

Offaly M. Furlong; M. Ryan, P. McCormack, M. O'Rourke; E. Mulligan, N. Clavin, M. Heavey; W. Bryan, K. Claffey; J. Cooney, K. Kilmurray, T. McTague; J. Gunning, S. Evans, M. Connor
Subs J. Smith for Claffey, P. Fenning for Gunning

Hurling

6 September 1981, All-Ireland hurling final, Croke Park
Offaly 2–12 Galway 0–15

Distilling history into a single moment might seem to do a disservice to the entirety of the process. But the goal by Johnny Flaherty, three minutes from the final whistle, that helped to seal Offaly's first All-Ireland senior hurling triumph is one of those moments that is frozen in time.

It was Offaly's first final and only the second championship where they had reached the All-Ireland stages, and they were facing the defending champions. As brave as their steady climb up the rankings had been, and as dreamlike their ambitions, few outside Offaly really believed that they had the wherewithal to go all the way.

And when Galway led by seven points four minutes into the second half, nobody could have predicted what was to come. For the next half hour, Offaly snipped away at Galway's lead, reining in the 1980 champions with ever-increasing momentum and authority. Could Offaly possibly complete the remarkable recovery? Yes, they could.

Flaherty's winning goal encapsulated Offaly's defiance and determination. His palming of the ball past helpless Galway goalkeeper Michael Conneely was the conclusion of a movement that had begun with Joachim Kelly and involved Pat Delaney and Brendan Bermingham before reaching Flaherty, who supplied the killer touch.

It was a performance that defied the critics, as expressed in the pages of the *Offaly Independent* by Eddie Rogers.

'Beyond the confines of the county, Offaly entered the fray as rank outsiders. The GAA 'experts' were unanimous in tipping the holders to retain their crown. Their post-match diet of humble pie proved indigestible, resulting in some Monday morning papers doing less than justice to Offaly's performance. To suggest that the winners were handed the title on a plate is the height of nonsense.'

Offaly D. Martin; T. Donoghue, E. Coughlan, P. Fleury; A. Fogarty, P. Delaney; G. Coughlan; J. Kelly, L. Currams; P. Kirwan, B. Bermingham, M. Corrigan; P. Carroll, P. Horan, J. Flaherty
Subs B. Keeshan for O'Donoghue, D. Owens for Kirwan

ROSCOMMON

Football
24 September 1944, All-Ireland final, Croke Park
Roscommon 1–9, Kerry 2–4

Roscommon's progress from relative obscurity in the 1930s to the summit of Gaelic football in the first half of the 1940s was one of the biggest stories of the period. Two All-Ireland minor titles – in 1939 and 1941 – with an All-Ireland junior title sandwiched in between, provided the impetus and talent for the senior breakthrough in 1943 when they beat Cavan to win the Sam Maguire Cup for the first time.

But, as voiced by their charismatic captain Jimmy Murray, known as 'Jamesie' in his native Knockcroghery, the true measure of a team's standing was how it fared when paired against Kerry. And such thinking added to the allure of the meeting between the two teams in the 1944 final.

Roscommon endured a shaky start to the defence of their title when they needed a replay to beat Sligo in the Connacht semi-final. But they upped the pace thereafter, eased past Mayo in the final before enjoying an unexpectedly comfortable win against Cavan in the All-Ireland semi-final.

As was their custom, Roscommon came together for two weeks of full-time training in preparation for the final, staying in the Old Infirmary in the county town, which now houses the County Library. Team trainer Sergeant Billy Keogh had devised special tactics for the final to counter the aerial power of the Kerry defence, led by Joe Keohane.

Signs carrying the letters K.T.B.L. were placed around the dormitories – Keep The Ball Low was Keogh's message. It worked.

Over 65,000 had attended the 1943 final, a figure regarded as extraordinary given the difficulties with travel at the time. For the 1944 final, the gates of Croke Park were closed when the numbers through the stiles reached 79,245 and thousands were left outside, depending on the radio for news of the game. The attendance was a new record for an All-Ireland final, bettering the 68,950 for the drawn Kerry–Galway final in 1938.

The news came in a constant stream. Kerry's Denis Lyne and Roscommon's Frankie Kinlough traded early goals and, at half-time, Roscommon led by 1–4 to 1–2. An Eddie Dunne goal eleven minutes into the second half gave Kerry the lead, 2–4 to 1–5. Aided by the roving Murray, the Roscommon midfield pairing of Eamon Boland and Liam Gilmartin began to dominate the game and, remarkably, Kerry did not score again.

Donal Keenan levelled the game with two points, one from play, one from a free – he ended the final as top scorer with 0–7 – and Kinlough restored Roscommon's lead four minutes from the end. Keenan's final point from another free sparked wild celebrations.

'The champions gave a polished display of high-class crafty football,' was the verdict of *The Kerryman* newspaper. 'On Sunday's form,' added the unnamed reporter, 'Roscommon are as good a side as ever I have seen in action.'

Words that were music to the ears of everyone in Roscommon.

Roscommon O. Hoare; W. Jackson, J.P. O'Callaghan, J. Casserly; B. Lynch, B. Carlos, P. Murray; E. Boland, L. Gilmartin; F. Kinlough, J. Murray, D. Keenan; H. Gibbons, J. McQuillan, J.J. Nerney
Sub D. McDermott for Nerney

Hurling

3 October 1965, All-Ireland junior final, St Coman's Park
Roscommon 3–10 Warwickshire 2–11

Gerry O'Malley's status as a footballer brought him fame and respect on a national scale during almost two decades of service from 1947 to 1965 but he always admitted that 'hurling is my first love'.

So, while an All-Ireland title eluded him as a footballer – he went closest when Roscommon reached the All-Ireland senior final in 1962 – he did become a champion as a hurler when Roscommon won its first championship, beating British champions Warwickshire in a thrilling final played at the old St Coman's Park in Roscommon town.

O'Malley was then thirty-eight years old and had retired from football the previous autumn. He was persuaded to give one more year exclusively to hurling and was initially rewarded when Roscommon comfortably beat Armagh, 6–8 to 1–3, in the All-Ireland 'home' final in Croke Park.

For what was billed as the final proper, Warwickshire fielded a team of exiles from six different counties, including Henry Shefflin Senior from Kilkenny, and contributed generously to a thrilling final. The teams were level with just two minutes remaining, but Roscommon finished strongly, team captain Mick Hoare securing victory with a point in the last minute. Séamus Cormican was Roscommon's top scorer on 1–4.

Roscommon T. Gavin; T. Moylett, P. Lyons, T. Murphy; B. Mitchell, J. Kenny, M.J. Keane; M. Laffey, S. Cormican; G. O'Malley, J. Boland, R. Fallon; M. Hoare, T. Boyle, J. McDonnell
Sub M. Glennon for Boyle

SLIGO

Football
20 July 1975, Connacht final replay, MacHale Park, Castlebar
Sligo 2–10 Mayo 0–15
With a sense of trepidation that was entirely understandable, Sligo football supporters made the trek to Castlebar almost resigned to their fates. Their footballers, forty-seven years without a Connacht championship title to celebrate, had let slip a six-point lead in the drawn game on their home ground two weeks earlier, and were fortunate to escape defeat.

With fifteen minutes remaining in MacHale Park in the replay some of those supporters were preparing for an early exit, that old familiar feeling deep in their stomachs of what might have been. Mayo led by two points and looked set to extend their advantage. As reported in the *Sligo Champion*, the Sligo team 'looked a dejected, demoralised outfit'.

Then, midfielder Tom Colleary hoisted a high and hopeful ball towards the Mayo goal. Mickey Kearins, fourteen years in pursuit of a provincial title, got a touch and the ball dropped into the path of Dessie Kerins. Without hesitation, he fired low and hard into Ivan Heffernan's net.

What had been a fairly mundane affair up to that point became an absorbing drama.

Mattie Hoey excelled in the Sligo forward line and kicked two points to put them three ahead. Seán Kilbride and J.P. Kean struck back for Mayo to cut the lead to a point. The kick-out after Kean's point was crucial. Sligo goalkeeper Tom Cummins drove it towards the centre of the field, Sligo's player-coach Barnes Murphy, ignoring the pain of a badly bruised ankle, won possession.

Sensing that referee Tommy Moran was ready to blow the final whistle, Murphy drove the ball over the sideline. Moran did, indeed, bring the game to an end and Sligo were the Connacht champions for the first time since 1928. A day that would be forever etched in Sligo folklore.

Mickey Kearins, recognised as one of the greatest players of all time and an All-Star in the first year of the awards scheme in 1971, was the centre of attention but there were others who stood out too, as journalist Jim Gray noted in the *Sligo Champion*.

'As the final whistle sounded, the unbearable tension mellowed to uncontrollable emotion as players and supporters jumped and embraced each other. Mickey Kearins was carried shoulder-high from the pitch.

'In a game of this nature, heroes tend to spring up like bees on a flower bed, and while it would, perhaps, be unfair to single out any of the Sligo players, I feel John Stenson must get my 'man of the match' tag. It's true that in the emotion following the game, Sligo supporters probably felt that the entire team should be nominated as All-Stars, but, in retrospect, it was Stenson's tenacity that was the difference between victory and defeat.

'This was a hard, physical battle and there was no place for the weak-hearted. Stenson revelled in this setting. When Mayo threatened to shatter Sligo's dream in the dying stages, it was the long-haired, bearded, Curry midfielder who kept the clockwork ticking through sheer determination.'

Sligo, who had beaten Galway by ten points in the Connacht semi-final, were unable to match the Connacht final heroics in the All-Ireland semi-final and bowed out tamely to eventual champions Kerry. Still, they had ensured that their names will always be fondly recalled in Sligo football folklore.

Sligo T. Cummins; R. Lipsett, J. Brennan, T. Carroll; M. Brennan, B. Murphy, P. Henry; J. Stenson, T. Colleary; M. Laffey, M. Hoey, F. Henry; D. Kerins, M. Kearins, J. Kearins
Sub B. Wilkinson for Laffey

Hurling

3 August 2008, Nicky Rackard Cup final, Croke Park
Sligo 3–19 Louth 3–10

Paul Seevers was a sixteen-year-old goalkeeper when he first played at Croke Park in 1986 as a member of the Sligo team that won the county's first All-Ireland minor hurling title in the B championship. Twenty-two years later – at the age of thirty-eight and wearing the number twelve jersey – he returned to the completely revamped stadium to taste glory once again.

His team-mate from those underage days, Mickey Galvin, was team manager and he had put together a team of widely varying ages to progress through the group and knockout stages of the Nicky Rackard Cup to reach the final against Louth.

In the final, Seevers contributed 1–4 of Sligo's 3–19 total, but he was first to sing the praises of his young team-mate Keith Raymond, who lined out at centre half-forward. The twenty-year-old scored 1–8 from play and prompted Seevers to say 'he'd walk into any team in the country and I'm including the very best in that'.

Raymond's own reaction reflected the mood of the squad. 'I'm just living the dream. It was one of those days when everything just fell right for me. But it is something I will always remember.'

Sligo C. Brennan; F. Coyne, W. Gill, R. Cox; D. Clarke, M. Burke, L. Reidy; J. Mullins, D. Colleary; M. Gilmartin, D. Burke, P. Seevers; J. Bannerton, K. Raymond, L. Cadden
Subs C. Herity for Cadden, M. Shelley for Bannerton, C. O'Mahony for Gilmartin

TIPPERARY

Hurling

2 September 1951, All-Ireland final, Croke Park

Tipperary 7–7 Wexford 3–9

It wasn't exactly a classic All-Ireland final, but context is everything. Tipperary have had more dramatic wins but none that carried the history-making dimension attached to the 1951 final.

This was the day they secured the All-Ireland three-in-a-row, a treasured prize that they had previously won in 1898, 1899 and 1900, a period when counties were, for the most part, represented by individual clubs.

The scene was much different by the time they tried to win their third successive final in 1951. Having beaten Laois easily in the 1949 final and Kilkenny by a point in the 1950 final, they were fiercely determined to complete the three-in-a-row.

The Munster championship draw certainly wasn't kind to them. Drawn against Waterford in the first round, it meant they would have to win three games to retain the provincial title. Waterford tested them all the way, but Tipperary held their nerve and won by three points.

Next up in the semi-final was Limerick, who were also seen off, 3–8 to 1–6. It left Tipperary facing a final date with Cork, who would have liked nothing better than to dethrone their great rivals.

They made a strong attempt too, before losing by two points in a contest described in the *Irish Independent* as 'supercharged hurling, worthy to rank with the best the storied southern past can have ever seen'.

The game earned record gate receipts (up to then) with the 42,337 crowd who packed into the Limerick venue paying a total of £6,280 (equivalent to €7,975).

Tipperary had a bye into the All-Ireland final, while Wexford beat Galway in the semi-final. Tipperary were hot favourites going into the final, a tag that appeared to weigh heavily on them in the early stages when they fell 2–3 to 0–4 behind after fifteen minutes. It presented them with a real challenge, one which they met in a manner that befitted such great champions.

Goals from Séamus Bannon, Tim Ryan and Ned Ryan got them into a familiar routine and, by half-time, they led 3–6 to 2–6.

Two significant moments in the thirteenth and fourteenth minutes of the second half, when Tipp were leading by 4–6 to 2–8, were turning points. Wexford were awarded two twenty-one-yard frees, and Nicky Rackard opted to go for goal with both, only to have his efforts blocked and cleared by the Tipp defence. Wexford's challenge wilted from there on and Tipperary increased their advantage, eventually winning by twelve points.

The elusive three-in-a-row had been secured, ensuring that 1951 would always be recalled as a special year in Tipperary history. Their bid for a four-timer in 1952 ended in the Munster final when they lost to Cork.

Tipperary T. Reddin; M. Byrne, T. Brennan, J. Doyle; J. Finn, P. Stakelum, T. Doyle; P. Shanahan, J. Hough; E. Ryan, M. Ryan, T. Ryan; P. Kenny, M. Maher, S. Bannon
Sub S. Kenny for P. Kenny

Football

22 November 2020 Munster final, Páirc Uí Chaoímh

Tipperary 0–17 Cork 0–14

The irony of it! Tipperary waited eighty-five years for a Munster senior football title and when it came, the only sound in the stadium was the delighted whoops from the ecstatic players. They made plenty noise too as they celebrated in Páirc Uí Chaoímh after beating Cork on a dreary winter Sunday.

Covid restrictions kept supporters away, but as Tipperary people watched the drama unfold on television, there was no doubt that it provided a welcome lift for the county. There could be no coming together to celebrate the success, which was a pity as this really was a special day for Tipperary.

Cork, who had beaten Kerry in the semi-final, were warm favourites, but Tipperary refused to accept the underdog role, and produced a fine performance that fully deserved to land the big prize. While the result may have stunned the wider football world, it came as no surprise to Tipperary players or management.

'We always believed we could beat Cork. I didn't have to say that because the players knew they had beaten Cork at minor and Under-21 level, so there was total belief that we could be successful,' said team manager David Power, who also had the distinction of leading Tipperary minors to All-Ireland glory in 2011.

There was an added poignancy to the 2020 seniors' triumph as it came exactly 100 years after Tipperary footballer Michael Hogan was shot dead in Croke Park during the Bloody Sunday killings in 1920. Tipperary wore green-and-white jerseys similar to the 1920 colours to mark the occasion, and did them and Hogan's memory proud.

Tipperary E. Comerford; C. O'Shaughnessy, A. Campbell, J. Feehan; B. Maher, K. Fahey, R. Kiely; S. O'Brien, L. Casey; C. O'Riordan, M. Quinlivan, Conal Kennedy; B. Fox, C. Sweeney, Colman Kennedy
Subs L. Boland for Colman Kennedy, P. Feehan for Fahey, E. Moloney for Fox, P. Looram for Kiely, P. Austin for Casey

TYRONE

Football
28 September 2003, All-Ireland final, Croke Park
Tyrone 0–12 Armagh 0–9

Mickey Harte didn't publicly describe it as destiny, but he sounded very much like a man who believed it was. Even as thousands of Tyrone people lingered in Croke Park and its environs after the game, absorbing a sense of joy never previously experienced by the county's supporters, the manager was offering a personal perspective to the media.

'I just felt we were made for this day. We had worked so hard, poured our hearts into it and there was so much goodwill towards us. All the [Tyrone] people lit candles and visited relatives' graves. That's what the spirit of the GAA is all about. It's about real people who have a passion for the game and don't divorce it from real life.

We had a team meeting last night and you could sense that all the players were really touched by this.'

A year earlier, Tyrone had watched enviously as Armagh had won the All-Ireland title for the first time – now it was their turn to sample the same elation as they became the nineteenth county to land football's biggest prize. They took a long route to glory, requiring five games to win the Ulster title (draw and replays with Derry and Down, with a win over Antrim in between) before moving on to Croke Park and wins over Fermanagh (quarter-final), Kerry (semi-final) and Armagh (final).

They conceded only 0–20 in their last three games, which was the equivalent of the 4–8 they leaked against Down in the drawn Ulster final. Switching Cormac McAnallen from midfield to full-back for the replay proved a masterstroke by Harte, as it solidified the Tyrone defence in a manner few thought possible.

McAnallen went on to become a key figure in the replay and grew to such a degree with the All-Ireland challenge that he later won an All-Star award at number three. Sadly, he died suddenly in March 2004 at the age of twenty-four – his untimely death making the 2003 success, and the role he played in it, all the more poignant for Tyrone people. He represented a new sense of self-belief among a younger generation in a county that had previously reached only two senior finals, losing to Kerry in 1986 and Dublin in 1995.

The 2003 semi-final win over Kerry, the honours-laden aristocrats of Gaelic football, was especially pleasing for Tyrone. Their gameplan and its clinical execution didn't make for easy viewing but was hugely effective, displaying a self-confidence that wasn't always evident among previous Tyrone teams.

It was a clear declaration that they were doing things differently and didn't care what anyone thought. Restricting Kerry to six points in the semi-final was a remarkable achievement, but it would have counted for little if they didn't complete the All-Ireland quest some weeks later.

That the final was an all-Ulster affair for the first time added to its appeal, especially as Armagh were the defending champions. Almost inevitably, it was going to be a war of attrition between two squads and management teams who knew each other so well, which indeed turned out to be the case.

Just as they had done all season, Tyrone found a way to solve problems, with none more influential than Peter Canavan whose exceptional career finally took him into the exclusive club reserved for players who had captained their counties to All-Ireland titles.

Frank Rodgers, writing in the *Ulster Herald*, summed up what the win meant to Tyrone people. 'Where were you when Tyrone won Sam? In Croke Park, home in Tyrone, or in New York, Sydney or Toronto – it was all the same if you had a Tyrone connection. A new date had been added to milestones in your life.'

Tyrone J. Devine; C. Gourley, C. McAnallen, R. McMenamin; C. Gormley, G. Devlin, P. Jordan; K. Hughes, S. Cavanagh; B. Dooher, B. McGuigan, G. Cavlan; E. McGinley, P. Canavan, O. Mulligan

Subs S. O'Neill for McGuigan, B. McGuigan for Canavan, C. Holmes for Gourley, P. Canavan for Cavlan, C. Lawn for Gormley

Hurling
9 July 2009, Lory Meagher Cup final, Croke Park
Tyrone 5–11 Donegal 3–16

A first Lory Meagher Cup final and a first national championship win for Tyrone hurlers – it was quite a day in Croke Park, and also quite a game.

Wins over Warwickshire, Leitrim and Longford earned Tyrone a place in the final against Donegal, who had beaten them in both the National League and Ulster championship.

The pattern seemed set to continue when Donegal led by nine points after forty-five minutes, but all changed dramatically after that. Tyrone out-scored Donegal by 4–4 to 1–3 from there to the end, leaving them a point ahead.

The honour of becoming the first Tyrone captain to accept a national trophy in Croke Park fell to Stephen Donnelly on an afternoon of high emotion for the small band of loyal followers who had travelled to watch the final.

Tyrone D. McCabe; S.P. Begley, D. Maguire, M. Kelly; T. McIntosh, S. Donnelly, C. Gallagher; J. Kelly, T. Hughes; D. Lavery, P. O'Connor, S. McKiver; C. Grogan, R. O'Neill, G. Fox

Subs P. McMahon for Fox, A. Kelly for O'Connor

WATERFORD

Hurling

4 October 1959, All-Ireland final replay, Croke Park
Waterford 3–12 Kilkenny 1–10

'We have the MacCarthy Cup' screamed the banner headline across the front page of the *Waterford News & Star* in its joyous account of the most famous victory in Waterford hurling history.

It told how a recording of the last ten minutes of Michael O'Hehir's All-Ireland final commentary on Raidió Éireann was played over loudspeakers at the post-match dinner in the Grand Hotel in Malahide, with guests cheering wildly every time Waterford scored or Kilkenny shot a wide.

'After the recording, the team and supporters were shown a film of the 1957 All-Ireland final between Waterford and Kilkenny – in slow motion,' the paper reported.

Waterford lost that game by a point, so watching a rerun would normally have been a painful exercise. Not anymore. The team had learned from that defeat and, two years later, won the county's second All-Ireland title. Securing it by beating Kilkenny added to the sense of satisfaction, which was further increased by winning it in a replay.

The *Kilkenny People* graciously acknowledged the merit of their neighbours' success.

'Waterford were the better side, and their superior speed gave them an advantage which Kilkenny could never counter. They fought hard for the past couple of years for honours which they now deservedly carry.'

There were many who thought that the advances Waterford had made in 1957, when they reached the All-Ireland final, had been surrendered after a dismal performance in the 1958 Munster final when they had lost to Tipperary by thirteen points.

'It must be admitted that they surrendered their Munster crown in a manner most unbecoming to champions. Gone was the speed and dash of last year and instead a listless fifteen, which seemed to accept defeat as inevitable, offered but token resistance to Tipperary,' reported a downbeat *Waterford News & Star*.

That background made the 1959 success all the more joyous for Déise supporters. A renewed sense of determination, allied to the efficiency they displayed in 1957, enabled them to beat Galway and Tipperary by twenty-four (7–11 to 0–8) and seventeen points (9–3 to 3–4) respectively before edging out Cork by three points (3–9 to 2–9) in the Munster final.

Kilkenny were left in no doubt about what they could expect in the final but were confident they could repeat their 1957 success.

They struggled in the first half and were six points behind early in the second. Displaying all their traditional qualities, Kilkenny fought back and were three points clear late on before Séamus Power rescued Waterford with the equalising goal.

Waterford had to come from behind in the replay too, albeit with more time to do it. Kilkenny led by six points in the first quarter but, by half-time, Waterford were ahead 3–5 to 1–8 – two of the goals having been scored by Tom Cheasty. They restricted Kilkenny to two points in the second half while adding seven to their own total.

Thus ended a historic day for Waterford.

Despite defeat, it had a special significance for Kilkenny too as they gave Eddie Keher, who had played in the minor final four weeks earlier, a senior championship debut as a sub. He would, of course, go on to be one of hurling's greatest players.

Waterford E. Power; J. Harney, A. Flynn, J. Barron; M. Lacey, M. Óg Morrissey, J. Condon; S. Power, P. Grimes; M. Flannelly, T. Cheasty, F. Walsh; L. Guinan, T. Cunningham, J. Kiely
Subs M. O'Connor for Lacey, D. Whelan for Cunningham

Football

2 June 1957, Munster semi-final, Waterford Gaelic Field
Waterford 2–5 Kerry 0–10

It still ranks as one of the most sensational results in championship history as Waterford stunned Kerry, who had run Galway, the 1956 All-Ireland champions, to five points in the National League final two weeks earlier.

Admittedly, Waterford's task was made easier by a chaotic Kerry camp, where internal wrangling had left them with only sixteen players. John Barrett, a reporter with *The Kerryman* and a good club player, was added to the Kerry bench in case they ran out of subs.

Despite the problems, Kerry led by six points after forty minutes before Waterford took over and marched to an unexpected victory, the winning point scored by Tom Cunningham.

Mick O'Dwyer, who went on to become one of the best players and managers in GAA history, made his championship debut that day. 'That game has gone down in Waterford and Kerry folklore for very different reasons,' he wrote in his autobiography.

It raised hopes in Waterford that they might win the Munster title for the first time since 1898, but it didn't materialise. Cork were on high alert and beat them by eleven points.

Waterford G. McCarthy; M. Prendergast, M. Lonergan, C. Crowley; M. O'Connor, T. Cunningham, J. Power; S. Power, S. Forde; G. Whyte, N. Power, W. Kirwan; J. Timmons, J. White, T. Power
Subs W. Daniells for Forde, S. Roche for Daniells

WESTMEATH

Football
24 July 2004, Leinster final replay, Croke Park
Westmeath 0–12 Laois 0–10
When Westmeath beat Dublin in the 2004 Leinster quarter-final, it was such a surprise that there was more emphasis on the losers than the winners. This didn't bother Westmeath, who were busily working on new targets. They rightly ignored claims that they had been lucky against Dublin.

It was a shallow assessment, based essentially on history and the fact that, prior to 2004, Dublin hadn't lost to Westmeath in the championship since 1967. In the real world, Westmeath were making real progress. And they weren't about to stop.

Underage success in the 1990s had paved the way. Westmeath had won the All-Ireland minor title for the first time in 1995, beating Derry in the final. Four years later, they had won the All-Ireland Under-21 title for the first time and, in 2001, had been unlucky not to reach the All-Ireland senior semi-final for the first time. A late goal had earned Meath a draw in the quarter-final and they went on to win the replay.

Two years later, Meath had again beaten Westmeath in a replay – this time in the Leinster quarter-final. It was frustrating for Westmeath, but there had been clear signs that an ambitious group were zoning in on a big break.

After beating Dublin by two points in 2004, Wexford were seen off in the Leinster semi-final, setting up a final against defending champions Laois. This was super-confident Laois in the Mick O'Dwyer era, having re-emerged as a major force in 2003, winning the Leinster title for the first time in fifty-seven years.

Not to be outdone, this was Westmeath in the Páidí Ó Sé era, O'Dwyer's former protégé who had led Kerry to All-Ireland success in 1997 and 2000. Four years later, he was steering Westmeath on a historic course. The rivalry was box office, boosting interest in the 2004 Leinster final far beyond what might normally have been expected.

As defending champions, Laois were favourites but, in truth, Westmeath should have won the game – but a late point from Laois captain Chris Conway earned a draw. The result was largely misinterpreted by even seasoned observers.

The general view held that Laois would have the edge in the replay, but that really wasn't based on anything more than an assumption that favourites are usually better second time around. Westmeath certainly didn't accept it and, on a Saturday evening of high drama in Croke Park, they landed Leinster football's biggest prize for the first time.

If the game wasn't particularly memorable, the aftermath certainly was. The outpouring of emotion when captain David O'Shaughnessy lifted the trophy will always have a special place in the Westmeath memory bank.

Páidí Ó Sé, whose playing career had yielded dozens of titles, summed up the importance of Westmeath finally landing the Leinster title 115 years after their first championship game.

'The players had a choice between joining the losing brigade or becoming winners and ambassadors, names that would never be forgotten in Westmeath football.'

As for the occasion, its essence was colourfully captured by Kieran Galvin in the following week's *Westmeath Independent*.

'Quite simply, last Saturday was the greatest day in the history of Westmeath GAA. Indeed, the county has never experienced a more glorious day since it broke away from the ancient province of Meath in 1542.'

Westmeath G. Connaughton; J. Keane, J. Davitt, D. Healy; D. Heavin, D. O'Donoghue, M. Ennis; R. O'Connell, D. O'Shaughnessy; B. Morley, P. Conway, F. Wilson; A. Mangan, D. Glennon, D. Dolan **Subs** J. Fallon for Wilson, G. Dolan for Conway, S. Colleary for Glennon

Hurling

22 June 1975, All-Ireland B final replay, Croke Park

Westmeath 3–23 London 2–7

Westmeath have beaten stronger opposition over the years, the most recent being the famous win over Wexford in the 2023 Leinster round robin, but none of them yielded a title. They were all special on the day, but one-off wins don't register on the record books, unlike the All-Ireland B final in 1975, the second year of a championship for lower-ranked counties.

That it came in a replay made the win all the more satisfying, having snatched a late point to bring the game level a week earlier – 4–16 to 3–19. It was all very different in the replay when Westmeath raced to victory, thanks to a powerful second-half surge.

The *Westmeath Examiner* had no doubts about the significance of the victory, classifying it as arguably the county's greatest hurling day. 'The Westmeath lads carved a special niche for themselves in the hurling annals by virtue of this win, their first success in this competition and perhaps the most prestigious triumph by a Westmeath senior hurling side.'

Westmeath O. Gallagher; F. Shiels, P. Jackson, M. Cosgrave; S. Fagan, M. Fagan, W. Shanley; G. Whelan, P. Curran; C. Connaughton, J. Keary, M. Kilcoyne; E. Fagan, M. Flanagan, E. Clarke

Sub N. Fitzsimons for Clarke

WEXFORD

Hurling
23 September 1956, All-Ireland final, Croke Park
Wexford 2–14 Cork 2–8

Wexford's retention of the All-Ireland senior hurling title and their first championship victory over Cork are the most significant storylines of this epic contest. But there were so many other tales to tell after this encounter that makes it one of the most memorable and talked about finals of them all.

Defeated finalists in 1954, losing to Cork, Wexford had won their first All-Ireland senior title since 1910 when they had beaten Galway in the 1955 final. A three-week delay to the staging of the 1956 final, due to an outbreak of polio in Munster, added to the sense of expectation about the rematch with Cork.

An attendance of 83,096 illustrated the extraordinary interest generated by a final where Cork legend Christy Ring was bidding to win his ninth senior championship. On the Wexford side, Nicky Rackard was establishing himself as an exceptional talent on his way to becoming arguably the greatest full-forward of all time. Cork full-back John Lyons later described him as 'the best full-forward I played in my career, the finest gentleman'.

There would be another hero whose exploits are still feted in Wexford. Goalkeeper Art Foley made a save that not only changed the course of the game but is still regarded as one of the greatest ever seen in Croke Park or anywhere else. That it was from Ring, and that it may well have been the deciding factor in an absorbing contest, ensured it would have legendary status in GAA history.

Early in the second half, Wexford enjoyed a seven-point lead – 1–9 to 0–5 – but Cork staged a ferocious comeback and goals from Ring and Paddy Barry levelled the game in the forty-ninth minute. Ring then gave Cork the lead for the only time when he handpassed a point. It was to be their last score. Wexford pulled two points ahead and, with three minutes remaining, Foley made the stunning block from Ring. Wexford's quick counterattack yielded a Nicky Rackard goal, and the Liam MacCarthy Cup was on its way to the southeast.

More than fifty years later, from the home he made in Machin, Long Island in New York with his wife Ann and six children, goalkeeper Foley recalled what happened next. In an interview originally published in the *Irish Echo* newspaper in 2011, he gave his version of events. 'I can still see it clearly. There was a long clearance from Cork and Christy won the ball. He took off on a long solo run, cutting across the field. He came straight down the middle and stopped at the twenty-one. Why he didn't keep going, I didn't know. I'm still surprised.

'Well, he shot and I blocked it straight up in the air. This is where they always get it wrong. They always say I caught it and cleared it, straight to Nicky [Rackard] and he scored the goal. But I blocked it out and Pat Barry [Cork] doubled on it, and it hit the outside of the net. I pucked it out to Jim English and he passed it to Tom Ryan, and he got it to Nicky and Nicky got the goal, and we went on to win.'

It was a drama that had a profound effect on all who saw it. The *Irish Independent* GAA writer John D. Hickey captured its essence. 'From the twelfth minute of the second half to the end it was a fusillade of hurling fury, the likes of which I cannot recall having seen and one that I will also carry with me as one of my greatest memories.'

Wexford A. Foley; B. Rackard, N. O'Donnell, M. Morrissey; J. English, W. Rackard, J. Morrissey; S. Hearne, E. Wheeler; P. Kehoe, M. Codd, T. Flood; T. Ryan, N. Rackard, T. Dixon

Football

16 February 1919, 1918 All-Ireland final, Croke Park
Wexford 0–5 Tipperary 0–4

Wexford, the first team to win four successive All-Ireland senior football titles, contested seven finals, including a replay, between 1913 and 1918. They lost to Kerry in the finals of 1913 and 1914 (a replay) and then went on an unbeaten run that brought them the title in 1915 (against Kerry in the final), 1916 (against Mayo) and 1917 (against Clare). Could they complete the four-timer?

The 1918 championship schedule was badly disrupted by an outbreak of Spanish flu throughout the island, and the final between Wexford and Munster champions Tipperary was delayed until February 1919.

On and off the field, Seán O'Kennedy was renowned as a natural leader and he had captained the team to the first three titles. Jim Byrne, a tenacious defender, succeeded O'Kennedy for the 1918 championship decider in which Gus O'Kennedy, Seán's brother, was the primary creator and provider in a low-scoring game.

Wexford J. McGrath; N. Stuart, P. Mackey, J. Byrne; T. Murphy, T. Doyle, M. Howlett; W. Hodgins, J. Doran; J. Crowley, R. Reynolds, P. Todd; A. Doyle, G. O'Kennedy, J. Redmond

WICKLOW

Football

18 July 2009, All-Ireland qualifier series, Round 3, Aughrim
Wicklow 1–15 Down 0–17

On some days, there is no need for silverware to adorn an occasion. A sense of achievement, a caress of the soul, is sufficient to satisfy the most earnest of desires.

Wicklow's summer of contentment, a welcome if rare experience, reached its dramatic climax on a Saturday evening in July, a month rarely associated with All-Ireland championship action in the county.

Mick O'Dwyer, the football evangelist from Kerry, had been sprinkling his magic dust over Wicklow for three seasons, a period in which interest in the county team had soared. His arrival was a massive lift for Wicklow, boosting self-esteem, as football's most successful manager set about raising their fortunes and their profile.

Wicklow's pre-season games in 2007 became akin to festivals, drawing big crowds, and even TV cameras, to Aughrim. Interest in Wicklow's progress extended well beyond the county boundaries.

By August, the Tommy Murphy Cup – a competition for lower-ranked counties – had been secured with a thrilling win over Antrim in extra-time in Croke Park.

In 2008, another important milestone was reached when Wicklow beat Kildare in the Leinster championship in Croke Park.

The 2009 Leinster championship ended for Wicklow with a loss to Westmeath in extra-time in the quarter-final. It was a big disappointment, but far from having a deflating impact, it fuelled them for a shot at the All-Ireland qualifiers.

The drama, the fun, the excitement and the memories were on their way. For three successive weekends, Aughrim became a football hotspot. Favourable home draws attracted big crowds, and Fermanagh and Cavan went home chastened by their experiences.

When the draw for Round 3 of the qualifiers was made, Wicklow were paired with Down. Even the romantics felt that the end was nigh for the Garden County.

Six minutes into the game Wicklow's dual-jewel Leighton Glynn scored a goal and Wicklow began to believe. Twice they led by five points and the decibel levels continued to rise. Down responded and were level near the end before Tony Hannon, Wicklow's deadly accurate free-taker, stroked over the winning point from a forty-five.

The county's hills and mountains reverberated to the sound of the cheering masses – Wicklow were in the last twelve in the All-Ireland race, having beaten three Ulster counties, all of whom had been ranked much higher after the National League.

O'Dwyer was ecstatic. 'It was a fantastic kick by Tony. He was under huge pressure, and he was kicking into the wind. But I had great confidence in him, as he is the kind of player who copes very well with pressure.'

Comparing that success with everything else he had achieved in football, O'Dwyer added: 'I don't think anything ever felt as good, in my life anyway. It was a marvellous victory.'

Next up was a Round 4 clash with Kildare, another county that had been enriched by O'Dwyer in the past. Sadly for Wicklow, the exertions of the previous three weeks took their toll and, while they played well at times, they lost by four points. The magical adventure had ended but the memories remained.

Wicklow M. Travers; C. Hyland, D. Ó hAnnaidh, S. Kelly; P. McWalter, B. McGrath, D. Hayden; J. Stafford, T. Walsh; J.P. Dalton, T. Hannon, L. Glynn; D. Odlum, S. Furlong, P. Earls

Hurling

3 June 2023, Nicky Rackard Cup final, Croke Park
Wicklow 1–20 Donegal 3–12

In Wicklow's hurling history, there are a few notable successes: an All-Ireland junior title in 1971 and an All-Ireland B championship win in 2003 among them. The latest addition to that roll of honour, the Nicky Rackard Cup success of 2023 is, arguably, the most notable of all.

Wicklow hurling was in limbo at the start of the 2023 season. Losing the Christy Ring Cup finals in 2011 and 2012 had been heartbreaking; losing Christy Ring status in 2022 had followed relegation to Division 2B in the league.

They needed a boost – and quickly. Manager Casey O'Brien targeted a Rackard Cup success, which was duly delivered when they narrowly defeated Donegal in a thrilling final. This was after winning all five games in the group section.

Wicklow trailed by four points at half-time in the final – 0–10 to 2–8 – and changes were needed. They introduced Daniel Staunton and Matthew Traynor, and the team became more competitive. The vital moment came in the forty-seventh minute when Andy O'Brien whipped the ball into the net for Wicklow's only goal.

Wicklow were level – 1–12 to 2–9 – and the momentum shifted. As the clock neared seventy minutes, they led by five points – 1–20 to 2–12. Donegal goalkeeper Luke White scored a goal from a free to cut the deficit to just two points. But Wicklow defended brilliantly for three minutes of added time and held on for a memorable win.

Wicklow C. McNally; B. Kearney, A. Kavanagh, M. O'Brien; P. Doran, J. Henderson, Sam O'Dowd; D. Masterson, J. Doyle; M. Boland, C. Moorehouse, E. McCormack; D. Maloney, A. O'Brien, L. Evans
Subs S. Germaine for Boland, D. Staunton for Masterson, M. Traynor for O'Dowd, G. Weir for O'Brien, P. Doyle for Evans

5 CHAMPIONSHIPS AND CHANGE

There is no allowing for the sense of bewilderment for players, who after months of training have been dumped out of the championship in the first round by one point. Counties should be given a second chance.
Current GAA president Jarlath Burns, speaking as Players' Committee chairman at the Special Congress in 2000 when the football championship format changed for the first time.

The Royal Lancaster Hotel in London was an unlikely venue for the GAA to take one of the most momentous decisions in the history of its competition structures, but, by the mid-1990s, a definite mood for change was blowing hard across the association's landscape.

It applied particularly to hurling where there was a sense that the game's massive public appeal hadn't been exploited to anything like the degree it should. Too few games in the summer, top teams eliminated as early as mid-May in a competition that didn't end until September and the awkward question of how to fit Galway into the All-Ireland championship, were among the issues concentrating minds.

The unevenness of the championship was underlined by the contrast between Clare and Galway, neighbouring counties with vastly different summer experiences. Three successive years – 1989, 1990 and 1991 – provided the perfect illustration of how lopsided the All-Ireland championship really was.

In 1989, Clare were eliminated from the Munster championship – and by extension the All-Ireland series – on 21 May. A year later, they were gone by 13 May and, in 1991, their exit date was 19 May.

By contrast, Galway didn't have their first championship game in 1989 until 6 August. Their entry date in 1990 was 22 July and, a year later, it was 4 August.

Since they qualified directly for the All-Ireland semi-finals in 1989 and 1991 – and lost both – it left them with only one championship game per year. In alternate years, as in 1988 and 1990, they had quarter-final games against London, but they weren't played until late July, by which stage most other counties had been eliminated.

In 1987 and 1988, Galway won an All-Ireland two-in-a-row by winning a total of five games, one of which was against London – All-Ireland B winners, who were out of their depth at the higher level.

It was deeply unsatisfactory on a number of fronts.

Despite the apparent flaws in the championship system, getting agreement on changes was never going to be easy. An open-draw,

All-Ireland format was totally out of the question as Munster and Leinster jealously guarded their championships, as they still do.

There was also reluctance among players to in any way downgrade the role of the provincial championships. In an interview in 1987, Wexford's George O'Connor, one of the big stars of that era, said that while players didn't begrudge Galway the success they were enjoying at the time, it was unfair that they got an automatic pass to the All-Ireland stages without playing a game.

'Counties like Clare, Waterford, Laois, Dublin and Wexford cannot help but be envious of them. Galway would probably suggest that an open draw is the answer. Both the Leinster and Munster championships have a great appeal so why scrap them? Instead, why not put Galway into Munster?' he said.

It was a suggestion that would have horrified Galway if it had got official backing. They had spent a miserable eleven seasons (from 1959 to 1969) in the Munster championship, during which time they won only one of twelve games. It had left them with bad memories from a misguided venture. A return would not have been countenanced, even if their stature was altogether higher than it had been in the 1960s.

Their move to Munster in 1959 came a year after they had qualified directly for the All-Ireland final. The same had applied in 1955 when they were waved through to the final, while Wexford and Limerick, respective Leinster and Munster champions, played in the semi-final. Wexford beat Galway by eight points in the final, having trailed by two at half-time.

Despite the apparent incongruity of the decision taken by congress to allow Galway, Connacht's only championship representatives, directly into the All-Ireland final every three years, there was no mood to change when it was next due to be discussed in 1958.

Tipperary beat Limerick, Cork, Waterford and Kilkenny to reach that final against a Galway side that had had no competitive game since losing to Clare in the National League in March. It was an utterly bizarre system and came to be regarded as such by the public. That was proven when the 1958 All-Ireland final attracted a low attendance of 47,276 – more than 6,000 fewer than for the Kilkenny–Tipperary semi-final.

Tipperary beat Galway by ten points, a margin that flattered the Tribesmen who were never really in with a chance. 'An embarrassing farce' was Mick Dunne's cutting description of the game in the *Irish Press*.

The decision to despatch Galway to the Munster championship a year later was designed to put them on an even footing with other counties in the All-Ireland championship race and, in theory, it looked sound.

However, it never worked. It was as if Galway felt totally bereft in their new environment and, after losing twice to Waterford – by 7–11 to 0–8 and 9–8 to 4–8 in 1959 and 1960 respectively – many in the county wanted a quick withdrawal. It didn't happen. A win over Clare in 1961 briefly lifted the mood, but that was as good as it got. They lost every game from then until 1969, after which it was decided they should exit Munster. It was a lucky escape.

Their average margin of defeat in eleven games was just over eleven points. Cyril Farrell, who went on to lead Galway to All-Ireland wins in 1980, 1987 and 1988, recalled in his autobiography how his early hurling memories were of embarrassing defeats.

His father brought him to Limerick for the 1959 Munster championship clash with Waterford, which Galway lost by twenty-four points.

'Galway weren't so much beaten, as humiliated. It was an awful disappointment, not just to a ten-year-old from Woodford but to a county which believed that a spell in Munster would be beneficial,' he wrote.

At the end of the 1960s, the mood among Galway supporters was low but it turned out to be a case of the darkest hour being just before the dawn. All changed for Galway in the 1970s. An All-Ireland Under-21 win in 1972 was followed, in 1975, by a first National League title success since 1951, and a first appearance in an All-Ireland senior final since 1958. They lost to Kilkenny but the tide had turned – Galway were now a genuine force. By 1980, they were All-Ireland champions and two more titles followed in 1987 and 1988.

Galway's successes in the 1980s undoubtedly played a part in focusing attention on the All-Ireland format. So, too, did a special competition, played in 1984 as part of the GAA's centenary celebrations. Run in open-draw format, it offered a glimpse into a different way of doing things.

The progress made by Laois was among the highlights of the novel venture. They overcame Limerick, Tipperary and Galway, and while Cork beat them in the final, their confidence had been boosted in a manner not provided by the Leinster championship for many years.

Supporters of an open draw put the Centenary Cup forward as an example of what might be achieved by a breakaway from the Leinster and Munster championships as the main bedrocks of the All-Ireland series. That wasn't going to happen, but tweaks were possible.

With Galway and Offaly having won five All-Ireland titles between them in the 1980s and Antrim reaching the final for the first time in forty-six years in 1989, mindsets began to change. The break from traditional powers dominating all competitions was encouraging and prompted further discussion on how best to advance the game.

It would still take some years for the first big breakthrough – allowing beaten Leinster and Munster finalists back into the All-Ireland championship – to emerge.

The plan envisaged Galway and the Ulster champions joining the beaten Munster and Leinster finalists in quarter-finals, while the Leinster and Munster winners qualified directly for the semi-finals. Given the many changes the All-Ireland championship has undergone since then, the arguments put forward for not allowing re-entry for any beaten team might appear flimsy today, but there was still quite a lobby group for retention of the 'one strike and you're out' format.

Liam Mulvihill, then director-general of the GAA, had proposed amending the format a few times in the early 1990s, but initially his ideas got little traction. In his 1994 Annual Report, he suggested that allowing the beaten Leinster and Munster finalists to re-enter the All-Ireland series would benefit Galway and the Ulster champions, while also increasing public interest.

'Most importantly, it would be more equitable, as it would be much more likely that the two best teams in the country would meet in the final,' he wrote.

At the 1994 Congress, Nickey Brennan, then Kilkenny County Board chairman and who later went on to become GAA president, delivered a stirring speech, during which he asserted that hurling 'is dying on its feet'.

Among his concerns was the promotion of the game, especially by comparison with football.

'For a number of years, hurling has fallen behind football in terms of support and appeal – that must be a matter of great concern for both the strong and weak counties. The overall state of hurling is being eroded and serious action is needed.'

Allowing beaten Leinster and Munster finalists back into the championship might not appear like a major response, but it did help on the promotion side.

Decision-day was 6 April 1996 at the Annual Congress, which was held in London as part of their 100th anniversary celebrations. The proposal was carried on a show of hands, but not before some strong opposition was expressed.

Brendan Ward, Offaly County Board chairman, insisted it was not in hurling's best interests.

'It will not be right to let losers in the back door. We hear people saying that hurling is going downhill. Is it because Galway, Offaly and Clare have come to the fore? I hope not.'

Oliver Kelly, Antrim County Board chairman, described the proposal as 'an absolute downgrading' of hurling in Ulster. The Cork County Board favoured the proposal but one of the county's best-known administrators put forward a strong argument against change.

Former GAA president Con Murphy predicted that allowing beaten provincial finalists back into the All-Ireland race would damage the championships and argued that it was being proposed to provide two extra 'live' games for television.

Most congress delegates disagreed with his assessments, although there was no doubt that the prospect of extra TV coverage made the proposal more attractive for hurling enthusiasts who felt their sport was overshadowed by football exposure.

As the debate progressed, it became clear that the mood for change was decisive. That was reflected in the vote, which was carried on what was estimated to be a 75–25 per cent majority. The hurling championship would never look the same again.

The honour of playing the first game under the new format fell to Ulster champions Down and beaten Munster finalists Tipperary, who met in the 1997 quarter-final in Clones. Tipperary won decisively – 3–24 to 3–8.

A day later, beaten Leinster finalists Kilkenny edged out Galway by two points in Thurles in one of the best games of that season's championship. Tipperary went on to reach the final, where they lost to Clare.

A year later – in 1998 – Offaly became the first beaten provincial finalists to win the All-Ireland title. It was the ultimate irony, given their opposition to the introduction of the new format seventeen months earlier.

Championships and Change

Unsurprisingly, pressure began to mount to change the system again, this time allowing all teams beaten in Leinster and Munster to re-enter the All-Ireland race, via qualifiers. Introduced in 2002, it ended the one-chance format for all counties.

The next big change came in 2009, and saw Galway and Antrim enter the Leinster championship. It had been mooted previously, with Nickey Brennan a major supporter during his term as Leinster Council president, but it took quite some time to come to fruition. There was scepticism in Galway about whether it would bring any benefits to them, while some Leinster counties were not enamoured by the prospect of such a strong force muscling in on their championship.

However, such was the apparent logic of the move, that it eventually attracted enough support at a Special Congress in October 2008. On 31 May 2009, history was made when Galway played their first game in Leinster – beating Laois by 5–29 to 0–17. Antrim followed a week later, but their first outing ended in a ten-point defeat to Dublin.

The next big championship change came in 2018 when the Leinster and Munster championships were run off on a round-robin system, with the top two qualifying for the finals. The winners qualified directly for the All-Ireland semi-finals, with the losers playing either third-placed in either province or Joe McDonagh Cup finalists in the quarter-finals. That format still applies today.

The original change in the hurling format in 1997 impacted football too. When the principle of losing teams being readmitted to the hurling championship became acceptable, it was only a matter of time before football began to examine its structures.

The long-established model of a straight knockout championship based on the provinces had tradition on its side. However, there was also a clear anomaly in that despite all four provinces having a different number of counties, they each had the same representation in the All-Ireland semi-finals.

In years when the Leinster and Ulster champions met in the semi-final, the winners were representing twenty-one counties, compared to eleven for the Connacht–Munster winners.

Also, a Leinster or Ulster county might have to win four games to reach the All-Ireland semi-finals, whereas a Connacht or Munster county could get there with two wins. Indeed, there were occasions when one win was enough to reach the semi-final.

In 1965, Galway, the reigning All-Ireland champions, were given a bye into the Connacht final against Sligo because their two-legged National League final against New York in Gaelic Park wasn't completed until 4 July.

The circumstances surrounding Kerry's bye to the 1980 Munster final were even more bizarre. They beat Clare by thirty-six points in the 1979 semi-final, a game dubbed the 'Miltown Malbay Massacre'. It prompted a review by the Munster Council, who decided that Cork were Kerry's only viable opposition in the province and that it was damaging for the others to take heavy beatings every year.

In 1980, Clare, Limerick, Waterford, Tipperary and Cork played off for the right to meet Kerry in the final. Despite Kerry being well ahead of the rest, the idea that they would get a bye to the final every year didn't sit well, and they returned at the semi-final stage from 1981.

Kerry had won the previous year's All-Ireland final by winning only three games, just as Galway did in 1965. Such a short campaign would be unheard of nowadays.

By the late 1990s, there was a groundswell of opinion calling for a revamp of football structures. President Joe McDonagh appointed the Football Development Committee (FDC), chaired by Noel Walsh (Clare) and also included several other heavy hitters. Their brief was wide and they responded accordingly.

Indeed, they surprised large swathes of the GAA membership when they issued their report in November 1999. Not only did they recommend the abolition of the National League, they also proposed a radical overhaul of the championship, including the dilution of the provincial campaigns.

The outline was as follows: the country was to be divided into three sections – Connacht/Ulster; Leinster/Munster and a third entity (B), comprised of so-called weaker counties.

The top seven counties in Ulster and the top four in Connacht would form one group; similarly with Leinster (seven) and Munster (four). The remaining B counties would form the third group.

It offered every county ten games each (five home, five away), played off in league format between early March and late June. Based on finishing places, the top four counties in Leinster and Munster qualified for their own provincial championships; similarly with the top three in Munster and Connacht.

In the B section, the top four would play-off, with the winners qualifying for the All-Ireland quarter-finals against two provincial winners. The other two provincial winners would go straight to the All-Ireland semi-finals.

The committee's reasoning was that it guaranteed every county ten championship games, while also retaining the provincial campaigns, albeit with only four in Leinster and Ulster and three each in Connacht and Munster.

Reaction was mixed.

Guaranteeing counties ten games between March and June was seen as positive, but removing nineteen counties from the provincial championships did not go down well. Nor did the fact that each provincial semi-final line-up would be influenced by counties from other provinces, depending on results over the ten games.

There was also unease about removing the National League from the calendar. By the time the proposals came before congress in April 2000, it was clear they had no chance of being accepted. It was decided to defer consideration and, a month later, another committee was established by new president Seán McCague.

Chaired by Páraic Duffy, who went on to become director-general eight years later, it also featured some of the FDC members as well as provincial secretaries and various others. Having noted how the FDC plan had run into trouble because of the proposal to interfere with the provincial championships and scrap the National League, they took a different route.

They proposed retaining the provincial championships in traditional form, while also ensuring that all counties were guaranteed at least two championship games. This was to be achieved by introducing All-Ireland qualifiers for all the teams beaten in the provincial championships.

It was to be done on a round-by-round basis depending on what stage a team exited the provincials, with the four survivors joining the provincial winners in the All-Ireland quarter-finals. Coming after the complicated formula proposed earlier in the year, this was the essence of simplicity and, with the mood for change still strong, it received strong support at a Special Congress.

Galway and Meath led the opposition, claiming that giving beaten teams a second chance would devalue the championship.

'If you win, you go on – if you lose, you go out,' said Galway delegate Jack Mahon, an All-Ireland medal winner in 1956.

Meath's Mick O'Brien claimed the proposed system would downgrade the championship and do nothing for weaker counties. He concluded with a colourful analogy. 'We're sending a man to his deathbed while he's in the peak of his health.'

Séamus Aldridge, chairman of the Leinster Council, joined the opposition too, suggesting that if the only benefit was to ensure every team got two championship games, it wasn't worth discarding a system that had worked for decades. 'If you ask children whether they want two plates of jelly or one, they'll always opt for two,' he said.

Several speakers, including the current president Jarlath Burns, who was then chairman of the Players' Committee, gave enthusiastic backing to the proposal, which was passed by a large majority for implementation in 2001.

Introduced on a two-year experimental basis, it was evident after a very successful start in 2001 that there would be no going back. The days of the straight knockout championship were over

– and only returned in 2020 and 2021 when the Covid pandemic required a truncated season.

Ironically, Galway won the All-Ireland via the qualifiers in 2001. Having opposed their introduction, they gratefully accepted the second chance after losing to Roscommon in the Connacht semi-final. They beat Wicklow, Armagh, Cork, Roscommon, Derry and Meath to take the title for a ninth time. Tyrone (2005 and 2008), Kerry (2006 and 2009) and Cork (2010) also won the title, despite having been beaten in the provinces.

The next big football adjustment came in 2018 when the quarter-finals were played on a round-robin basis, featuring two groups of four, comprising the four provincial winners and four qualifiers.

More changes emerged in 2022 when the qualifier rounds were reduced to two and the Tailteann Cup was introduced for teams that didn't make the top sixteen.

Qualification for the top sixteen and a place in the All-Ireland series was changed to include the provincial championships (winners and runners-up) and finishing places in the National League.

The addition of the Tailteann Cup, which carries an automatic place in the Sam Maguire Cup tier for the following season, has been a great success, as have the Joe McDonagh, Christy Ring, Nicky Rackard and Lory Meagher cups for the tiers below Liam MacCarthy level in hurling.

The tiered system has seen the introduction of several new competitions in the new millennium.

The Tommy Murphy Cup, an earlier equivalent of the Tailteann Cup, lasted only five seasons (2004–2008) while the All-Ireland

B football championship, another competition for lower-ranked counties, ran from 1990 to 2000 before being abandoned. Fermanagh won it twice, with one win each for Antrim, Carlow, Clare, Laois, Leitrim, Louth, Monaghan, Tipperary and Wicklow.

Bigger competitions fell out of favour over the years, including the Railway Cup interprovincials in football and hurling and the Oireachtas Cup (hurling).

The interprovincial series originally ran for three years (1905–1908), after which it went into abeyance. In 1926, Cork proposed a motion at congress calling for it to be revived, with the finals to be played in Croke Park on St Patrick's Day. It was an inspired idea. Sponsored by Great Southern Railways – hence the Railway Cup tag – the players and public responded enthusiastically.

The series grew in stature over the years, peaking in the 1950s when attendances at the finals regularly beat the 40,000 mark. A crowd of 41,416 attended the 1952 finals and, two years later, a record crowd of 49,023 watched Leinster complete a double over Connacht (football) and Munster (hurling).

The Railway Cup finals in Croke Park became an essential part of the St Patrick's Day experience for GAA supporters, an opportunity to see the top players from all over the country playing each other in provincial jerseys.

The players relished it too. Indeed, being selected for your province was a real badge of honour for players and the games were just as competitive as inter-county action. The announcement of the provincial teams was the first big GAA event of the new season and usually generated heated debate as media and supporters teased through the various selections.

The Railway Cup also provided a great opportunity for players from weaker counties to get well-deserved recognition. The stronger counties dominated most selections but there was usually a few from lower-ranked counties too. It was extra special for them, offering a chance to play with the best and have a decent chance of winning a title in Croke Park.

Mickey Kearins (Sligo), Packie McGarty (Leitrim), P.T. Treacy (Fermanagh), Eddie Webster (Tipperary), Senan Downes (Clare) and Andy Philips (Wicklow) are prime examples of players from lower-ranked football counties whose profiles were raised by the Railway Cup.

The same applied in hurling, with some players beyond the established county powerhouses being given an opportunity to prosper with their provinces. Kildare's Pat Dunney was a prime example. A dual-player of the highest quality, he was competing at the top level with Kildare footballers but with the hurlers not going as well, his opportunities to test himself against the best were largely confined to the Railway Cup. It wasn't easy to break into a Leinster team dominated by Kilkenny, Wexford and Dublin but he managed it over a sustained period in the 1970s, winning four titles.

Offaly's Paddy Molloy was equally impressive in the 1960s at a time when his county wasn't challenging for major honours.

The Railway Cup's boom time of the 1950s continued into the 1960s when the average attendance at the finals in 1960, 1961 and 1962 was almost 39,000. Over the next five years, the average dropped to 26,000. The decline was steep and got even steeper. By 1972, it was down to 16,241 and, five years later, only 8,034 turned out.

Championships and Change

Various reasons were put forward to explain why a competition, held in such esteem for so long, lost its lustre so quickly. One explanation was the decision to show the finals live on Telefís Éireann, as it was known at the time.

Coverage started in 1962 when the second half of the Leinster–Munster hurling final and the entire Leinster–Ulster football final were screened live. All of both finals were shown live from then on.

That the decline in attendances mirrored television coverage was no coincidence. Live coverage of sport was a novelty at that time, making it all the more attractive whenever it happened. So instead of heading for Croke Park on St Patrick's Day, it was much easier – especially for people outside Dublin – to congregate in each other's houses and make an event of watching the Railway Cup finals on television.

Smaller crowds at semi-finals and finals began to impact players. Up to the early 1970s, being selected for your province was the equivalent of an All-Star award. With attendances decreasing, the GAA decided to take the finals out of Croke Park and spread them around provincial venues. The first such venture in 1981 saw the finals played in Ennis before a crowd of 7,017. Only 3,011 turned out in Tullamore for the 1982 finals.

Breffni Park in Cavan hosted the 1983 finals and while the official attendance was given as 4,400, many exited after the Ulster–Leinster football final, leaving the Connacht and Leinster hurlers to play their game on a badly cut-up pitch in front of a tiny crowd. It was to become a clear symbol of a dying competition.

Between then and 2015, a whole range of initiatives designed to reignite interest were undertaken, mostly without success. Playing the semi-finals and finals in the same county over one weekend and taking finals to Rome, Boston, Paris, Abu Dhabi and London were all tried, but to no avail.

The All-Ireland club finals took over as the St Patrick's Day attraction in Croke Park and with player interest in the interprovincials having dropped to such a degree that managers found themselves struggling to put panels together, it was clear that the competitions had no future.

The last finals were played in 2016, when Munster beat Leinster (hurling) and Ulster beat Connacht (football). The hurling final was played in front of 592 spectators in Thurles on a Thursday night nine days before Christmas.

The football final was played in Carrick-on-Shannon two days later, before a crowd of around 500. The Railway Cups had run off the tracks and would not be coming back.

Their demise had been well underway by the time the All-Ireland club championships were added to the calendar in 1971. Informal championships had been played in the late 1960s, but it wasn't until Congress 1970 that they were finally accepted into the official fold.

Such is their popularity now across all grades that a younger generation find it difficult to understand why there was considerable opposition to their introduction. Galway and Wexford led the call for them, making a strong argument about why they would be a welcome addition.

Bertie Coleman, a leading advocate for their introduction and a man with considerable experience of the club scene with Dunmore MacHales in Galway, spoke of how invigorating it would be for players to test themselves against counterparts from other counties.

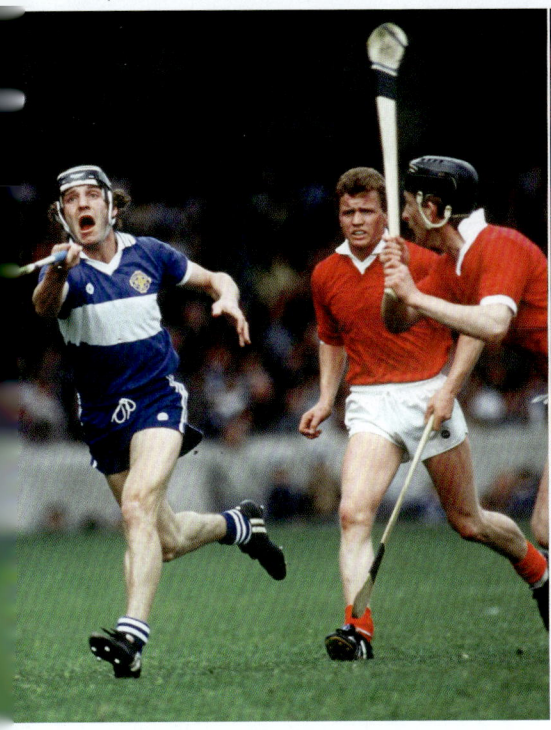 

Pat Critchley, seen here in action against Cork, is the only Laois hurler to have been selected as an All-Star having been chosen at midfield in 1985.

His skills and a fierce competitive streak have made Davy Fitzgerald one of the most familiar figures in modern hurling.

Seánie McMahon, the first Clare player to be named as Hurler of the Year, in 1995, in action against Offaly's Joe Dooley.

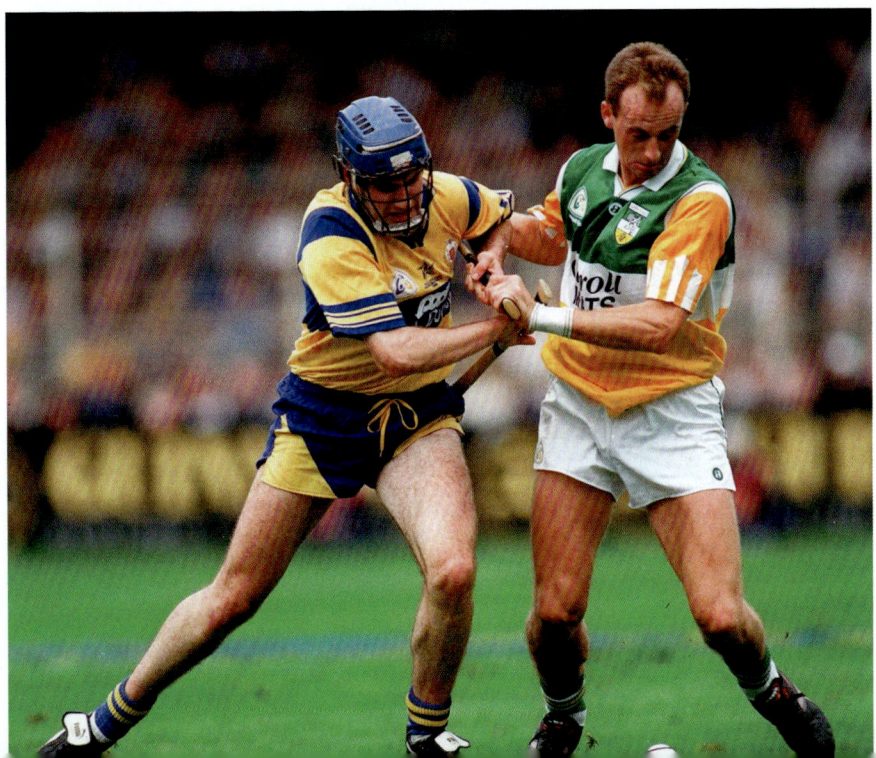

Terence 'Sambo' McNaughton was one of the most popular personalities in hurling during a long career with Antrim and was honoured as an All-Star in 1991.

Ken McGrath celebrates after Waterford won the 2002 Munster senior hurling title, the county's first provincial triumph since 1963.

Eoin Kelly lifts the Liam McCarthy Cup aloft in September 2010 after leading Tipperary to glory. It was his second All-Ireland triumph.

Aaron Gillane has been one of the most prolific score-getter of the modern era and a major contributor to Limerick's record-breaking exploits.

Two legends: Limerick's Pat Hartigan and Cork's Charlie McCarthy together at the 2014 Munster final. Hartigan was an All-Ireland winner in 1973 and is the only full-back to have won five consecutive All-Star awards. McCarthy won five All-Ireland titles between 1966 and 1978.

Jimmy Barry Murphy, closely marshalled by Offaly full-back Eugene Coughlan in the 1984 All-Ireland hurling final, won his first major title as a footballer with Cork in 1973.

Liam Currams was at midfield on the Offaly hurling tram that won the county's first All-Ireland senior title in 1981 and, a year later, he lined out with the footballers as they captured the Sam Maguire Cup.

Mick Holden became famous as a footballer and was an All-Ireland winner in 1983, but hurling was his first love and he won underage honours with Dublin and a Railway Cup with Leinster.

Cork's Teddy McCarthy, surrounded by P.J. Gillic, Brendan Reilly and Brian Stafford from Meath in the 1990 All-Ireland final when he became the only player to win All-Ireland hurling and football medals in the same year.

Regarded nationally as one of the all-time great footballers, Greg Blaney also won an Ulster hurling title with Down in 1992.

Dublin camogie legend Kathleen 'Kay' Mills.

As a player, pundit and administrator, Liz Howard has been a trailblazer throughout her life in the GAA.

Kilkenny captain Angela Downey lifts the cup after defeating Cork in the 1991 All-Ireland senior camogie final between Kilkenny and Cork, Croke Park.

Kilkenny captain Ann Downey lifts the cup following the 1994 All-Ireland senior camogie final between Kilkenny and Wexford, Croke Park.

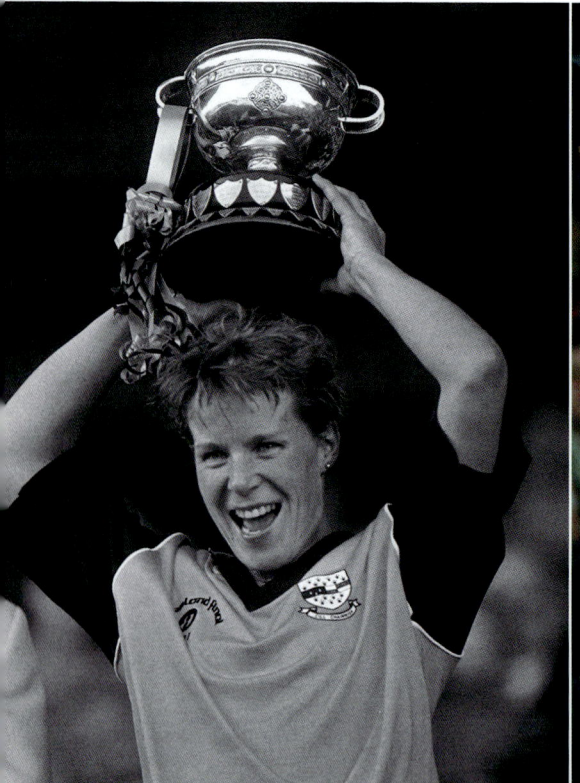

Louise Ní Mhuircheartaigh of Kerry with former Kerry ladies footballer Mary Jo Curran after their side's victory in the 2024 All-Ireland ladies football final between Galway and Kerry, Croke Park.

Cora Staunton – a Mayo legend, regarded as one of the greatest players in ladies football.

Carla Rowe has been one of the outstanding players on the Dublin ladies football team that won four All-Ireland titles between 2017 and 2020 and was captain when Dublin returned to the victory podium in 2023.

Briege Corkery of Cork has seven All-Ireland camogie titles and eleven All-Ireland football titles.

History – on a memorable and emotional evening on 24 February 2007, Ireland and England played their Six Nations clash for the first time in Croke Park. An inspired Irish team won 43–13.

Tony Kelly enjoys that special feeling as he raises the Liam MacCarthy Cup after Clare beat Cork in the 2024 All-Ireland hurling final.

The look of joy – team captain, Aidan Forker hoists the Sam Maguire Cup in front of equally delighted supporters after Armagh won the 2024 All-Ireland football title.

He had been active in organising unofficial championships, involving a small number of clubs, in the late 1960s and had seen the excitement they generated.

In 1970, he presented a solid case to congress in Galway and was supported by Wexford chairman Jim Roche, but Cork were quick off the mark to oppose them. Members of the Cork delegation argued that All-Ireland championships would be difficult to organise, as experienced in Munster where unofficial versions had fallen behind schedule in previous years.

Cork also insisted that it would require a two-thirds majority to pass the Galway–Wexford motion but president Pat Fanning ruled that a simple majority would suffice. His decision proved crucial as the motion was carried on a 92–74 majority. If the two-thirds requirement had applied, it would have fallen short by nineteen votes.

Instead, a new and exciting competition was added to the schedule. Roscrea (Tipperary) and East Kerry were the respective hurling and football winners in 1971 and though it took some time for the competition to build up serious momentum, it went on to become a vibrant part of the scene – a position it enjoys to this day.

Its growth was in almost direct proportion to the Railway Cup's decline, a fate also suffered by the Oireachtas hurling tournament. Featuring the top hurling counties, it was introduced in 1939 and ran until 1999.

As with the Railway Cups, the Oireachtas Cup enjoyed its best years in the 1950s and 1960s when big crowds attended the final. They were usually played in October and November and, as they often featured the All-Ireland winners, the public responded.

In 1956, the attendance for the Wexford–Kilkenny final in Croke Park was 37,172; a year earlier the same pairing attracted 29,352 fans. Crowds in excess of 25,000 were common for several years, including 1961 when 28,034 attended the Tipperary–Wexford replay. That was 9,000 more than for the drawn game, which was played on a day high winds and heavy rain lashed the country.

Another competition that thrived for a time in the 1960s before losing impetus was the Grounds Tournament, which was set up to raise funds for stadium development work. Launched in 1961 and also played in October and November, it featured the four All-Ireland football semi-finalists, with the parings changed from the championship line-up in August.

The semi-finals were played as double-headers in Croke Park, with the final also at GAA HQ. Both days proved very popular, in the early years at least.

The 1963 semi-finals (Dublin–Kerry and Galway–Down) attracted a crowd of 43,337, with the Dublin–Galway final drawing 30,020. Two years later, the Down–Kerry and Galway–Dublin semi-finals had a crowd of 36,612.

An interesting feature of the competition was the similarity between the teams that played in the All-Ireland semi-finals and final and the Grounds Tournament line-ups. There were years when the semi-finals were played two weeks after the All-Ireland final, a time when winners might be expected to still be in celebration mode and not interested in renewing rivalry with teams keen to knock the gloss off their big success. However, that never proved to be the case, with most teams at full strength – hence the large attendances.

There was drama in 1964 when Meath, having named their team on the Tuesday night before the final against Galway, objected on Wednesday to the appointment of Kerry's Séamus Garvey as referee.

They were unhappy with Garvey's handling of the All-Ireland semi-final, which Meath lost to Galway by two points. They declared their intention to withdraw from the grounds tournament final unless Garvey was replaced, leaving the GAA's power brokers in a very difficult position. They couldn't allow a county to dictate who would referee their games and asked Meath to withdraw their objection.

Meath refused, thereby placing the game in doubt right up to Friday.

When it became clear that Meath were not for turning, the GAA asked Dublin to replace them. The 1963 All-Ireland champions agreed and, despite the short notice, acquitted themselves well against the new champions before losing by three points in front of a crowd of 19,192.

Meath were unhappy that Dublin agreed to replace them, but Dublin took the view that it was an opportunity for a good test. Besides, Meath's dispute with the GAA had nothing to do with them.

As with the Railway Cups, public interest in the Grounds Tournament waned as the 1960s progressed. By 1971, the attendance at the final was down to 8,516 for the Offaly–Galway match, a repeat of the All-Ireland final. The competition was abandoned after the Offaly–Tyrone final in 1973, having run for twelve years.

6 BY ORDER OF MANAGEMENT

There are five pieces of advice I would dispense after my long years in management. Be your own person; trust your instincts; take calculated risks; give your players confidence; never select a player who is carrying an injury irrespective of how talented he is.
Record-breaking manager Mick O'Dwyer in his autobiography Blessed and Obsessed.

When Dublin County Board chairman Jimmy Gray persuaded Kevin Heffernan to undertake a revival mission for Dublin football in the late summer of 1973, he could not have envisaged that it would have such a seismic impact on the how all county squads were run.

Prior to this, management all over the country was largely by committee, with varying numbers of selectors in charge of teams. One or two tended to take a lead, especially when it came to training and devising tactics, but in the matter of team selection, they all had a vote.

Selection panels could be quite large. At one stage during their All-Ireland football three-in-a-row successes from 1964 to 1966, Galway had no fewer than eleven selectors. John 'Tull' Dunne, who had won two All-Ireland medals in the 1930s, trained the team and was also board secretary, so he had a more front-of-house presence than the others, but everyone's view counted. It worked because Galway had such good players available in the 1960s that it made selection meetings quite easy most of the time.

In Kerry, Dr Eamonn O'Sullivan, a man renowned for his deep knowledge of the tactical side of the game, trained teams that won eight All-Ireland titles between 1924 and 1962. Fr Tommy Maher was probably the highest-profile coach in hurling, presiding over seven All-Ireland wins with Kilkenny.

So, while counties always had recognisable figureheads, they weren't classified as managers until Kevin Heffernan took over in Dublin for the start of the 1973–1974 National League season. He did so at a time when the county team was well down the national rankings.

It might have been only ten years since Dublin had won an All-Ireland title and eight years since they were Leinster champions, but the subsequent decline had been quick and steep. Between 1967 and 1972, they won only three championships games, so when Gray persuaded Heffernan to take over, they agreed that a new approach was urgently needed.

Heffernan wasn't described as manager at the time of his appointment, but it was clear from an early stage that he was in control. His two fellow selectors – Donal Colfer and Lorcan

Redmond – were shrewd football men so the new arrangement worked well from the start.

So well, in fact, that by September 1974, Dublin were All-Ireland champions. The rise in interest throughout Dublin as the championship campaign progressed changed the face of football in the capital forever. Heffernan became very much identified as the main orchestrator, a revered figure in song and story. A blue wave washed across Dublin, powering up the hype as it went.

In a tribute song released by The Memories showband to mark the revival, Heffernan was the only part of the team referred to by name:

Oh the Dubs are back, the Dubs are back
Let the railway end go barmy
'Cause Hill 16 has never seen
the likes of Heffo's Army.

The cult of the GAA manager had been launched.

That Dublin turned their fortunes around so quickly after vesting extensive power and authority in one man was noted all across the country, including Kerry. In fact, most of all in Kerry.

They had last won the All-Ireland title in 1970 and impatience had set in after watching Offaly (twice), Cork and Dublin land the big prize. The 1973 and 1974 seasons had been particularly disappointing for Kerry, having lost to Cork in the two Munster finals by a combined total of sixteen points. Cork had also beaten them in 1971. It was the first time since 1906–1909 that Cork had won three of four Munster titles. Worrying times in the Kingdom.

Unpalatable as that might be in normal circumstances, it was amplified by Dublin's return to the top. Kerry still headed the All-Ireland table, but Dublin had now cut the lead to four. There were genuine concerns in Kerry that their decline still had some way to go. They needed an immediate reset.

Johnny Culloty had stepped down as Kerry team trainer after the 1974 Munster final defeat to Cork, but it was a departure two months earlier that proved even more significant. Mick O'Dwyer finished his eighteen years as a player in May and was available to move on to the next phase of his career.

Ger McKenna, county board chairman, was impressed by how the Kerry Under-21s had performed under O'Dwyer in 1974. Even though they had lost the Munster final to Cork by a point, they had played with a method and structure that looked innovative and interesting.

During his playing days, O'Dwyer had served as a selector at various times so McKenna approached him. Would he be interested in the senior role?

'I told Ger that if I was to take the job, I would have to be allowed do things my own way. He let it be known from the start that I would have his total backing and that I wouldn't have to be looking over my shoulder all the time,' O'Dwyer wrote in his autobiography, *Blessed and Obsessed*.

By the end of the 1975 season, O'Dwyer's first in charge, Kerry were All-Ireland champions and the concept of having a main man had been advanced significantly throughout the country. First Heffo, then Micko – other counties, both in football and hurling, looked on and decided the all-powerful boss was the way forward.

With the top two football counties embracing change so enthusiastically, the knock-on impact was quick and widespread. In many – although not all – counties, managers were given authority to choose their own selectors. It all added to the excitement heading into the 1980s, which turned into a decade of change in so many ways.

In hurling, Galway were among the first to experience the benefit of giving one man all the power he required. Having been team trainer when Galway lost the 1979 All-Ireland final to Kilkenny, Cyril Farrell was appointed coach and team manager in 1980, with Bernie O'Connor and 'Inky' Flaherty as selectors.

Aged thirty, Farrell was the youngest manager to be handed so much responsibility, but it's what he wanted. Having managed the Galway Under-21s to All-Ireland success in 1978, he was convinced the senior breakthrough could be achieved. He was disappointed by the seniors' setback in 1979 and frustrated by his lack of influence as team trainer. He vowed that if he got the chance to manage the side, he would be very much his own man. He felt the approach used by Dublin and Kerry football could also be applied in Galway hurling.

Granted, Dublin and Kerry had a history of winning All-Ireland football titles, whereas Galway hurling did not, having taken their only title in 1923. Farrell refused to believe tradition was a factor throughout the decades of drought.

'I knew that Galway's failure to win an All-Ireland was not simply down to a lack of skill or strength. No, it had more to do with attitude and, on a few occasions, fitness. It was a time of change. Kevin Heffernan and Mick O'Dwyer had pushed the fitness frontiers through new horizons in football. Hurling was slow to react, operating on the basis that it had different requirements, and that hi-tech fitness was not all that important. I disagreed. A good, ultra-fit hurler is far more valuable than a good hurler,' he wrote in his autobiography, *The Right to Win*.

By September 1980, Galway were All-Ireland champions, and they went on to win two more under Farrell's stewardship in 1987 and 1988. By that stage, Galway's biggest challengers were Tipperary, who had appointed Michael 'Babs' Keating as manager in 1986.

'Babs' was very much in the new wave of thinking when he took over in Tipperary. He had been on the last Tipperary team to win an All-Ireland title in 1971, after which they went into serious decline. Without a Munster title since 1971, the county was wrapped in pessimism when 'Babs' took over. It was their longest spell without a Munster championship win since the foundation of the GAA.

Keating realised that a new approach was required, one that involved the whole of the county – and indeed Tipperary people living abroad. An early priority was to make the players feel good about themselves, which he believed would be reflected in performances. A Supporters' Club was established and other fundraising schemes were also introduced to ensure that the squad wanted for nothing.

'Money was needed. These were different times. The pressures on young lads were much greater than when I was playing. They had greater commitments, tougher jobs, or sometimes no job at all, mortgages, car loans. We had to make sure they were never short, that financial worries did not affect either their private lives or their hurling,' he wrote in his autobiography.

The new approach worked. Tipperary went on to win Munster titles in 1987, 1988 and 1989, a year in which they also added the All-Ireland title. They added another All-Ireland in 1991. The much-talked-about Tipperary famine was over.

However, the biggest hurling story of the 1980s wasn't the return to the top table of Galway and Tipperary, but rather Offaly's double breakthrough in 1980 and 1981. Winning the Leinster title for the first time in 1980 was a huge achievement but even greater peaks were reached a year later when they won the All-Ireland title.

Andy Gallagher, a famous name in Offaly hurling for decades, was manager but Offaly looked outside for a coach, stopping off in Kilkenny to recruit Dermot Healy. It was an inspired move. Healy brought a new perspective, injecting a Kilkenny attitude into an Offaly squad that, for all its talent and ambition, had enjoyed little success.

Goalkeeper Damien Martin, one of their most experienced and committed performers, said in an interview many years later that Healy's biggest contribution lay in his ability to change mindsets. He worked on convincing the squad that they were as good as the very best rivals in every area except self-confidence. Fix that and all would change.

'He talked us into winning matches we had no right to win,' Martin said.

The degree to which Offaly's self-belief had soared was best exemplified by their second-half performance against Galway in the 1981 final, when they recovered from a seven-point deficit to win by three. Four years later, Offaly won their second title, again beating Galway in the final.

In between, the Offaly footballers had achieved what many regarded as mission impossible – stopping Kerry winning the All-Ireland five-in-a-row in 1982. An outsider was hugely influential there too.

This time, Offaly's recruitment took them no further than Longford where they had persuaded Eugene McGee to take over in late 1976. His successes with UCD, which he led to two All-Ireland club successes in 1974 and 1975, had convinced Offaly that he was the man to get the best out of an improving squad.

They were right. The challenge was huge at a time when the great Kerry and Dublin squads were at their peak, but McGee was in for the long haul and believed Offaly would finally reach their destination. They hit their first target in 1980 when they ousted Dublin in the Leinster final, and though Kerry beat them in the All-Ireland semi-final and in the following year's final, a determined squad and manager never lost confidence.

Still, they were long-odds outsiders going into the 1982 final against Kerry, who were attempting to become the first county to win the five-in-a-row. It has gone down in history as one of the most dramatic finals as Offaly hung on gamely when the flow was very much against them in the second half before unleashing a driving finish, culminating in a spectacular winning goal by Séamus Darby.

Apart from ensuring that every Offaly player would always be a revered name in the county, it sent McGee's stature as a manager soaring into the stratosphere. Offaly hadn't just won an All-Ireland title, they had beaten a team who had taken five of the previous seven titles and who went on to win three of the next four.

In the same month as Offaly won the 1982 title, a rookie manager was beginning his journey with a sceptical Meath squad, whose confidence was rock-bottom after some miserable years.

Seán Boylan would remain in charge of the Royals for twenty-three years. In those years, he led Meath to four All-Ireland titles, one more than the combined total won by the county since the championship was launched in 1887.

Meath's initial breakthrough under Boylan came in 1986, when they won the Leinster championship for the first time since 1970, followed a year later by a first All-Ireland title in twenty years. They completed the two-in-a-row in 1988. By the mid-1990s, a squad rebuild was required and Boylan undertook it with as much enthusiasm as before. The rewards followed as they won two more All-Irelands in 1996 and 1999, cementing his place as one of the greatest managers.

The 1980s closed with a new name on the managerial roll of honour as Billy Morgan led the Cork footballers to their first All-Ireland title for sixteen years. It brought him the rare distinction of having captained (1973) and managed (1989) a team to ultimate glory. Cork completed the double in 1990, when the hurlers beat Galway by three points.

If the 1980s saw the influence and stature of managers grow rapidly, the 1990s brought a further expansion in both codes. It came about through first-time All-Ireland wins or counties ending long periods without a title.

In football, Brian McEniff (Donegal, 1992) and Eamonn Coleman (Derry, 1993) were in the former category, while Pete McGrath (Down, 1991 and 1994), Pat O'Neill (Dublin, 1995), Páidí Ó Sé (Kerry, 1997) and John O'Mahony (Galway, 1998) completed the second group. O'Mahony also hit a notable provincial high in 1994, steering Leitrim to their first Connacht title since 1927. It was quite an achievement as they beat the province's three powerhouses: Galway, Mayo and Roscommon.

In 1992, O'Mahony's fellow-Mayoman John Maughan steered Clare footballers to a first Munster title for seventy-five years; Tommy Lyons led Offaly to a first Leinster title for fifteen years in 1997 and to a first National League title a year later; Tommy Breheny managed Sligo when they won the Connacht title for the first time in thirty-two years in 2007; and Martin McHugh presided over Cavan's 1997 Ulster title win, their first for twenty-eight years.

In hurling, Ger Loughnane (Clare, 1995 and 1997) and Liam Griffin (Wexford, 1996) imposed their flamboyant personalities as they oversaw famous All-Ireland wins. Clare's 1995 triumph was their first since 1914, while Wexford ended a twenty-eight-year wait in 1996. Limerick's Eamonn Cregan and Galway's Michael Bond joined an exclusive club of managers who led counties other than their own to All-Ireland success. Offaly were the beneficiaries on both occasions (1994 and 1998).

Few would have predicted at the start of the new millennium that hurling was about to enter a phase where one county and one manager would exert a level of control never previously seen.

Kilkenny, with Brian Cody in his first year as manager, lost the 1999 All-Ireland final to Cork before going on to win eleven of the next sixteen titles.

It was an extraordinary level of dominance, expertly presided over by Cody and his single-minded devotion to the challenge of setting and maintaining the highest standards that helped yield eleven All-Ireland titles in sixteen seasons. Nicky English (Tipperary), Donal O'Grady (Cork), John Allen (Cork), Liam Sheedy (Tipperary) and Davy Fitzgerald (Clare) were the five other managers to win All-Ireland titles during Kilkenny's glory period between 2000 and 2015.

There were many years during that period when Limerick must have wondered if their day would ever come. Between 1999 and 2016, they had no fewer than nine managers, a turnover that typified the lack of a clear vision in the county.

Everything changed in September 2016 when they set out with the latest recruit, John Kiely. The rest is glorious history for Limerick, who have enjoyed their greatest era since Kiely's appointment. His first season was more frustrating than disappointing, for while they lost their two championship games to Clare and Kilkenny, there were obvious signs that solid foundations were being put in place. A year later, Limerick were All-Ireland champions for the first time in forty-five years, beginning a run that has taken them to extraordinary heights.

Kiely and Cody aren't the only managers to have led their counties into a dream world over the past twenty-five seasons. In 1992 and 1993, McEniff and Coleman had taken Donegal and Derry respectively to first-time All-Ireland football wins – and this was matched by Joe Kernan and Mickey Harte, who repeated the feat with Armagh and Tyrone respectively in 2002 and 2003.

That four counties won the title for the first time over a ten-year period was most unusual. It was put in context by the fact that the previous first-time winners were Offaly in 1971.

It's safe to assume that a substantial part of the successes of Donegal, Derry, Armagh and Tyrone were down to the advanced strategies deployed by their managers, all of whom brought various innovations to the quest for ultimate glory.

Unsurprisingly, the arrival of new champions brought a reaction from Kerry, who appointed Jack O'Connor as manager after Páidí Ó Sé's departure in 2003. A year later, they were All-Ireland champions for the thirty-third time. O'Connor went on to become one of the most successful managers in history, in three separate terms with Kerry. He also spent a season with Kildare.

Dublin's response to the emergence of new Ulster powers was much slower. Indeed, it wasn't until 2011 that they finally regained top spot under Pat Gilroy. When they lost the All-Ireland semifinal to Mayo in 2012, doubts arose about whether they were one-hit wonders, but they quickly banished that theory by winning again in 2013.

It was Jim Gavin's first season in charge and the start of an era that took Dublin into the record books. By the time Gavin departed in November 2019, Dublin had won another five All-Ireland titles, all consecutively between 2015 and 2019. It was the first time any county – in football or hurling – had won the five-in-a-row, a sequence Dublin extended to six under Dessie Farrell in 2020.

Gavin's achievement ensures him of a place in managerial history, his five-in-a-row set a record that was generally thought to be unattainable in the modern game. The shape, structure, general sense of know-how and calmness under pressure, which were all so evident in the run, typified Gavin's forensically detailed approach to his role as strategist.

The first twenty-five seasons of the new millennium had other managerial highlights too: Jim McGuinness bringing a fresh approach to possession football, which was so crucial to Donegal's 2012 All-Ireland success; Conor Counihan's quiet leadership which led Cork from troubled times to All-Ireland glory in 2010; Páidí Ó Sé's flamboyant sojourn in Westmeath, during which they won a first Leinster senior title in 2004; Malachy O'Rourke overseeing Monaghan's first Ulster title success for twenty-five years in 2013; David Power's stewardship in Tipperary as they won the Munster title for the first time in eighty-five years in 2020, which was also the year that Mickey Graham skilfully plotted Cavan's route to their first Ulster title for twenty-three years.

And who could forget Mick O'Dwyer, proving yet again that he brought magic dust wherever he went? Having done it for so long in Kerry, he spread more all over Kildare in 1998 when they won the Leinster title for the first time in forty-two years.

Five years later, he helped end an even longer famine in Laois, who won the Leinster title for the first time in fifty-seven years. Wicklow became the third Leinster county to benefit from his expertise when he took them on their best championship adventure.

Wicklow's three All-Ireland qualifier wins over Fermanagh, Cavan and Down in Aughrim on successive Saturdays in 2009 energised Wicklow like never before. It lifted them into exalted company as one of the top twelve counties in the championship and even though Kildare blocked their path to the quarter-final, it was still a memorable summer in the Garden County.

That O'Dwyer did so well in Kildare, Laois and Wicklow increased his claims to be regarded as the best football manager of all time. He was dealing with extra-special talents for most of his fourteen years as Kerry manager but showed he was equally adept when dealing with players and counties that hadn't enjoyed success for a very long time or, in Wicklow's case, not at all.

There's no doubt that the change in management structures, specifically giving extensive powers to one individual, was a largely positive development in football and hurling. However, as the years passed and managers became ever more powerful, problems emerged which have remained unsolved.

Specifically, there's the issue of the training loads imposed on players, plus the control that managers exert in so many other ways. Effectively, players are expected to live their lives as professionals, a demand that presents serious challenges for the GAA as it battles to preserve its amateur ethos. The pressure is building like never before.

7 A TOUCH OF CONTROVERSY

The important point is that sport in Ireland has taken on a new look, one which should benefit every code.
Irish Independent editorial after the removal by GAA Congress of the Ban in April 1971.

In an organisation that touches virtually every parish in the country, it's hardly surprising that the GAA runs into controversies from time to time.

Unlike many sports – including soccer and rugby, where rules and many of the regulations are set by a controlling body at European and/or world level – the GAA is completely self-governing. This is both an advantage and a disadvantage.

It enables the GAA to react to issues in a manner that's specific to itself, rather than being controlled internationally.

However, there's a downside too.

Because of its local nature, there's always a risk of getting caught up in petty squabbles that ignore the bigger picture. Many of the biggest controversies in the GAA's history have been of its own making, arising either from entrenched policy positions or failing to spot the possible consequences of a decision.

The following are examples from both of these categories.

THE BAN

No Foreign Games Here

On Easter Sunday 1962, Carlow attempted to have arguably the most controversial regulation in GAA history removed from the rulebook. Rule 27 – the Ban – decreed that it was a violation of GAA rules to play, attend or promote soccer, rugby, hockey or cricket games or associated events.

The punishment for breaking Rule 27 was suspension. In place since 1902, the rationale behind it was that as an organisation committed to all things Irish, it should work to limit the influence of sports perceived to have a strong English leaning.

The Ban had given rise to intense arguments over the years, with more moderate opinion holding that it went too far and reflected badly on the GAA. Still, even at the start of the swinging sixties, there was no real mood for change as Carlow discovered at Congress 1962.

Their motion calling for the abolition of Rule 27 was beaten on a 265–7 vote. During a speech on why it should be retained, a Cork delegate pointed out that Queen Elizabeth II had honoured Jack Kyle, one of Ireland's all-time rugby greats, for his services to the sport but ignored Christy Ring's achievement in winning eight All-Ireland hurling medals.

It was scarcely a direct comparison but, together with some other impassioned contributions opposing change, it underlined how entrenched most delegates were in their opinions. A Dublin motion to direct Central Council to set up a committee to examine all aspects of Rule 27 was beaten on a 180–40 vote.

Three years later, Dublin sponsored another motion calling for a deletion of Rule 27 and though it was beaten comprehensively, there was a modest shift in voting patterns with fifty-two in favour and 227 against.

In 1968, the majority in favour of retention remained sizeable (220–88), although not quite as high as three years previously. Gradually, attitudes were changing, and it was decided to establish a special committee to examine all aspects of Rule 27. Players were especially vocal in their opposition to the rule, arguing that it was unfair and unsustainable to restrict their sporting choices in such a draconian manner.

The committee took two years to report, by which time there had been a significant swing in opinion across all strands. In the run-up to Congress 1971, thirty of the thirty-two counties pledged to support the deletion of Rule 27.

Its formal removal came at congress in Belfast, following a proposal by Con Shortt (Armagh), seconded by Tom Woulfe (Dublin), who had been a consistent campaigner against the ban for years. Jack Rooney, Antrim County Board chairman, registered his county's support for the rule but did not propose its retention.

It was over quickly and cleanly – the Ban was gone.

In the space of nine years, calls for its removal went from a mere seven votes to an overwhelming majority, marking a dramatic turnaround that had seemed utterly unthinkable in the early 1960s.

The decision was met with widespread approval throughout Ireland.

'We must be grateful to the congress in Belfast for the decision it made yesterday, and to the counties which asked for such a decision,' stated an *Irish Independent* editorial.

'The decision represents a social and political watershed in our history,' noted an *Irish Press* editorial.

Rule 27 had, without doubt, been a consistent source of controversy for decades, especially when its intransigent interpretation impacted directly on individuals – including Dr Douglas Hyde, who served as President of Ireland from 1938 to 1945.

In November 1938, after attending a Republic of Ireland–Poland soccer match in his official role as president, Dr Hyde was removed from his position of GAA patron, a position he'd held since 1902. It was the toughest of hardline stances by the GAA towards a man who had a deep affinity and connection with Irish culture and games.

The GAA's decision was roundly criticised, but they held steadfastly to the belief that Dr Hyde had broken Rule 27. Nor could they be persuaded that since he had attended the game in his official capacity as president, he was exempt from GAA rules. It was an example of intransigence in its severest form, and was deeply resented in his native Roscommon. Decades later, they ensured that his name would forever be linked with the GAA in the county by naming the county ground Dr Hyde Park in his honour.

Some high-profile players also fell foul of the rule. In 1957, Down footballer Paddy Doherty was banned for twelve months for playing soccer. Six years later, the Waterford hurler Tom Cheasty incurred a suspension in bizarre circumstances.

He was deemed guilty of breaking Rule 27 after attending a dance run by a soccer club. It was a very harsh decision. That a player would be banned from playing the sport he loved for attending a dance angered many in the GAA.

They felt it was an intrusion too far, and while it took another eight years for the rule to be deleted, the Cheasty affair almost certainly played a big part in the movement to have Rule 27 removed.

RULE 42

No Foreign Games in Our Fields

When it was announced in 2006 that Lansdowne Road was to close a year later for redevelopment, the eyes of the sporting public turned towards the GAA and its state-of-the-art stadium across the River Liffey.

It made perfect sense on every front for rugby and soccer internationals to be played in Croke Park while Lansdowne Road was closed. The alternative was to play Ireland's 'home' games in Britain, which would have been deeply unsatisfactory.

As well as being a disadvantage for Irish teams, it would greatly inconvenience supporters and also be a serious economic loss for

Dublin. The alternative was to switch to Croke Park, the capacity of which was 30,000 greater than Lansdowne Road, thereby offering an opportunity for more people to attend the rugby and soccer games. Renting the ground would also provide a welcome cash injection for the GAA.

It looked a win–win situation and would have been except for GAA regulations. They included a rule which stated:

Grounds controlled by Association units shall not be used, or permitted to be used, for horse racing, greyhound racing or field games other than those sanctioned by Central Council.

At face value, it appeared as if Central Council could decide on whether to make Croke Park available for soccer and rugby while Lansdowne Road was closed, but the GAA had always interpreted the rule in a manner that required annual congress to make the decision.

The use of Croke Park had been on the agenda long before the Lansdowne Road announcement. As far back as 1992, when the GAA brought forward plans to redevelop Croke Park, the question of whether it should be made available for other sports moved up the agenda. Opinion was divided within the GAA membership.

Those in favour insisted that it made no sense to restrict such a big, modern stadium to only hosting Gaelic games when it could generate substantial income for the GAA by renting it to other sports bodies.

Those opposed to any change contended that it was the responsibility of rugby and soccer to provide their own facilities and that if the rule was amended for Croke Park, it was only a matter of time before pressure mounted to open up county grounds too.

Congress 2001 brought a significant development when a proposal to give Central Council ultimate power to decide on the use of Croke Park was carried by a 176–89 majority.

However, since it was one vote short of the required two-thirds majority, the motion was lost. The vote was conducted on a show of hands – scarcely the most scientific means of reaching such a big decision, especially when it was so close. A call for a second vote was rejected by GAA president Seán McCague.

There had been a significant development the night before the vote when the government announced a €60 million allocation for the Croke Park redevelopment. In return, the GAA agreed to support a government proposal to build a national stadium in Abbottstown, promising to play 'a substantive programme in Stadium Ireland when it is completed in five years'.

That included playing championship games, including All-Ireland semi-finals, in the new facility. There were various interpretations of what it all meant. Some saw it as the government trying to apply pressure on the GAA to open up Croke Park, thereby making the national stadium project unnecessary. Others interpreted it as a move by government to persuade the GAA to retain Rule 42, which would have made the need for a national stadium all the greater.

Whatever the background machinations, Seán McCague and the GAA regarded the national stadium plan as complementary to Croke Park, rather than being a competitor, saying, 'We have agreed with the government to play a programme of games in Stadium Ireland when it is completed in five years' time.'

Many members were confused by the developments. Why should the GAA agree to play some games – up to and including All-Ireland semi-finals – in Stadium Ireland while, six miles away, a redeveloped, and larger, Croke Park lay idle?

The impact of the government's €60 million promise for Croke Park, coming so close to the debate on whether to open it up, was – and has always remained – unclear. In any event, the proposal for change lost by the narrowest of margins.

Curiously, when a similar motion came before Congress 2002, it was heavily defeated – 197 to 106. The loss of support was somewhat surprising, but then the €60 million government grant had largely removed the financial argument for opening up Croke Park.

Undeterred, advocates for change, such as Noel Walsh (Clare), Tommy Kenoy (Roscommon) and Anthony Delaney (Laois), pressed on with the campaign, and when Seán Kelly took over as president in 2003, it brought a significant shift.

He was very much in favour of opening up Croke Park, particularly while Lansdowne Road was closed, but a strong lobby remained vehemently opposed. They claimed that it would be wrong to bring moral pressure on the GAA to open up so that international teams didn't have to play in Britain. The GAA kept Croke Park open during its extensive redevelopment work – why couldn't Lansdowne Road be kept open too?

The exchanges in the run-up to the 2005 Congress were tetchy, tense and quite divisive. So too was the debate at congress, which ran on expected lines. Those in favour argued that Rule 42 was no longer in keeping with a modern Ireland; those opposed contended that the GAA had a right to do whatever it wanted with its own property and should not be subjected to moral pressure from outside.

Seán Quirke (Wexford), speaking in favour of change, offered a simple analogy: 'If a neighbour's house went on fire, you wouldn't leave them without a room.'

Former GAA president Con Murphy was very much in the opposite camp. 'If you support this [opening up Croke Park], you are supporting the formation of a new association which caters for everything and counts for nothing.'

The vote, conducted by secret ballot, returned a 227–97 majority in favour of opening up Croke Park while Lansdowne Road was being developed. It was almost another two years (11 February 2007) before the first international rugby game – Ireland v France – was played there. It was followed in March by the first soccer international when Ireland played Wales.

Croke Park continued to host rugby and soccer internationals until 2010, generating €36 million in rental income for the GAA.

LIAM MILLER BENEFIT GAME
A Bruising Time for the GAA

If the depth of a controversy can be measured by its long-term impact, it's accurate to describe the row over a charity soccer game in Páirc Uí Chaoímh in 2018 as the real deal.

As often happens with controversies, they start out small and with no obvious signs that they have the capacity to escalate rapidly.

A Touch of Controversy

When it was announced in the summer of 2018 that the organisers of a tribute game for Liam Miller, a soccer player from Cork who had died at the age of thirty-six, had asked for the use of Páirc Uí Chaoímh there was no immediate reaction.

The aim of the venture was two-fold: to honour a local man who had established a big reputation as an international star – he'd played with several top clubs, including Celtic and Manchester United – and to raise funds for his family and some local charities.

With a capacity of 45,000, Páirc Uí Chaoímh was by far the most suitable venue for the venture but, unfortunately, there was a problem. Under GAA rules, grounds other than Croke Park could not be used for games except those under the control of the association.

The GAA also pointed out that since rules could only be changed at annual congress, which takes place in February, it would not be possible to make an exception, even for a benefit game where some of the proceeds would go the family of a man who had died of cancer at such a young age.

Suddenly, the GAA were sucked into a controversy cauldron. They claimed the rules precluded them from making Páirc Uí Chaoímh available – public opinion demanded that they find a way around their own regulations. Political pressure mounted too, with some senior figures raising the question of whether the GAA were entitled to stick by their rules after receiving €30 million from the government for the stadium's redevelopment.

With public and political opinion lined up against the GAA, it had little choice but to find a compromise that would allow the soccer game to be played in Páirc Uí Chaoímh. The solution was eventually reached with a reclassification of the occasion: it was to be deemed a community event, featuring soccer and Gaelic games. The immediate crisis was over, the event went ahead and proved to be a great success, but the fall-out dragged on for the GAA.

Director-General Tom Ryan returned to the matter in his 2019 Annual Report:

Much of the clamour that arose amounted to demands for us just to ignore our own standards and indeed our decision-makers. To ignore the rule and find a loophole and host the game. As a body charged with trying to uphold standards, we should not be in the business of finding ways around our own rules.

The overwhelming sentiment being that we felt we were being bullied into a course of action that we might well have taken anyway, if given the chance. We are permitted, under certain circumstances, to use the grounds where it's not in contravention of the aims of the Association. We'd reached a stage where the groundswell of opinion was such that by not holding the game, you were actually compromising the aims of the Association in terms of goodwill and reputation.

Having found a way of circumventing their own rules to avoid severe reputational damage, the next step was to ensure that a similar scenario could not arise in the future.

Accordingly, a motion was brought to Congress 2019 calling for Central Council to be given the power to decide on applications to use GAA county grounds for non-GAA games. Nobody spoke against and it was passed on a 91–9 per cent majority.

A similar motion, proposed by Clare in 2016, had been beaten on a 67–23 per cent majority. The bruising events of summer 2018 had obviously changed mindsets. A benefit game for a deceased soccer player had, in effect, led to a fundamental change in GAA rules.

THE RDS AFFAIR
Distinct Absence of Christmas Cheer

How could something as straightforward as two games played at the same venue ten days before Christmas develop into a major controversy?

It was a question that occupied many in the GAA in December 1991, as they tried to figure out why their organisation had become trapped in a public-relations nightmare. There were no satisfactory explanations then, or indeed later.

The unfortunate saga arose from a novelty promotion planned by Dublin club Clanna Gael-Fontenoys as part of their centenary celebrations. It involved a football–soccer double-header at the RDS, featuring Down, the reigning All-Ireland champions, in a challenge game against Dublin, and a Shamrock Rovers–Shelbourne League of Ireland game.

The GAA's Games Administration Committee initially refused to grant permission on the basis that the RDS was not vested in the association, but members later relented. Clanna Gael-Fontenoys launched a major publicity campaign and all seemed to be progressing smoothly until the GAA's Central Council met on 7 December, eight days before the proposed event.

After it had conducted its ordinary business, journalists were asked to leave the meeting as a matter had arisen that needed to be dealt with in private.

It was later announced that permission for the Down–Dublin game had been withdrawn. The reasons given were vague, with references to violations of conditions previously laid down. There were also concerns over the financial arrangements.

Suddenly, a novelty event had become a major news story. Moving from back to front pages, it sparked claims that the GAA's decision was down to an unwillingness to have any dealings with soccer.

Paddy Downey, the *Irish Times* GAA correspondent, described the decision as the blackest day in GAA history. 'Over the weekend gone by, the great and the glorious times were not just devalued but virtually degraded.'

As the controversy rumbled on, GAA president Peter Quinn and director-general Liam Mulvihill conducted interviews with Sunday newspapers where they insisted that the decision to withdraw permission for the RDS venture was based on practicalities and not on an antipathy towards soccer.

'If people want to see me in that light [anti-soccer] there is not a whole lot I can do about it. I am not anti-anything, not anti-sport in any way,' Quinn told the *Sunday Independent*.

Mulvihill was equally adamant that the GAA's concerns were based solely on the circumstances as they saw them. He told the *Sunday Press*:

We had major reservations that, from a financial viewpoint, there was no way the club's ambition could be realised and that despite the excellent PR job they had done, it was unlikely to attract enough spectators to pay all the costs. Our decision to withdraw backing for the game was taken on practical rather than idealistic grounds. There were certain aspects of the whole deal we found disturbing, and these had nothing to do with an anti-soccer attitude.

However valid the explanations put forward by Quinn and Mulvihill were, the PR damage had been done. December should have been a quiet month for the GAA but instead they were mired in a controversy which could have been easily avoided.

LIFFEY DIVIDE
Two Teams for Dublin

It came like a bolt from the blue. And this time it literally was blue as a high-powered committee proposed a north–south split for Dublin GAA. The River Liffey was to be the dividing line.

It was the most eye-catching proposal contained in the 2002 Strategic Review Report and caught everyone – most of all Dublin – by surprise. It recommended that Dublin would field two minor football teams in the championship from 2003, followed by two senior teams in 2004. This was no attention-seeking intervention by a lightweight group, but rather the considered deliberations of a high-powered, sixteen-man committee, chaired by former GAA president Peter Quinn.

Established by Seán McCague when he took over as president in 2000, the committee also included Joe McDonagh, another former president, as well as senior provincial officials and representatives from business, politics, the Irish Sports Council and RTÉ. Players were represented by Mayo footballer James Nallen.

The rationale for the Liffey divide was that with over one-third of the Republic's population living in Dublin, it had a bigger population than two of the provinces combined. The report pointed to the administrative challenges arising from the size of Dublin's population and felt that a practical solution would be to create two counties. The report noted:

> *For too long, the rest of the country has viewed Dublin's problems from a distance, as if they had no relevance to the other county units. That view has to change. Dublin's importance to the GAA nationally is such that the entire Association must take some ownership of the resolution of Dublin's problems. It is not enough to leave their problems to be sorted out internally.*

News that they were being asked to undergo such a seismic change stunned Dublin, who only heard of the proposal on the day the report was launched. They hadn't been consulted, which further irritated them.

They had concerns too over comments by Peter Quinn at the launch of the report when he said that while Dublin's views on the proposal were important, they would not have the final call. 'We don't want to override Dublin but this is a national matter. It's a matter for everyone in the GAA. One way or the other, we must make progress in Dublin.'

It quickly became clear that even if there was logic in the two-team proposal, based on demographics, the emotional ties could not be broken.

Kevin Heffernan, the most instantly recognisable name in Dublin football, told the *Irish Independent* that while a separation might make sense from an administrative viewpoint, it was different from a playing perspective. 'It wouldn't be quite the same for a Dublin player to be chosen for North or South. It would weaken the sense of identity.'

John O'Leary, who had captained Dublin to All-Ireland success in 1995, said that more and better-organised clubs were what the county required. Jimmy Keaveney, a star performer in the Dublin revival in the 1970s, said players and fans would struggle to get used to the two-team idea and that it simply wouldn't work.

Mick O'Dwyer, who had led Kerry in so many famous battles with Dublin in the 1970s and 1980s, described the proposal as 'plain daft' and said it shouldn't be taken seriously. 'Dublin are Dublin, and you don't start tinkering around with them. I'd hate to see Dublin divided and I hope it never happens.'

It never did. In fact, it didn't get any further than a proposal in the Strategic Review Report as it quickly became apparent that Dublin were lining up the strongest possible resistance. And despite Peter Quinn's insistence that it was a national matter, other counties were not prepared to even contemplate discussing Dublin's future.

The two-county proposal died quickly, but it did raise fundamental issues about the challenges caused by a demographic shift to the east, and to Dublin in particular. Twenty-two years later, those challenges are even greater.

RULE 21
No British Army or RUC

It was only forty-five words long, but they were mighty impactful on GAA history:

> *Members of the British armed forces and police shall not be eligible for membership of the Association. A member of the Association participating in dances or similar entertainment, promoted by or under the patronage of such bodies, shall incur suspension of at least three months.*

Rule 21 lasted for nearly one hundred years and while it went unchallenged for much of that period, it gradually became a source of controversy and its relevance questioned, especially as the political landscape in Northern Ireland changed. Even some of those who had favoured its retention for many years began to wonder if it served any purpose, other than portraying the GAA as a quasi-political organisation.

Nevertheless, there was nervousness within Leinster, Munster and Connacht counties to address an issue that didn't directly affect them. They tended to take a lead from Ulster counties, where there was a far greater reluctance to remove the rule.

Stories of harassment of GAA members by police and British army were many and varied, with players telling how they were often stopped and delayed for ages on their way to training or games. They believed that, in the main, it was deliberatively provocative – harassment for harassment's sake.

There was also the British army's occupation of part of the Crossmaglen GAA ground as a military base for many years from the mid-1970s. It was deeply irritating for the club and had wider ramifications too, with supporters of Rule 21 arguing that it would be outrageous to lift the ban on British army personnel joining the GAA while they still occupied part of a club ground.

Congress passed motions every year calling for the immediate withdrawal of troops from Crossmaglen. Pressure was applied on the Irish government to raise the matter with their British counterparts as often as possible. However, it wasn't until 1999 – a year after the signing of the Good Friday Agreement – that a withdrawal process was announced.

At Congress 1998 – eight days after the Good Friday Agreement had been signed – an attempt to have Rule 21 abolished failed. Driven by GAA president Joe McDonagh, who believed its time was up, a Special Congress was called for 30 May. A lengthy debate took place behind closed doors and while there was considerable support for change, many delegates from Ulster counties were more reticent.

They believed that it was too soon after the Good Friday Agreement to make such a big decision. Rather than take it to a vote, which probably wouldn't have got the required two-thirds majority for abolition, the matter was deferred, and a statement was issued.

'Cumann Lúthchleas Gael pledges its intent to delete Rule 21 from its Official Guide when effective steps are taken to implement the amended structures and policing arrangements as envisaged in the British–Ireland Peace Agreement.'

It was more than three years later when the GAA was satisfied that the time to abolish Rule 21 had come. In November 2001, Special Congress voted it out of the rulebook by a large majority. Five Ulster counties – Armagh, Derry, Antrim, Tyrone and Fermanagh – were mandated to oppose the deletion but there was no rancour or recriminations.

It was appropriate that an Ulsterman, Seán McCague, was president for the abolition of the rule. 'We have deleted an exclusion rule – that's really all we did. We consulted our membership and found they were in favour of change. The timing was right.'

His predecessor, Joe McDonagh, said the abolition reflected the change in the GAA and in society generally. 'It has been a long process but is all the healthier for that,' he said.

CORK TURMOIL
Three Strikes but Not Out
Between 2002 and 2009, Cork squads went on strike three times in an unprecedented demonstration of player power.

Strike One
In November 2002, Cork hurlers announced they were withdrawing their services in protest at the way they were being treated by the county board. Grievances relating to training facilities, travel, food, gear and medical backup were all outlined in detail. As far as

the players were concerned, they had reached breaking point and were not prepared to take any more.

The footballers joined the protest a few weeks later. Talks followed and a deal was struck but the seeds of discontent had been sown. The players were seen to have won, but there was still a long way to go.

Strike Two

In October 2007, Cork County Board voted to change the manner in which selectors were chosen. For the previous five years, the county managers had been allowed to name their own selectors – after the change, the power would revert to the board.

It might not have looked a particularly serious issue initially, but it escalated rapidly when the board appointed Teddy Holland to replace Billy Morgan as football manager. Four selectors were also chosen.

The footballers and hurlers made it clear that they would not play under the new management, contending that they had been put in place using a flawed mechanism.

A stand-off ensued and, as 2008 dawned, it became clear that Cork's participation in the national leagues was in doubt. Kieran Mulvey, chairman of the Labour Relations Commission, was brought in as an arbitrator but despite his vast experience in industrial relations, he found untangling the Cork mess very challenging.

Ultimately, the departure of Holland and his selectors was seen as the only viable option and they were duly removed by the board in mid-February. They had found themselves in an invidious position, trapped in a row between the board and the players. And since the players held the upper hand – Cork would have no senior teams in 2008 unless the squads got their way – Holland and the selectors were sacrificed. It was an unedifying end to a bitter row that damaged Cork GAA on a number of levels.

Strike Three

Peace didn't last long after the second strike. In October 2008, the hurling squad objected to the extension of Gerald McCarthy's term as manager. He had been in charge for two years and while the board were happy for him to continue, the players took a different view.

Despite that, the board ratified McCarthy. They insisted it was their job to appoint managers without having to consult the players.

This was the norm everywhere else but Cork was different. Player power was rampant.

McCarthy, a revered figure in Cork from his playing days and a man of considerable managerial experience, stood his ground. He had been ratified by the county board, giving him a mandate to continue and he wanted to act on it.

If only it were that simple.

Once again, the players withdrew their services, leading to a protracted period of strife that dominated Cork GAA and also had implications further afield.

Cork started the 2009 season without the 2008 squad, fielding a new-look team that couldn't possibly be ready for the big demands being placed on them. As the pressure mounted, McCarthy eventually stood down in March, signing off with a statement that carried the chilling revelation that he had been subjected to death threats. He wrote:

> *A few days ago, my father, who is in his mid-eighties, pleaded with me to step down after one of my sons, in my absence abroad, received the latest threat against me. The threat against my life, which has been referred to the gardaí, is the latest in a sequence of threats and abuse, random or organised I do not know, which I and my family members have had to endure over the past few months.*

He also insisted that if the players had been willing to discuss what they perceived as problems, a resolution could have been found early on. Instead, they had pressed the strike button.

> *The players' modus operandi has been simple: strike, issue ultimatums, refuse to speak and raise the temperature by carefully choreographed public events. No amount of these can disguise the fundamental truth, however. No dispute was ever resolved in the absence of dialogue.*
>
> *My reasons for taking the stand I did four months ago are as valid today as they were then. Hurlers should not have the right to appoint their own manager, veto the appointment of a manager, interview their own manager or pursue commercial interests at the expense of the broader GAA family.*

Denis Walsh replaced him as manager and the 2008 squad returned.

MONEY FOR WASHING DIRTY LINEN

It was Kerry like they had never been seen before. Some dressed in shorts and jerseys, others just in shorts, a few with towels draped around them, all standing near a washing machine.

In the middle of them was manager Mick O'Dwyer, a stern look on his face as if to say: Here we are, Croke Park, what have you got to say about this?

It was the day of the 1985 Dublin–Kerry All-Ireland football final, and the full-page advertisement for Bendix washing machines had a striking presence in the *Sunday Independent*. The caption ran: 'Only Bendix could whitewash this lot.'

Those outside the GAA would have had no appreciation of the significance. They would have seen it as just another advertisement, using well-known sportspeople as a selling point. GAA members knew it wasn't quite that simple.

Kerry had won six All-Ireland finals since 1975 (and would go on to win two more in 1985 and 1986) and were very much the glamour boys of that era. Inevitably, they attracted commercial interests and were happy to engage with them, much to the unease of the Croke Park power brokers, who feared it might be the next phase of a challenge to the GAA's amateur status rules.

Four years earlier, Adidas contributed to a Kerry holiday fund in return for using their gear. That contravened GAA regulations, which stipulated that squads could only use Irish-made gear.

Croke Park applied pressure on the Kerry County Board but O'Dwyer still found a way to use Adidas gear during the championship. He recalled in his autobiography, *Blessed and Obsessed*, how a Croke Park official came into the dressing room before the All-Ireland final clash with Offaly to inspect the gear.

'Presumably he was expecting to find Adidas tags on the jerseys. There wasn't any to be found because we had cut them off. We got £20,000 from Adidas for our holiday fund that year and the county board was fined £500 for so-called gear violation, so we made a nice profit,' wrote O'Dwyer.

By 1985, O'Dwyer and his squad were viewed suspiciously by the GAA authorities and when the Bendix advertisement appeared they saw it as another example of defiance. That deal was organised by the county board and while the players were happy to pose in front of a washing machine if it helped swell the holiday coffers, O'Dwyer felt it was worth a lot more than the £5,000 reputedly paid by the advertisers.

'Had I been involved, I would have looked for at least £20,000 and even more later on because Bendix got a massive amount of publicity from the ensuing controversy,' wrote O'Dwyer.

There's no doubt that O'Dwyer and Kerry pushed the boundaries in the 1980s, but he has always insisted that it was a progressive move, one that the GAA should have been driving, as indeed they did later.

'It was sad that instead of noting how many opportunities were out there, the GAA [in the 1980s] took the narrow view that raising money for team funds and holidays was a stepping stone to a form of professionalism. It was far from it. All we wanted to do was get as much as we could for the players. What was wrong with that?'

Antrim try to Have Kerry Disqualified

On 18 August 1946, Kerry beat Antrim by 2–7 to 0–10 in the All-Ireland football semi-final in Croke Park.

'Antrim made a valiant effort but their forwards carried hand-passing to extremes when direct methods would have yielded a more fruitful return,' reported the *Irish Independent*.

'The match provided a great contrast of styles – Antrim depending solely on hand passing with practically no footwork,' noted the *Cork Examiner*.

There was no mention of foul tactics in either report. Antrim had a very different perspective, convinced that Kerry had effectively intimidated their way to victory. The Antrim County Board were so incensed that they decided to lodge a formal objection to the result. It was a sensational development.

The objection was based on the following grounds.

'That members of the Kerry team continually indulged in rough play and repeatedly made deliberate and unwarranted assaults on our players.'

'That those members of the Kerry team were guilty of conduct calculated to bring the Association into disrepute.'

Antrim further asserted that 'the majority of these attacks, which resulted in serious injury to many of our players, were when they were not in possession of, or playing, the ball'.

They named eight players who, they claimed, were victims of

'deliberate attacks' and offered to submit evidence regarding the extent of the injuries. They also referred to 'brutal methods' and warned that players would opt out of the game if this were to become the norm.

Pointedly, Antrim included the wording of the rule relating to bad behaviour by players. 'A whole team may be disqualified for rough play, even though it won the match.'

Kerry were disgusted by Antrim's actions, claiming that it was outrageous to insult the county's pedigree by alleging their team were guilty of such bad behaviour.

Objecting to the result of an All-Ireland semi-final was a big decision by Antrim and, having lodged it, they set about making as strong a case as possible. The Central Council meeting to hear the objection was set for Saturday, 31 August, the week after Roscommon had won the second semi-final.

But who would be their opponents in the final?

Central Council debated the Antrim objection for more than two hours, with heated contributions for and against it. A vote was finally taken, resulting in the rejection of the Antrim proposal on a 19–10 majority.

It was later claimed that most of the Antrim players hadn't wanted to object on the basis that it would have made them look like bad losers. However, the county board proceeded, believing that they had a strong case for a rematch at least. Central Council decided otherwise.

The whole affair left a sour taste as the view across the wider GAA held that it was bad for football's reputation to have an objection to an All-Ireland semi-final result, especially one based on claims of 'deliberate attacks' and 'brutal methods'.

A relieved Kerry simply got on with training for the final against Roscommon. It finished level before Kerry won the title for a sixteenth time with a four-point win in the replay.

8 THREATS AND CHALLENGES

We recommend that live TV coverage of All-Ireland semi-finals and provincial finals should not be allowed. They should be taped and transmitted subsequently.
The McNamee Commission, which reported in 1971, was fearful that live coverage of GAA games would reduce attendances.

The recommendation was unambiguous – reduce 'live' coverage of GAA games. It came after one of the most forensic reviews ever undertaken by the association at a time when Ireland was undergoing rapid change in economic, social and sporting life.

Conscious that it needed to assess where it stood – and where it was headed – the GAA established a commission in 1969 to look into all areas of its activities. Chaired by Pádraig McNamee, a former Ulster Council chairman, and comprising twenty members (dozens of others made submissions), it took two years to complete the report. Published on 1 December 1971, it stretched to 90,000 words.

Among the report's many recommendations were that: the All-Ireland football and hurling championships be run on an open draw; a three-tier development plan for hurling, tailored to further strengthen it in the traditional counties, step up promotion in weaker counties and provide special support for smaller pockets in other areas; acceptance of sponsorship; floodlighting of main county grounds; major changes in coaching structures; restructuring of administration systems at national and local level; and a new system of training and grading referees.

All of the proposals catered for areas where, with the exception of the open draw, the commission members were satisfied that they were on solid ground. One other recommendation dealt with a more-vague issue, where there was no evidence-based means of helping them to reach a conclusion. Judging from their assessment of how to cope with the impact of television, it presented more of a threat than an opportunity.

As far back as April 1960, twenty months before the launch of Telefís Éireann, GAA president J.J. Stuart had warned that the association needed to be mindful of television's possible impact on Gaelic games. Speaking at congress, he said the GAA should be vigilant and prepared.

'Those of you from northern and eastern counties who are familiar with this most potent modern instrument of entertainment, education and propaganda for good or evil, know the extent to which is has revolutionised sport by bringing it to the very fireside.'

Stating that it was vital the new Irish television service would do as much for Irish sport as its British counterpart had done for English games, he warned of the need for vigilance.

'Day after day and night after night, they [British television] have loaded their television programmes with exhibitions of their various codes of football, their race meetings, their cross-country runners, their boxers. All that is very good for the English people, but it has a vital lesson for us who are about to embark on the great experiment.'

Telefís Éireann began broadcasting on 31 December 1961 and, eleven weeks later, it screened a live GAA match for the first time. The Railway Cup interprovincial finals on St Patrick's Day were chosen and, while there was a sense of excitement in the GAA at the move into this new medium, there was also some apprehension. Would it be good or bad for the national games?

For some reason, it was decided to launch coverage by showing the second half only of the Leinster–Munster hurling final, followed by the entire Leinster–Ulster football final. Joining a game halfway through was a strange way of introducing the public to television coverage and underlined the uncertainty of the GAA's approach to the new arrival.

A second example of the confused thinking came five weeks later when congress passed a Tyrone motion stating that permission for future live television coverage would only be granted if at least half of the commentary was in Irish. This was after an Armagh motion calling for the entire commentary to be in Irish was withdrawn.

Another strange move, which didn't go down well with viewers, was when dual commentary was used for the All-Ireland semi-finals and finals in 1962, with Seán Óg Ó Ceallacháin (English) and Micheál Ó Muircheartaigh (Irish) alternating every ten minutes. It was the ultimate compromise, one that drew sharp criticism in the *Irish Independent*.

'It is in no anti-Nationalist vein that I suggest that a very large proportion of the viewers were 'at sea' when the play was being described in Irish. It would have been more satisfactory to have the entire commentary of actual play in the English language and good summaries in Irish at the interval and at the conclusion,' wrote Barry Nolan.

In 1963, the dual role was replaced by Michael O'Hehir's single commentary, which went out simultaneously on radio and television. O'Hehir's exceptional commentating skills were widely recognised, but having the same commentary on radio and TV was unsatisfactory as the requirements for each are very different. Despite that, the dual model continued until 1970.

The GAA had bigger concerns than commentaries. As the 1960s progressed, they became fearful that live TV coverage would impact negatively on attendances, so the McNamee Commission set about assessing its future role.

The recommendations were stark: no more live coverage of All-Ireland semi-finals or provincial finals (earlier rounds of the championship weren't even considered). Recorded games could be shown later. The commission clearly regarded television as a serious threat. As the report noted:

Television has presented the Association with one of its major problems, for which no final solution has been so far forthcoming. Live TV transmission of games is of constant concerns to GAA legislators, but no definite policy line has been laid down.

One the one hand, it is argued that live coverage sells the games to the public. On the other hand, it is argued that live TV results in reduced attendances and, in some cases, e.g. the All-Ireland semi-finals, it interferes considerably with club championships.

It suggested that even if broadcast fees covered the loss of gate receipts resulting from lower attendances, it would still have a detrimental long-term impact. The conclusion reached was that only All-Ireland finals and Railway Cup finals should be shown live. The proposal was later rejected by Special Congress, but a degree of unease remained about TV's influence on attendances. Indeed, it's highly probable that televising the Railway Cup finals led to a dramatic decline in crowds in the 1970s.

Soccer's growing popularity was also presenting challenges for the GAA. McNamee referred to the impact of England's 1966 World Cup soccer triumph on Ireland's sporting outlook, suggesting it had strengthened the development of the game here.

Other TV-related issues were also worrying the GAA. Jimmy Gray, Dublin County Board chairman, told the 1972 Dublin County Convention that exposure to English soccer might have been partially responsible for the decline of the county's senior football team.

The type of football being played in Dublin at inter-county level and at club level is not Gaelic football, and the system and tactics being used are copies of those employed in soccer as seen on television.

Those methods, which are used in English soccer as a means of not losing, detract from Gaelic football and have the effect of making it boring as a spectacle and completely negative from a results point of view. There must be a new thinking about the game by clubs and coaches, but particularly by the players. They must think for themselves and use techniques which are appropriate to Gaelic football.

There were wider concerns too that the influence of *Match of the Day* on BBC on Saturday nights and *The Big Match* on ITV on Sunday afternoons would popularise soccer at the expense of Gaelic games. Manchester United, Liverpool, Arsenal, Everton, Leeds United, Chelsea, Celtic and various other soccer clubs were attracting an ever-increasing fan base in Ireland, and with Rule 27 (the Ban, which barred GAA members from playing 'foreign games') deleted in 1971 there were fears for the association's future well-being, especially in Dublin and other cities and towns. The big soccer action, albeit watched through a grainy haze in many parts of the country, was regarded as new and glamorous, and very attractive to a younger generation in particular.

It was also consistently available every weekend from August until May. This came at a time when the GAA was dealing with the aftermath of the removal of Rule 27, allowing players to test themselves in other sports. There were early gains for rugby.

Threats and Challenges

Within thirteen months of the removal of the Ban, three of the Galway football team that had completed the All-Ireland three-in-a-row in 1966 starred for Galway Corinthians when they won the Connacht senior rugby cup for the first time in eighteen years.

Jimmy Duggan was at full-back, with Enda Colleran, Galway captain in the 1965 and 1966 All-Ireland wins, and Martin Newell paired in the centre as Corinthians beat University College Galway 10–3 in the final. Colleran, who scored two penalties in the game, and Newell were no longer on the Galway football panel, but Duggan was still a key member of the squad and would remain so for many more years.

That he was playing competitive rugby the month before lining out for Galway in the Connacht football championship underlined how much had changed in just over a year.

Meanwhile, the decline of Dublin football was a growing cause for concern, not only for the county's administrators but also the Croke Park authorities. Combined with the removal of Rule 27 and the growing influence of English soccer, questions were being raised about the association's future in the capital.

Yes, it would always survive but that was never going to be enough. The GAA needed a vibrant Dublin, especially on the football side, challenging for top honours.

It wasn't happening – certainly not between 1966 and 1973 when Dublin were eliminated from the Leinster championship in the first round four times and reached no final. Kildare (three times), Longford (twice) Westmeath, Laois and Louth all took turns at beating Dublin, with only one (Longford in 1968) going on to win the provincial title. It put the state of Dublin football in sharp perspective. Even when they won a game, they were rarely impressive.

'One would have to be reminded that this was a championship game as the thirty players plodded their mistake-laden way through as dull and unexciting an hour as one could wish to witness,' wrote Michael Fortune in the *Irish Press* after Dublin's win over Westmeath in the 1972 Leinster quarter-final. They lost the semi-final to Kildare.

A year later, less than 2,000 spectators turned out for Dublin's win over Wexford in Wexford Park, before they lost a second-round tie to Louth.

Given that depressing background, what happened in 1974 was quite remarkable – the revolution under Kevin Heffernan took Dublin from virtual no-hopers to All-Ireland winners in four unforgettable months.

The impact was just as seismic. The GAA's popularity had not only been re-established in Dublin but it had a momentum that would enable it to resist whatever challenges came its way.

Concerns over Dublin had passed, but TV coverage continued to present challenges for the GAA. Still unable to quite figure out whether it was a plus or minus, evidence supporting the latter emerged in the early 1980s when attendances dropped alarmingly.

In his review of 1982, Director-General Liam Mulvihill described the decline as a 'most pressing concern to all members of the Association'.

It wasn't a one-off either. 'The problem did not suddenly appear this year; indeed it has been evident for a number of years and has accelerated since the advent of television coverage,' he continued.

Mulvihill also listed economic problems – cost of transport, accommodation and catering, increased admission charges, standard of games, issues with facilities at games and counter-attractions on Sundays – as other contributory factors.

He outlined how aggregate attendances at the two All-Ireland football semi-finals – always regarded as a key indicator – had halved between 1979 and 1982, down from 85,000 to less than 43,000. The latter figure was the disappointing total in 1982 for Armagh v Kerry (17,523) and Galway v Offaly (25,111).

The figures prompted suggestions from various quarters that both semi-finals should be played on the same day in order to create a better atmosphere. Mulvihill's list of possible reasons were all valid but there was another factor too – Kerry's overwhelming dominance.

Having won four-in-a-row All-Ireland titles (1978–1981), there was an air of inevitability ahead of many of their games, including All-Ireland semi-finals, which they won by an average of thirteen points between 1978 and 1982. Many Kerry supporters had stopped travelling to Croke Park for semi-finals, believing them to be a formality, while neutrals weren't interested in what they expected to be one-sided games.

Attendances increased for the 1983 semi-finals, boosted by Dublin's return for the first time since 1979 plus Cork's presence for the first time since 1974, and held reasonably well for a number of years. However, Mulvihill returned to the topic in his review of 1989, pointing to a 'significant drop in attendances' and stating that it left the GAA short of the financial targets it had set for the redevelopment of Croke Park.

This was to be the major project for the 1990s, so big that when the full details were announced in 1992, the scale of the undertaking sent worried tremors across large swathes of the association. This was no mere revamp, but rather a grand plan to turn Croke Park into one of the most modern stadiums in the world.

Initially costed at just over £100 million (€127 million) and targeting an increase of capacity to 79,000 (it eventually rose to 82,300), the inclusion of corporate boxes on three sides of the ground was one of the features that attracted most attention.

Would the business sector respond? This was a new concept in Ireland and since a sizeable portion of the funding depended on the sale of boxes and long-term tickets, there was scepticism over whether it was an overstretch that would leave the GAA with financial problems for decades.

Peter Quinn, then GAA president and a man with vast financial experience, was a major driving force behind the ambitious plan; so too was Mulvihill. They believed that notwithstanding the volatile economic situation, the time was right for such an ambitious undertaking and that redeveloping on a more modest scale would be a lost opportunity, even if it made it easier to manage in the short term. Clearly, if corporate boxes weren't included in the original design, they could not be added later, thereby preventing the stadium from being a state-of-the-art facility as well as seriously reducing its income capabilities.

Despite the upbeat approach of the leadership, there were

Threats and Challenges

many GAA members who feared it was too much of a financial risk.

They were proven wrong.

Work began on the redevelopment the day after the 1993 All-Ireland football final, starting with the Cusack Stand, continuing through the Canal End (now Davin Stand), onto the Hogan Stand and finishing with Hill 16, now named after Frank Dineen, who bought the ground on Jones' Road in 1908 and held it in trust for the GAA before selling it to them in 1913. In all, it took twelve years to complete the work.

The redevelopment wasn't without its difficulties but proceeding with it on such a large scale proved to be one of the GAA's best decisions.

Other challenges, whether rooted in history, ethos or demographics, were far more intractable. Indeed, quite a few still remain on the GAA's agenda.

One that proved very difficult on a number of levels arose from the H-Block prisoners' hunger strike in 1981. Maintaining a clear line between sport and politics became very difficult for the GAA at a time of incredible tension in Northern Ireland.

The GAA came under enormous pressure from many of its members in Northern Ireland to show tangible support for the hunger strikers. Clubs were asked to join protest marches, GAA grounds in the north were used for rallies, and protests at half-time were commonplace during the 1981 Ulster championship. There were calls for black flags to be flown in Croke Park on All-Ireland final days.

The GAA at central level were anxious to avoid any connection with the protests, not because they weren't sympathetic to the suffering of the hunger strikers but because they didn't want to become involved in anything that might be seen as overtly political.

GAA president Paddy McFlynn admitted in his memoirs, published many years later, that he feared the GAA would split on the issue.

Following his retirement in 2008, Liam Mulvihill also referenced the period around the 1981 hunger strikes as among the most difficult of his twenty-nine years as director-general. It was outside the control of the GAA, so all they could do was tread warily. So too with some other issues which overlapped between sporting and political.

Other areas that came under their direct jurisdiction proved just as difficult. Indeed, some of them are still problematical, including amateur status and player relations.

As far back as the early 1970s when P.J. Carroll & Company became sponsors of the All-Stars scheme, it was clear that the GAA held an attraction for the corporate world. That cigarette manufacturers were accepted as sponsors underlined the different attitudes that applied at the time. Many other sports also had deals with cigarette companies, so it wasn't as if the GAA was on its own. Still, a certain wariness remained in the GAA about commercial arrangements of any kind up to the 1970s.

The GAA's approach to sponsorship loosened considerably throughout the 1980s and, by the early 1990s, they were ready to take a major step by allowing company logos to be used on jerseys. Dublin's motion to that effect was carried on a 194–96 vote at Congress 1991, but not before objections were raised.

Threats and Challenges

Cork county secretary Frank Murphy was among those who opposed the motion, warning of the risk of 'cheap and commercial emblazoning of jerseys'. Others complained that jersey sponsorship would widen the gap between stronger and lower-ranked counties, with the former able to generate far more lucrative deals. However, a two-thirds majority backed the proposal, subject to restrictions on the size of the branding allowed.

As the GAA centrally began to embrace sponsorship across a wide range of areas, generating sizeable incomes in the process, it became much more difficult to hold the amateur line. Since players were being used as advertising mediums, pressure increased for better collective conditions, as well as allowing individuals to arrange their own deals.

In addition, rugby was heading out on the professional road in the mid-1990s, which had its own significance for the GAA. Up to then, it could always point to rugby as a sport that, despite having a major international presence, held the amateur line. With rugby going professional, another brick loosened on the GAA's amateur wall.

The first test came, not from players, but from the management world, where reports of under-the-counter payments emerged regularly. Stories of payments to managers swept the country but since they couldn't be verified, there was nothing the GAA leadership could do. The same applies to this day.

As far back as 1992, Liam Mulvihill wrote of 'persistent allegations about payments to coaches at club and county level'. He warned there were 'enough indications to warn us all that they could be a fundamental threat to our amateurism if we are not more vigilant'.

He returned to the subject in 1993 ('the Association cannot accept a situation where there is dishonesty in the administration of our affairs'), 1994 ('disturbing allegations continue to come from various quarters') and 1998 ('there have been persistent rumours about payments to coaches and managers').

By the time he retired ten years later, little had changed. His successor, Páraic Duffy, was equally concerned about the apparent blatant disregard of a rule that was supposed to be one of the GAA's cornerstones.

'The least acceptable option is to continue to proclaim a value and, at the same time, ignore it. I believe the time has come to call on all the expertise available to examine the current situation with a view to bringing forward proposals later in the year that will allow a debate throughout the Association on the best way to deal with this difficult situation,' he wrote in his 2010 Annual Report.

Despite his best efforts, which included producing a position paper outlining various options, he acknowledged in his final annual report in 2018 that the problem persisted.

> *I wrote in 2010 that the choice facing the Association was a simple one; either we do nothing in the certain knowledge that nothing will change, and that in five or ten years we would still be lamenting the damage to our ethos and values, or we decide that it would be irresolute and defeatist not to*

confront directly a practice that we proclaim to be a blemish on the Association. The choice is the same now and the need to address it is even greater.

Duffy's successor, Tom Ryan, referring to amateur status in his 2024 report, wrote of 'the failure on the part of the Association in espousing one thing and doing the exact opposite'.

The obvious conclusion is that maintaining the amateur ethos is as challenging now as it was forty years ago. In fact, it's probably even more difficult.

Interestingly, a report compiled in 2018 by a committee tasked with providing a roadmap for the GAA leading up to its 150th anniversary in 2034 had some interesting suggestions on how to balance financial rewards for inter-county players and managers with maintaining amateur status. Entitled 'Towards 2034', the report was never published but leaked details did emerge. Among them was a predicted hybrid solution on how players and managers might be rewarded.

> *By 2034 the GAA will have developed a model to recognise the time and effort contributed by senior inter-county players and their managers. This will facilitate effective budgeting, where senior inter-county players and managers will retain their existing amateur status but have their value to the Association, and their enormous commitment to their sport, recognised by a defined and agreed allowance.*

It was an interesting perspective but since the report wasn't formally published there was no discussion on its merits.

Rewards for players shot to the top of the agenda in August 2000 when a £50,000 (€63,500) deal was announced between ten of the highest-profile stars and the Marlborough Group. It involved the players engaging in promotional work for Marlborough, in return for which they would receive £4,000 (€5,080), with the remainder going to the Gaelic Players Association (GPA), which had been founded a year earlier.

It was regarded as a defiant statement of intent and a challenge to the GAA's mechanism for sharing sponsorship/promotional money, earned by individual players. Under that arrangement, a player received 50 per cent of a fee, with the remainder divided between the rest of the panel (30 per cent), the county board and a hardship fund (10 per cent each).

Some of the 'Marlborough Ten' outlined why they had no qualms about stepping outside the official GAA scheme for sponsorship earnings. Cork's Brian Corcoran, one of the all-time great dual players, insisted that players were entitled to make their own arrangements.

> *The GAA are trying to rule what we do in our spare time. But we are amateur players who never get money for playing and, as an amateur player, I feel I'm entitled to do what I like in my spare time. I don't see how they could be controlling us as if we were a group of professionals.*

Within hours of the Marlborough deal being announced, the GAA's official player representative group, chaired by the association's current president, Jarlath Burns, voiced their objections in a statement.

> *On behalf of all players in the association, we would like to express our disappointment at this move which will obviously deprive the team-mates of those involved of their entitlements as team members.*
>
> *It would appear that those who have claimed in the past that the GPA is elitist and only representative of a greedy minority may very well have been proven right after today's announcement.*

A stern rebuke, but then tensions were running high at the time as the GPA began a muscle-flexing exercise. Some leading GAA figures believed the GPA would lose impetus over time, but the opposite proved to be the case. Indeed, it went from strength to strength.

It was a long journey, with frequent outbreaks of controversy, acrimony and strained relations with Croke Park that went on for nearly a decade. In his first year as president in 2000, Seán McCague accused the GPA of attempting to take credit for the work of the official players' committee. 'They [GPA] have no grounds to taking any credit in this regard and their public utterances are disingenuous to say the least,' he said.

In 2004, his successor, Seán Kelly, said that while the gap between the GPA and GAA was narrowing, much more needed to be done.

'I know that if we were starting from a green-field site, an arrangement could be reached with players without too much difficulty. Can the same be said for those that represent, or purport to represent, the players, namely the GPA? I'm not sure but maybe it's time to find out,' he said.

In 2006, Nickey Brennan, Kelly's successor, said that he felt pay-for-play in some form was on the GPA agenda, and two years later he questioned their general attitude. 'The GPA must understand and accept that a prerequisite to any meaningful relationship is mutual respect and understanding,' he said.

By November 2009, a deal had been struck, which involved the GAA formally recognising the GPA as the official players' representative group. In addition, the GAA were to provide €250,000 annually for administration costs as well as allocating €1.1 million for player-welfare projects in 2010.

'This is about moving things forward in a positive, constructive manner for the good of players and the GAA in general,' said president Christy Cooney.

'It's important that we remain as an independent voice a nd we intend to do just that,' said Dessie Farrell, GPA CEO. He had been a key driver in building the GPA from a position where it was seen by many GAA administrators as a short-term irritant that would go away, to being an influential force in the association.

The new arrangement still had to go before congress for ratification, which was duly achieved at the 2010 Congress in Newcastle, County Down.

It came nearly thirty years after the first attempt by players to have a direct line of communication with Croke Park. A Players' Association was formed in the early 1980s, with the rather modest target of providing a forum for input on various matters.

They regarded themselves as an advisory body, making submissions and raising issues that directly affected players. The response from the GAA ranged between cold and freezing. They obviously saw the group, as a threat to the status quo and had little interest in engaging with the players in any meaningful way.

That, coupled with the group being reliant on their own organisational capacity, with little back-up support, made it very difficult to establish any long-term momentum and it faded away over time.

John Callinan, then a star Clare hurler and a leading figure in the players' group, later reflected on its demise, which he described as 'a great loss to the GAA in general'. He couldn't understand the perceived hostility, insisting that its intentions were totally constructive.

'It was as if they [GAA leadership] saw it as a threat, a sort of union which would be constantly seeking changes. That was never the intention. The GAA authorities weren't enamoured by the idea of having a Players' Association although I have yet to meet an official who could explain why it was so frowned upon,' Callinan said in an interview in 1987.

One long-standing challenge, which is probably more pronounced now than ever before, centres on demographics, specifically population shifts to cities and towns. There's also the ever-increasing population bulge in Dublin and surrounding counties.

As far back as 1990, Liam Mulvihill wrote in his annual report about how population imbalances between counties were having a detrimental impact on competitions.

The appeal of our Association has been healthy rivalry and a strong competitive base to our games. At inter-county level, there is a danger that this will be eroded in all but the top six to eight counties which have a realistic chance of success in All-Ireland championships. If our Association really valued its democracy, we should be looking at ways of countering the imbalance and of giving more of a chance to the less successful counties to come to the top.'

Thirty-four years later, the disparities are just as wide – if not wider.

9 CONGRESS CLIPPINGS

A motion in the name of Sligo County Board that, in all inter-county matches, competing counties receive, as well as all travelling expenses, ten per cent of gate money was lost by a majority.
Irish Independent report of GAA Congress, April 1924.

Congress stands at the top of the GAA's administrative pyramid, the association's supreme ruling body, empowered to set, amend or abolish rules as well as determine broad policy outlines.

It is composed of representatives from counties, overseas units, players, past GAA presidents and various other groups. It elects presidents, oversees Central Council and subsidiary councils, considers motions submitted by counties and various groupings, and acts as the overall guardian of the association's policies and principles.

There are two categories of congress – annual and special.

Annual congress must be held before 1 March every year – a fairly recent development. In previous times, it had various timings, usually in March or April. For many years, it was held on Easter Sunday.

From time to time, a special congress is called – usually in autumn – to discuss matters that need to be addressed before the next annual congress.

A striking feature of congress has been the change in the subjects it discusses and the tone of its debates. They tend to be more focused today and discussion is usually quite muted, unlike the past when robust debate and oratorical flourishes ensured that journalists had lots of colourful copy to choose from.

Congress had an impact away from day-to-day activities too, with the president's address treated as a news event that nearly always made the front pages. That was particularly true in relation to non-games matters, such as the GAA's strict rule regarding 'foreign games', restrictions on who was permitted to join the association and policies regarding its basic aim of 'strengthening of the national identity in a 32-county Ireland through the preservation of and promotion of Gaelic Games and pastimes'.

There was also the use-of-grounds issue, which bubbled to the surface in the 1990s before becoming a major controversy early in the new millennium when pressure grew to open up Croke Park to rugby and soccer. Rule 42 – the long-established rule preventing the playing of non-GAA sports in GAA grounds – was abolished in 2005, and allowed Croke Park to be used for rugby and soccer while Lansdowne Road was under redevelopment.

Unquestionably, one of the biggest and longest-running issues was the Ban, which prevented members from playing or being associated in any way with rugby, soccer, cricket or hockey clubs or events. Discussed at congress on a regular basis up to 1971 when it was abolished, the debates gave a clear insight into just how embedded in the GAA psyche the rule was. This is reflected in many strident contributions, especially from those who regarded its retention as absolutely essential.

Congress addressed a broad range of other issues too, as demonstrated by the following snapshots taken from newspaper reports of the debates over the years.

1931

GAA president Seán McCarthy told congress that he regretted to have to say that some clubs were running 'foreign dances' for the purpose of raising funds, which was not in keeping with the spirit of the association. As for those who were fostering 'foreign games', they represented the 'outposts of Anglicisation'. 'The GAA never counted on them; they do not count on them now and it would be a sad day if they ever had to count on them,' he said.

1933

Teams travelling to games by lorry came up for discussion after the GAA received a letter from the Department of Local Government. President Seán McCarthy said he was glad 'this long-standing question' had been addressed in the Road Traffic Bill. He wanted it understood that the GAA had sought permission for travelling to games by lorry only when adequate alternative transport was not available. Lorries carrying players to games had previously been liable for a special tax.

1936

Cavan proposed that All-Ireland football and hurling finalists and officials be entertained at a banquet on the Sunday night of the finals, hosted by Central Council, pointing out that the social side of the GAA tended to be neglected. A Mayo delegate said issues would arise over the number of invitations. Laois suggested that winning the title was enough for all concerned and Cork claimed many players would be unable to attend as they had work commitments on Monday. The matter was referred to Central Council.

1937

Complaining about press coverage, GAA president Robert O'Keeffe said his main objection centred not on the amount of coverage given to Gaelic games, but rather on the 'daily boosting of foreign games and all connected with them'.

'It appears as if there's a well-planned campaign to laud and advertise foreign games to such an extent that we will be forced by persistent pressure to repeal some of the fundamental rules of our Association. Let them have no illusions regarding our rules. They are fundamental and there they will remain in spite of the anti-Gaelic virus and pro-British honey that the daily press can inject over its sporting pages. We will not compromise and, knowing well the imperial origin of the aggression, we will straighten our backs and stiffen our minds and go full tilt for an Irish Ireland.'

1938
Dublin asked that All-Ireland winners be given free admission to all GAA matches but withdrew it when there was no support. Meanwhile, president Robert O'Keeffe acknowledged there were too many incidents of rough and dangerous play. 'It's a blemish on our games. Practically all our players have to turn into work on Monday mornings and it is a serious prospect for them if they are not protected from rough and dangerous play in their games on Sunday afternoons. I would beg all referees to have no hesitation in enforcing the rules relating to rough and dangerous play,' he said.

1940
Louth proposed that congress call for the abolition of tax on Irish-dancing events run by the GAA, pointing out that if the Gaelic League ran a céilí, it was exempt from tax. The director-general Pádraig Ó Caoímh said they should 'not touch the subject at all' as GAA games were exempt from tax. Instead, he suggested that clubs form Gaelic League branches and, in that way, secure exemption from tax. His suggestion was accepted.

1941
Cork proposed that a club found guilty of playing an overage minor be suspended for twelve months. Laois argued that it was the player, not the club, who should be penalised. A Wexford delegate cited the case of a player who was invited to play minor, despite being overage. He was suspended and 'the rest of the club were smiling at the whole thing'.

1944

There was criticism of colleges for what was described by one delegate as their 'wilful and deliberate insistence on playing foreign games'. He said it 'fostered a spirit of snobbery and cultivated that pernicious atmosphere of imperialism which these foreign games engendered'.

A motion that the All-Ireland finals be brought forward to August was defeated.

1945

Director-General Pádraig Ó Caoímh said that 79,245 people had watched the Kerry–Roscommon final in 1944, giving rise to concerns about the capacity of Croke Park. It was envisaged that interest in attending the All-Ireland finals would increase to 100,000 if Croke Park had the capacity.

Mr L. Brady (Laois) said that with improved sea and air services into Ireland, they should look forward to a day when the finals attracted 150,000, saying that Croke Park would be no longer suitable and they would have to go to the Phoenix Park.

1946

President Séamus Gardiner said some people did not understand the GAA's attitude towards 'the imported games of another country', but it was important to hold the line.

'Rugby, soccer, hockey and cricket are games which, according to our rules, are banned to our members. These games were brought into the country by England. These games, with her language, have always followed her flag. Never have the British

Army of occupation, as far as I know, adopted the games of any country they conquered. They always played their own games and encouraged them. They did that in Ireland and when they left the twenty-six counties, their games stayed behind in certain towns and cities. Compare the treatment which our games receive in England with that which British games receive here. Across the water our games are treated with cold indifference, where they are denied support by a large section of the press. Here, their games receive prominence out of all proportion to their numbers by most of our press.'

1947

Down proposed that Rule 27 – the Ban – should apply to players only and not spectators. Unimpressed by the argument, a Kildare delegate said that 'spectators at foreign games would soon become players'. President Dan O'Rourke referred to 'the grave scandal of many prominent Gaelic players taking part in foreign dances'.

Rev. Bro. W.G. Collins, treasurer of the Central Colleges' Council, protested against the practice of some colleges fostering foreign games and even forbidding the playing of national games. He said the aims of those colleges seemed to be 'to make them good citizens of the empire'.

1950

A Galway motion proposing an open draw in the All-Ireland hurling championship was passed (107–73) but failed to get the two-thirds majority required to make it happen.

1952

Tyrone called on congress to 'condemn the spirit of semi-professionalism which has begun to creep into the Association and to be vigilant in suppressing private tournaments for which the prizes are money or articles having a commercial value'. President M.V. Donoghue said the rules already covered that.

A call by Galway and Antrim, which they made most years, for an open-draw hurling championship was beaten, with the strongest opposition coming from Munster counties.

1954

Congress voted 95–56 to ban full-time training for big games, which had been in place for many years. Kerry, Armagh and Roscommon led the call to retain it.

1955

Further reinforcement of the Ban came from president M.V. O'Donoghue. 'The GAA is as vigorous and uncompromising as ever, defending Ireland against the new aggression and the native weaklings who, unwittingly or otherwise, play the game of the wily Saxon.'

Cavan, Kerry and Roscommon sponsored a motion to allow each county to decide whether or not it wanted to use full-time training. It was beaten on a 76–63 vote. Roscommon submitted a broadly similar motion in 1956, which was well beaten.

1957

A different president this time – Séamus McFerran – but the message on the Ban was the same. 'As a counter measure, our ban rule was introduced to purify our membership and to preserve our games from infiltration. We have retained the ban and its existence should serve to remind us of a type by no means extinct in Ireland to this very day.'

McFerran was also unhappy with GAA press coverage. 'The odd sensational article continues to appear at the whim of certain sports editors who ought to know better. I condemn this approach to our affairs, knowing how much it is resented, apart entirely from the fact that it is the poorest form of scavenger journalism.'

1960

A Kerry proposal to allow football goalkeepers pick the ball directly off the ground in the square was passed but not without strong opposition, led by Cork. Kerry based their case on the need to provide better protection for goalkeepers and also contended that the proposed new rule would speed up the game.

Cork delegate Paddy O'Driscoll said that, in relation to goalkeepers, the change would make football too similar to soccer. Another Cork delegate, P.A. Murphy, questioned why the goalkeeper should get special protection, stating that football was 'no namby-pamby game'. The motion was carried on a 150–54 vote.

A Louth call to have goalkeepers wear distinctive jerseys, different to outfield players, was withdrawn. That change was introduced in 1963.

1962

A year before being elected president, Alf Murray voiced his view on the Ban. 'I hold firmly to the conviction that Rule 27 should be retained. The GAA owes its nationwide strength and power to the fact that it is more than a sporting or athletic body. It has taken its stand on the principle of native games only and because no one can give allegiance to two or more similar organisations, it asks its members for undivided loyalty.'

Kerry delegate Micheál Ó Ruairc was unimpressed by a comment to congress from Longford footballer Pádraig Gearty that a great many players and clubs favoured the removal of the Ban. 'It is evidence of the growing unrest at club level,' said Gearty.

Ó Ruairc gave a withering response. 'I hold that we are entitled to ignore the views of players in the same way as students and undergraduates are not consulted about the curriculum they have to study.'

1964

A Kerry motion calling for the holders of All-Ireland senior football and hurling medals to be allowed to purchase two tickets for finals got little support.

1965

There was little sign of a thawing in attitudes towards the Ban, certainly nothing to suggest that it would survive for only six more years. Dublin's call for its removal was backed by only fifty-two of the 282 delegates.

Down's motion to allow GAA members to attend 'foreign sports' without facing sanction fared better (eighty-one votes) but still fell well short of the requirement to be accepted.

1967

Roscommon called for live television coverage to be restricted to All-Ireland finals and Railway Cup finals, claiming that showing more games would seriously reduce attendances at club games. They were supported by Kerry and Louth, but Monaghan's Michael Duffy countered by pointing out that the GAA had been 'crying out for the televising of games and now that they were getting the service they were crying out that they didn't want it'. The Roscommon motion was beaten 106–98.

1968

A motion calling for the abolition of the Ban was beaten 220–88. It was the last time it survived a congress vote.

1969

Let's dance! Dublin, Tyrone, Kildare, Offaly and Mayo called for the deletion of the rule which precluded 'foreign dances' at GAA functions. It was defeated, but a Down motion stating that GAA units 'shall not organise any entertainment at which foreign dancing, other than old time waltzing, shall be permitted' was passed.

1970

A large majority backed a Rules Revision Committee proposal to extend provincial finals, All-Ireland semi-finals and finals from sixty to eighty minutes. The main argument put forward for the twenty-minute increase was that an hour's duration didn't do justice to such big games. Also, it was argued that sixty-minute games offered poor value for money for people travelling from overseas. It meant that teams who had played all National League games and provincial championships up to semi-finals over sixty minutes had to adapt to a one-third increase from there on.

It was quite a change, especially when implemented mid-championship. It applied for five seasons (1970–1974) before being reduced to seventy minutes in 1975.

1971

The end of the Ban, deleted without fuss or acrimony at congress in Belfast. A mood for change had swept the country in the late 1960s and, by 1971, counties were virtually unanimous on the need to abolish the rule. It was all over in four minutes – the Ban was gone. So too was the ban on all foreign dances at GAA functions.

1972

'GAA MUST INTRODUCE SOCCER SKILLS' screamed the headline in the *Sunday Independent* after Kerry delegate Micheál Ó Ruairc criticised the standard of Gaelic football. Responding to a comment in the annual report by Director-General Seán Ó Síocháin that 'the majority of our games fall far short of an acceptable standard', Ó Ruairc said it was a pity that Ó Síocháin hadn't gone further.

'I said a few years ago we were not giving our Croke Park patrons value for money. I think our standards have plummeted and this is true of club games in particular. Unless we bring skills into our games like soccer, we will not attract the youth.'

T.P. O'Reilly (Cavan) also expressed concerns about standards. 'With our games being televised to a large extent nowadays, our image is not improved when we see mentors running on to the pitch with refreshments for players. I wonder if our players are even remotely fit.'

1974

Roscommon proposed that, in view of the increasing price of gold, All-Ireland medals should be made of silver. They pointed out that gold medals cost £14 in 1972, £20 in 1973 and were likely to reach £36 by the end of 1974. The call was rejected, with the counter-argument being that rising gate receipts more than kept pace with the price of gold.

Ger McKenna, Kerry County Board chairman, was unhappy over coverage of GAA games.

'On picking up our Sunday newspapers, one could feel looking at the sports pages that one was is in an entirely different country. Our games are almost totally ignored and there are great splashes about games played across the channel.'

1975

GAA president Dr Donal Keenan expressed disappointment over what he regarded as a failure by rugby-playing colleges to embrace football and hurling, pointing out that it was four years since the GAA had removed the Ban. He said rugby-playing colleges 'made no move to lift their unwritten ban on Gaelic Games'.

'It is not sufficient just to put Gaelic Games on the curriculum; the facilities must be provided and those who want to play our games must be encouraged to do so in these schools,' he said.

Dr Keenan had attended Clongowes Wood College, where he played rugby, before going on to become one of Roscommon's best footballers, winning All-Ireland titles in 1943 and 1944.

At the same congress, Mayo called for a refusal to renew advertising contracts in Croke Park for alcoholic drinks and tobacco, arguing that no sports organisation should support the promotion of those products. They got nowhere – the overwhelming majority opposed the proposal, prompting the *Sunday Independent* to run the headline: 'Puff and Pint OK.'

1981

It took nearly three-quarters of an hour to decide not to conduct the 1984 Congress solely in Irish. Proposed by Galway, Clare, Sligo and Leitrim, Joe McDonagh, an All-Ireland hurling winner with Galway in 1980 and a future GAA president, said that marking the centenary year with an Irish-only congress would be a fitting tribute. However, there was considerable opposition on the basis that those who weren't fully conversant in Irish would be excluded from decision-making. The motion was withdrawn.

1986

Canvassing can disqualify! Armagh brought forward a rather unusual motion, calling for a suspension of not less than a year for any GAA member found to have canvassed for any official position. Proposer Gene Larkin was adamant that the practice had to be stopped. 'Some very capable people have refrained from going forward for positions because they refuse to prostitute themselves trying for votes,' he said.

Opponents of Armagh's call argued that it would be a pointless rule since there could be no definitive way of knowing what constituted canvassing. Despite that, the motion was passed by a large majority.

1987

In a policy-shift that had applied for the previous two years, congress decided to accept alcoholic drink companies as sponsors of competitions (it had been confined to social events). Those in favour of the change argued that the existing policy left the GAA at a disadvantage compared to other sports that had no such restrictions. Some speakers claimed the GAA should hold the line on drink-company sponsorship. In an impassioned speech, Mayo delegate Fr Leo Morahan urged delegates 'to put your hands up with me and prevent us from making a disgrace of ourselves'. He got some support, but not enough to prevent the motion being passed on a 159–79 vote.

1994

A Kilkenny man declaring that hurling 'is dying on its feet' was bound to attract attention. All the more so when the speaker was the county board chairman and a former All-Ireland winner. Nickey Brennan, who went on to become president eleven years later, stunned congress with his stark analysis.

'For a number of years, hurling has fallen behind football in terms of support and appeal. The overall state of hurling is being eroded and serious action is needed. There are major problems and even those of us in what are regarded as stronger counties have difficulty keeping the games alive.'

1995

A call to make helmets compulsory for players wasn't supported. One of the reasons put forward for rejection was that it would send out a message that hurling was dangerous. It was also suggested that it might lead to insurance liability. It was another fifteen years before helmets were made compulsory for all hurlers.

2000

Donal O'Neill, head of the Gaelic Players Association, which had been launched the previous year, was refused entry to congress in Galway on the grounds that he didn't have a pass. He explained that he was there 'on behalf of the players to see exactly how congress is run'. GAA antipathy to the GPA was running very deep at the time. 'We just want to give the players a voice,' said O'Neill.

2002

What a difference a year makes! In 2001, a proposal to make Croke Park available for rugby and soccer won a 176–89 majority (failing by a single vote to get the two-thirds majority required to change the rule) but the exact same motion was beaten 197–106 a year later.

2010

Director-General Páraic Duffy told congress that the long-standing tradition of pitch invasions after big games in Croke Park had to stop. 'We came at it too late last year. It's different this time. We're starting here at congress and now want our delegates to go back to their counties with the clear message that pitch invasions have to stop.

Con Hogan, head of the GAA's safety group, painted a stark picture. 'Do we want to be standing here sometime in the future observing a minute's silence in memory of people who died because we did not exercise due care and proper crowd control?' he asked.

2011

GAA president Christy Cooney threw out an interesting idea regarding competition structures, suggesting consideration should be given to the redrawing of provincial boundaries.

'So we need a more even spread of counties in each province? Should we dispense with the ancient geographical borders of the four provinces and seek instead to realign our provinces along more practical lines? Let's debate it and see what comes of it,' he said in his address to delegates.

2019

Congress voted by a 91–9 per cent majority to allow county grounds to be made available for rugby and soccer in certain circumstances and subject to Central Council approval. A similar motion had been beaten by a 67–23 per cent majority in 2016.

10 FROM PASTIME TO BIG TIME

The general standard of sporting behaviour which prevailed during the game was such that many of our sporting males could, and should, try to emulate.
Report in the *Offaly Independent* after Tipperary beat Offaly in the first All-Ireland ladies football final in 1974.

In fewer than a hundred words – sixty-five to be precise – an anonymous contributor to a major national newspaper in the summer of 1967 captured the scale of the fight still to be fought for women to be treated as equal in the world of Gaelic games and, indeed, sport in general.

Looking back on a letter published in the *Sunday Independent* on 27 August, many will be suspicious. Was it genuine? Or just a deliberate provocation to get a reaction?

Either way, it displayed a mindset which one would have thought no longer existed in Ireland as the swinging sixties were heading towards a colourful end. As broadcaster Myles Dungan commented when he interviewed historian Hayley Kilgallon on *The History Show* on RTÉ's Radio 1 in 2020, 'It sounds like something from 1967 BC.'

Kilgallon regularly uses the letter in her discourses on the evolution of ladies football, which in 2024 celebrates the fiftieth anniversary of both its founding as an association and its first All-Ireland championship.

The letter – headlined 'Keep Women Out Of Croke Park' – read:

Sir – Now that the All-Ireland finals are at hand again, let's hope the GAA will bar women from attending these games, taking up valuable space.

To me, there is nothing more revolting or unnatural than to see a pleasure-bent woman up in the city for fun and enjoyment, instead of being satisfied with her lot at home. The GAA is a man's organisation – for men only.
Co. Cork farmer.

Naturally enough, it generated a reaction.

A week later, the newspaper published a selection of responses. The following are a few examples.

Sir – So we still have them with us – the mothers who rear selfish sons in the belief that they are demigods because they happen to be born male. 'Farmer From Cork' seems to be a specimen of the latter, reared by the former.

Sir – I was shocked to read the letter from the 'Co. Cork Farmer'. He should be shot.

And a week later again, the following was published.

Sir – Congratulations to the Cork farmer who advocated that women should be barred from Croke Park.

I consider, however, he did not go far enough. Croke Park might be a good start, but I would follow it up by extending the bar to institutions, such as Dáil Éireann, County Councils and any other such place where females might congregate to conspire and plan the ultimate takeover of man's rightful place in this country.
Béal Dúnta, Dundalk.

Note the signature in Irish – 'Mouth Closed' – was at least being light-hearted about it all!

The irony of such a debate is that around the time the letter was published and over the next few years, men were central to organising what were essentially 'exhibition' games of ladies football that would eventually lead to the establishment of a national association and an All-Ireland championship.

While there are references in histories of Gaelic games to women playing football and, from time to time, sometimes earning the wrath of the authorities for doing so, there was a definite increase in activity during the 1960s. To describe this upswing as a surge would, however, be stretching things. Games were mainly organised for local festivals and, initially at least, were not taken very seriously.

Brendan Martin from Tullamore, County Offaly, a man whose name will forever be associated with ladies football, was central to the new and progressive movement. A successful businessman who had set up a construction company in Dublin, he became involved in the Offaly Association, which organised Gaelic football training sessions in the Phoenix Park.

In an interview some years ago with journalist Gordon Manning, then writing in the *Irish Sun*, Martin gave an interesting insight into the early activities. He recalls a number of women turning up to the Phoenix Park sessions, anxious to become involved. He told Manning: 'They wanted to train, so we trained them.'

His brother Tom, who had a house in Waterford, told him that a group of girls were playing football in the county. 'I asked him to get me a contact and he did, a priest called Fr Ahearne. We got in touch, and the Offaly Association in Dublin took a team down to Stradbally and played. That was my first involvement in any kind of match.'

In August 1973, he was also involved in organising a game between an Offaly selection and a Kerry selection in Tullamore. By then, it was obvious that an increasing number of counties were organising ladies' games. A meeting was called for 18 July 1974 in Hayes Hotel, Thurles, site of the founding of the GAA itself in 1884, to form a new association to govern ladies Gaelic football.

Men, including Martin, were well represented on the first executive. He was appointed assistant treasurer. Army man Jim Kennedy from Tipperary was the first president of what was named Cumann Peile na mBan. Roscommon's Marie Holland was vice-president; Mary Nevin from Offaly was secretary, with Joe Feighery from Offaly her assistant. Roscommon's Mary Flanagan was treasurer.

Reaction was hardly positive around the country. Martin explained to Gordon Manning: 'There was nothing but opposition. People thought we were crazy, girls playing this rough game, this rough men's game. There were people who didn't think it was right.

'But, despite everything, the enthusiasm and determination of the girls to play never diminished. People thought we were crazy, but the girls wanted to play. There was no funding, we had nothing. We had no pitches. We had to beg for everything.'

The first business conducted was the organisation of an All-Ireland championship. Laois, Offaly, Roscommon, Waterford, Kerry, Galway, Cork and Tipperary entered for the inaugural competition in 1974.

'We didn't have a cup,' Brendan Martin explained. 'At the time I was doing OK in business and I had a few bob, so I went down to John J. Cooke's [a jeweller in Fownes Street in Dublin] and bought a cup. That's how it happened.'

And the Brendan Martin Cup (the original trophy was replaced by Martin in 1999) has become the symbol of ladies football.

Without any fanfare, Tipperary and Offaly qualified for the first All-Ireland final, played in Durrow, County Laois, on 13 October 1974. Tipperary won by a point: 2–3 to 2–2. The event was largely ignored by the national media, although the *Irish Press* did send Dan Coen and a photographer to provide a 'colour' piece that featured on the front page the following day.

'From the moment the ball was thrown in, the women got stuck in and, by half-time, the teams were level with a goal and two points each. The enthusiasm was there with much umbrella-waving, shouting and calling on all the saints in heaven and sometimes even the devil to do something about the flagging fortunes of either side.

'It was a great day for women's football. With a bit of luck more than eight counties will take part in next year's championship and the All-Ireland final will be in Croke Park,' Dan Coen wrote.

The newspaper did not carry a match report; neither did the *Irish Independent* nor the *Cork Examiner*. Some of the local newspapers in Tipperary did carry a report, provided by the county PRO, while the *Westmeath–Offaly Independent* carried a substantial piece on the game the following week.

The battle for recognition had begun. But it would take many years before the game received the recognition its players and organisers deserved.

One rare, and divine, exception to the general apathy from the media towards the new championship came as early as the 1978 All-Ireland final, which featured Cavan and Roscommon and was played in Dr Hyde Park on 10 November. There was much interest about one participant – Roscommon's Pauline Gibbons, who had joined a convent in England after winning the Connacht title that summer.

Under the headline 'Big Match Prayers for Sr Pauline', the *Irish Press* carried four photos across the top of the front page on the day before the game, featuring Pauline in action, and also ran a significantly long piece down the side of the page.

A pair of football boots and a Roscommon jersey on a wall in an English convent will always remind an Augustinian postulant of the day she became the first nun to play in an All-Ireland women's final.

They will adorn St George's Convent, Burgess Hill, Sussex, which Sr Pauline Gibbons left this week to turn out for Roscommon tomorrow against Cavan at the Dr Hyde Park in Roscommon.

As Sister Pauline prepares for the kick-off, forty nuns and patients at the private nursing home, run by the Order, will be on their knees tomorrow praying that she will come back with a winner's medal.

Sr Pauline, a tall 18-year-old, learned her football at Carniska National school near Strokestown in Co. Roscommon and by kicking a football across numerous fields as she travelled twice daily from her Ballinafad home to their school.

Eighteen months ago, Sr Pauline came on as a substitute on the county side and played well enough to retain her place. Among the spectators at that game was the nun who was later to play a big part in Sr Pauline playing in tomorrow's final, Sr Leonie McDermott.

Sr McDermott, an aunt of Sr Pauline, is the Mother Superior of the English convent who gave the young postulant special leave to return for the game. She is an avid Roscommon football fan and will treasure the Roscommon hat and scarf Sr Pauline is bringing back to her.

Sr Pauline was a regular in the Roscommon side this year that won the Connacht title with wins over Galway and Mayo.

She left for Sussex before the All-Ireland semi-final and missed the game against Kerry. Roscommon also missed her, and the team manager appealed to Sr Leonie to give Sr Pauline special leave for the final.

'I was delighted when I was told I could play,' said Sr Pauline. 'Word soon got around. The nuns and patients asked me about the game and nicknamed me George Best.'

Sr Pauline scored a goal in the final but neither it, nor all the prayers, were enough to take the title. Cavan were winners by 4–3 to 2–3.

A year later, without their nun, Roscommon won the title for the first time when they beat Tipperary in the final in Ballinasloe. An article about the game, with a photo of the players celebrating in the dressing room, appeared in a general sports feature on page three of the *Irish Press*, but the newspaper did not carry a match report or the scoreline in the sports section.

Helen O'Rourke, a primary-school teacher in Dublin in the 1980s, was from a family that was immersed in the GAA and played football for Park Rangers in the Phoenix Park.

She was one of an estimated 10,000 young women playing ladies football and recognised the need to volunteer as an administrator and became involved with the Dublin Board.

In a very short period, she became the national PRO, and then, in 1994, the youngest president of the Ladies Gaelic Football Association (LGFA). Three years later, she became its first chief executive officer, working full-time originally in an office of her own before being provided with office space in Croke Park.

She has overseen the extraordinary growth in the game at every level. Today, membership is close to 200,000, there are almost 1,500 clubs in Ireland and the game is being played in countries all over the world. There are television contracts and lucrative sponsorship deals and big crowds watch their All-Ireland finals, which are now major events on the sporting calendar.

It hasn't been easy. When O'Rourke was national PRO, she endeavoured to tackle the lack of media coverage of ladies football. Her personality, persistence and ability to create and develop relationships with a predominantly male press corps met with some success, but it was hard work.

The men who were the lead GAA correspondents in the print media already had two mainstream sports to cover and were not inclined to increase their workload any further. They weren't getting any encouragement from their bosses to do so either, since space in the sports pages was already at a premium.

And although no one would admit it publicly, the male GAA media still wasn't taking ladies football very seriously.

O'Rourke was not deterred. With RTÉ the only game in town at the time, she targeted them for television coverage. The first All-Ireland ladies final to be shown live was the 1998 meeting of Waterford and Monaghan. O'Rourke and her association got lucky as it is still regarded as one of the greatest finals, with the scores finishing level amid high drama and excitement.

The CEO wanted more. She pressed RTÉ for increased coverage of the championships, specifying the All-Ireland semi-finals as the next target. Her powers of persuasion worked and, the following year, the semi-finals were broadcast.

By the start of the new millennium, the LGFA needed both a long-term TV deal and a sponsor. It was essential, the leaders believed, that there was both an expanse and stability to the TV coverage if they were to promote further growth. The more exposure they could get, the more funds they could generate to further promote the game.

TG4 was the ideal outlet. The station was looking for a unique partnership with a sport upon which they could pitch much of their sports coverage. LGFA officials, including O'Rourke, began discussions with the Irish-language station and a strong working relationship began to form. In an interview with *The Irish Times* in 2020, O'Rourke described the impact of the partnership with TG4.

'TG4 was a major turning point in our whole development. Because all of a sudden parents saw that this was a great game and they wanted to get their daughters involved. In schools, they became more aware of it as well because of TG4 and it appealed to them because here was a game that you could get fifteen girls playing. Before that, basketball was traditionally the biggest sport for girls in schools but there are only five girls on a basketball team. And once football started growing in schools, it was easier to set up underage competitions in every county in the country.'

The LGFA now has fifteen full-time staff and attendances at All-Ireland finals are high – the 50,000 barrier was broken in 2018 and an astonishing 56,114 witnessed Dublin complete the three-in-a-row in 2019 with a victory over Galway. A far cry from the early days.

That Dublin team achieved the sort of national recognition that the great Kerry team of the 1980s could not have visualised.

Between 1982 and 1990, Kerry won nine consecutive championships. The first three of the finals were played in Nenagh, Kilsheelan (Tipperary) and Timahoe in Laois. Attendances were not recorded and coverage was scant.

However, change was coming slowly. In 1985, Páirc Uí Chaoímh was secured as the venue for the All-Ireland final. Kerry beat Laois by 2–9 to 0–5. An attendance of 5,000 is recorded for that game, a figure some recall being achieved because the game was a curtain-raiser to the Cork club hurling semi-final between Blackrock and Glen Rovers. The first All-Ireland junior ladies final was also played that day, with Galway beating Cork.

Mary Jo Curran was one of Kerry's goal scorers (Del White was the other) and Curran went on to star in all of Kerry's nine successes. Her name became one of the first in ladies football to be recognised nationally. She added a tenth title in 1993.

Curran was selected as an All-Star eleven times, a record she shares with the Mayo legend Cora Staunton.

Moving the finals to Croke Park in 1986 would prove hugely significant, despite a slow start. It gave the event greater status, and it prompted the national media to provide coverage, which included match reports and photographs. By 1989, the *Irish Independent* assigned a staff writer to report on the final between Kerry and Wexford. The journalist was Cliona Foley, one of the first female sports writers employed in the industry in Ireland.

When Kerry recorded the nine-in-a-row in 1990, the *Independent* heaped praise on Curran, who had given a great display.

'Curran, who reminded many of another Kerry great midfielder, Mick O'Connell, with her high catching feats, was the outstanding player on the field. The complete athlete, she roved from end to end, and if her passes occasionally went astray, it was possibly due to the fact that she had assisted Marathon in a basketball match the previous night, but her undoubted ability was always ready to surface if the need arose.'

Kerry's domination was stifling at the time, but other teams were about to emerge. Waterford, Laois and Monaghan were prominent through the 1990s and players like Maire Crotty and Aine Wall (Waterford), Sue Ramsbottom and Tracey Lawlor (Laois) and Jenny Greenan and Brenda McAnespie (Monaghan) became well known to a growing audience.

The public's growing recognition of the individuals certainly contributed to the growth in crowds at finals, although attendances otherwise remained small. The media found players to latch on to, none more so than a youngster from Carnacon in Mayo, who would become known nationwide as simply Cora.

Cora Staunton was so gifted that she first played senior football for Mayo at the age of thirteen. Five years later, in 1999, she was due to play in her first All-Ireland final, against Waterford, but, in a training session the week before the game she broke her collarbone. The Mayo manager, John Mullin, decided she would start anyway although he would not take any chances. Her selection was completely ceremonial, and he took her off after a minute.

He explained his actions to *Irish Independent* reporter Shane Scanlon. 'We've had a great spirit all the way through and Cora Staunton is very much part of it. Whatever was going to happen, we decided that she could say she played in an All-Ireland final. She is a fabulous talent and the country will see that in the years ahead.'

Staunton became the game's biggest star in a team of stars led by Diane O'Hora, and she also conquered the Australian Rules game. She won four All-Irelands with Mayo and equalled Mary Jo Curran's haul of eleven All-Star awards.

In 2005, former Cork player and coach Eamon Ryan took over their ladies team and helped those players to become a major force. That first year they played in the first final to break the 20,000 attendance barrier (against Galway) and won eleven of the next twelve championships. Their players became household names – Valerie Mulcahy, Juliette Murphy, Briege Corkery, Rena Buckley, Bríd Stack and Nollaig Cleary were as familiar to Cork supporters as their male counterparts.

Cork's run of All-Ireland successes was interrupted when they suffered a shock defeat to Tyrone in the 2010 quarter-final, but they returned to the podium in 2011 and won six more titles, the final three against their newest rivals and eventual successors, Dublin. When Cork relinquished their position as number one in 2017, it was Dublin who won the title, but the rivalry was not over.

A year later, Cork were back in the final. It wasn't quite the mighty team of yore, but Dublin were still spooked. When they nervously edged a victory – 3–11 to 1–12 – a sense of relief and a new belief settled over the Dublin squad. Players of the quality of Lynsey Davey, Sinéad Ahearne, Sinéad Goldrick, Carla Rowe and Noelle Healy led Dublin's dominant run to four titles in succession.

Their bid for a fifth successive title was scuttled in 2021 by a new adversary. Meath, under the management of Eamon Murray, had been making steady progress in developing the game over the previous fifteen years but few outside the camp believed they had a chance when they faced the mighty Dubs in the All-Ireland final on 5 September.

But, in one of the biggest shocks in the history of the championship, Meath emerged as 1–11 to 0–12 winners.

On GAA.ie journalist John Harrington summed up the events and highlighted the heroes.

Not only did they [Meath] perform with great heart, they also possessed incredible poise. The game intelligence for a group of players with so little experience at this level was truly remarkable.

Time and again they made Dublin dizzy with their ability to retain possession by playing the ball patiently out of defence and before striking like cobras when they did make it into opposition territory.

It almost feels wrong to single out any individuals because this was the ultimate team performance by Meath, but some deserve extra-special mention.

There are very few sportspeople in Gaelic games who send a buzz around a stadium as soon as they get their hands on the ball, but Vikki Wall is one such person.

Dublin did their best to limit her influence, but you might as well have been trying to hold back the tide with a wall of sand.

Time and again she burst forward with great power and athleticism to leave Dublin defenders scattered like rag-dolls in her wake.

The effect was two-fold. Her team-mates were inspired by her example and so were the very vocal Meath supporters roared their team on from start to finish.'

New heroes continue to emerge.

11 TRAILBLAZERS

We will only begin to know our strength in Gaelic games, I believe, when we have this integrated organisation up and running. And then, watch out, it will be extraordinary.
Mary McAleese, former President of Ireland and now chairperson of the steering group overseeing the integration of the GAA, Ladies Gaelic Football Association and the Camogie Association.

Liz Howard never set out to be a trailblazer. She just followed her natural instincts and became one.

A camogie player with Clare, Tipperary and Dublin, she never contemplated conforming to what was assumed to be a woman's role in the GAA. 'I grew up in a house where equality was never mentioned, it just existed,' she once told an interviewer.

So, when RTÉ embarked on the production of a Sunday-night GAA championship highlights show in the summer of 1979, Liz Howard became the first and – until more modern times – only female pundit on *The Sunday Game*.

While it was unusual, it was not unexpected.

The following January, she broke down more barriers when she became the first female officer of a county board, winning the election for PRO in Tipperary.

Slowly, and not entirely steadily, since that time, women have taken on more prominent positions in GAA administration at all levels. A woman as county secretary or chairperson is no longer unusual. It has been a welcome change.

Howard spent her working life with Aer Lingus and it was a recruitment drive for that company that brought her to the RTÉ studios in Montrose during the 1970s for an interview. An interested listener to the programme was journalist and broadcaster Mick Dunne, who already knew Howard and her father Garrett, a five-time All-Ireland hurling medallist with Limerick and Dublin.

Dunne spoke to colleagues about an idea he had. Howard was extremely articulate and very confident. Dunne believed she would provide a new element to analysis on RTÉ Radio's All-Ireland finals coverage. Jimmy Magee was the programme presenter and was also enthusiastic about bringing Howard into the team.

After three years working alongside Magee, Howard was offered the opportunity to front her own show but said no. When *The Sunday Game* was being launched in July 1979, presented by Jim Carney alongside Bill O'Herlihy, the producer Mike Horgan suggested to Howard that she might join the team as an analyst. This time she said yes.

One or two newspaper columnists found a female analyst hard to accept but, in general, the reaction to her early appearances was positive.

The reaction to her election as Tipperary PRO the following January was muted. The *Cork Examiner*, as it was known at the time, sent Jim O'Sullivan, its GAA correspondent, to the county convention in Thurles and he naturally realised the significance and gave the election prominence in his report. Neither the *Irish Independent* nor *Irish Press* mentioned it.

Howard spent twenty years – with one interruption in 1983 – as Tipperary PRO and became one of the best-known officials in the country. She changed how PROs worked and how they were viewed generally in the GAA. Indeed, her profile and longevity helped significantly to change how the role of women in the GAA was seen.

Noreen Doherty's election as Donegal secretary in 1991 was another ground-breaking event. She had been secretary of her club – Seán MacCumhaills in Ballybofey – and, for some years, had been the only female delegate attending county-board meetings.

She was never fazed by the fact that she was the only female involved at county-board level.

'I never noticed I was in a man's world at all. I was never brought up in the sense that there was any difference between females and males anyway,' she said in an interview with the *Sunday Independent* in 2015. 'There was no resentment that I would have noticed anyway. As time went on, they saw you just as a person, not as a female. And you got no concessions by the way; you had to fight your corner.'

There were four candidates proposed for the position of secretary in 1991, Doherty and three men. She won by just one vote.

It was the start of a new trend in the GAA. Women like Margaret Doyle in Wexford and Kathleen O'Neill in Kildare served long stints as county secretary. And when Doherty stepped down in Donegal in 2005, she was succeeded by twenty-two-year-old Crona Regan.

Doherty later became the first woman to serve on the GAA's Central Council when she was selected in 2009, before becoming the county's full-time administrator.

On 9 December 2014, Roisín Jordan joined the ranks of the history-makers when she became the first female chair of a county board following her election in Tyrone.

A former camogie player, she got involved in administration with her club Eglish, in various roles, and served three years as vice-chair before being elected unopposed to the top position.

During her three-year term, another high-profile female official emerged. Tracey Kennedy from Killeagh in Cork had never played camogie or ladies football but she was closely involved with her club. She became a delegate to the county board and, in 2011, was elected PRO.

She became vice-chair in 2014 and, three years later, became chairperson. She serves as Cork's delegate to the Central Council and, in February 2024, became the first female member of the GAA's Management Committee.

In the modern world of television and streaming, the presence of a woman as a presenter or pundit on sports coverage is taken for granted. In Ireland, RTÉ, Virgin Media and TG4 have turned to female presenters to front or work as analysts on all the major events, national and international.

It is a phenomenon that no one would have predicted less than four decades ago. Liz Howard was a familiar face in the TV studio, but press boxes all over Ireland, whatever the sport, were essentially all-male environments. The only women who entered the press area were those making and handing out the tea.

As the 1970s came to an end, that began to change, slowly at first, then more rapidly. Maol Mhuire Tynan, a talented camogie player from Tipperary, started to work for the Irish Press Group in the late 1970s. Caroline Murphy, an all-round sportswoman from Dublin, joined the sports department in RTÉ around the same time.

But it took almost another decade for the ranks to grow. Cliona Foley's byline began to appear in the sports pages of the *Irish Independent* and *Evening Herald* towards the end of the 1980s. A native of Laois, she reported on Gaelic games mostly but covered other sports as well, and by the end of the decade she was well established and continues to enjoy a highly successful career.

Yvonne Judge joined the Irish Press Group and had become well known throughout the country by the time she moved to RTÉ following the closure of the *Press* in 1995. In RTÉ's headquarters, the number of female sports reporters began to grow when Clare McNamara, a native of Tipperary, joined the staff.

The arrival of female reporters in sports departments and press boxes helped change attitudes towards women in sport, albeit slowly. Before the late 1970s, camogie coverage in the national media was limited, although the sport had a powerful advocate in Agnes Hourigan who also used her Irish name, Una Uí Phuirséal.

An All-Ireland medal winner with Dublin in 1938, she had married the renowned GAA writer Pádraig Puirséal, and supplied copy to the *Irish Press* under her own name and used a non-de-plume 'Taobh Líne' when contributing to the *Irish Independent*. She also served as president of the Camogie Association from 1976 to 1979.

Maol Mhuire Tynan mixed playing camogie with Tipperary and working as a reporter and feature writer. She won a league title and was part of the team that reached the All-Ireland final and were hotly tipped to beat Antrim in 1979. However, they were beaten – 2–5 to 1–4.

At the end of a disappointing and unexpected defeat she trudged back from Croke Park to the *Irish Press* offices in Burgh Quay to write a front-page article about her experience. It cannot have been easy.

Under the heading 'Antrim's Sheer Talent Bests Premier County', she wrote:

> *After an All-Ireland, words are superfluous. The defeated are dejected, the victorious are elated and yesterday's final was no exception.*
>
> *It's only a game, say the well meaning. But, of course, it is much more. For the superb Antrim side, it is the resurrection of camogie in northern ranks while we in the Premier County, with our long, impressive tradition of hurling, must painfully carry out the post-mortem on our sister game.*
>
> *Yesterday's weather in Croke Park provided the perfect setting to an exciting duel. It was regrettable that these natural*

elements were not complemented by properly defined sidelines or freshly painted goalposts.

Yet this game was a cracking performance of speed and skill. The few thousand supporters, all confined to the Hogan Stand, showed their appreciation as enthusiastically as those who thronged it the previous week [for the hurling final] and neither side envisaged defeat.

The first twenty-five minutes were magical for Tipperary. We had complete control from goalmouth to full-forward and, by half-time, it seemed that the O'Duffy was southward bound.

But our confidence was unjustified; the scoreboard did not reflect the run of play. And, while our forwards were running through a crumbling Antrim defence, their efforts rarely came to a fruitful conclusion.

This was due to the incredible anticipation displayed by Antrim goalkeeper Carol Blaney who celebrated her twenty-first birthday in style. She obviously came of age on the camogie pitch a long time ago.

Spirits were high in the Tipperary dressing room at the interval and our rivals were more than slightly depressed with the two-point margin. But they were first back on the sod and, within minutes, supporters and players alike knew they were determined to satisfy their hunger for victory.

At last, they took a grip on the game and displayed such speed and grit that we no longer wondered why they had shattered super-team Kilkenny. But even when the lead slipped from us, we fought back, desperate to inscribe our name on an All-Ireland trophy.

> *But fate, or should I say Antrim's sheer talent and abundant stamina, interfered with our plans. Anyway, when the referee's whistle was heard all over Croke Park, the northern girls had joined that elite group of O'Duffy Cup winners.*
>
> *And Tipperary? Well, we did try. But it is no mean achievement to reach the Fiddler's Green of all GAA enthusiasts and, while it is no consolation at all, there is always next year. Meantime, Antrim have successfully overcome the restrictions the game has faced during the past decade. They are indomitable.*

Tynan never played in another final, calling time on her inter-county playing career because of the demands of journalism. She did, however, continue to play for her club Drom-Inch until the end of the 1980s.

From the earliest days of the GAA, hurling was the choice of Gaelic game for the women of Ireland. Using a smaller stick, smaller ball and playing on a ground of smaller dimensions than hurling, the game was given a different name – camogie, a derivative of the Irish word for the hurley, *camán*.

There are newspaper reports of camogie matches taking place in Dublin's Phoenix Park and in Navan in July 1904. 'The ladies handled their *camáns* in very good style,' was the opinion of the observer for the *Meath Chronicle*.

The Camogie Association was founded in 1904 but the first All-Ireland championship was not played until 1932, with the final between Dublin and Galway delayed until the end of July

1933. Dublin's success – 3–2 to 0–2 – was recorded in the *Irish Independent*. 'The first final of the Inter-County Cup was played at Galway yesterday and Dublin proved good winners over the home county.

'The Galway team had beaten Louth in the semi-final, but proved no match for Dublin, who were superior in hitting and finish, Miss Hannon, the Bray forward, proving her scoring worth.'

After the All-Ireland camogie championship was established, the game began to produce some great champions. It took time for the individuals to become noticed because of the fractures both within the association, which led to administrative disputes, and scant coverage of games.

Then, in 1941, a teenager living with her grandmother in Inchicore was selected to play for Dublin. Kathleen Mills, known as Kay to her friends, became one of the best-known sportswomen in Ireland over the next two decades, winning fifteen All-Ireland titles.

Her first title was won in 1942 when, in a replay, Dublin beat reigning champions Cork in Croke Park. 'Kay Mills did splendid work and it was unfortunate that she had to retire injured near the end,' the *Irish Press* reported.

As her career was coming to a close in the late 1950s, Mills attracted national attention. The 1958 All-Ireland final was scheduled to take place in Croke Park on the evening of the hurling semi-final between Tipperary and Kilkenny. With a 7.30 p.m. start, many supporters had left the ground, but thousands stayed on to get the first glimpse of this phenomenon.

She didn't let them down. The *Irish Independent* reported:

'For once, Kathleen Mills did not display her general all-round ability, but as a contribution to winning her eleventh All-Ireland medal she scored a wonder goal, which must rank with the greatest ever seen. From fully forty-five yards out, on the sideline, the CIÉ club girl, with deadly accuracy, gave Cathleen Carroll no chance.'

Mills played her last game for Dublin in the 1961 final when Dublin beat their great rivals Cork. Agnes Hourigan marked the occasion in the introduction to her match report. 'Kathleen Mills, the most-famed camogie player of all time, bade farewell to the game in a blaze of glory at Croke Park yesterday where she played a big part in Dublin's victory over Tipperary that gave her county their twentieth All-Ireland title while Kathleen herself won her fifteenth All-Ireland medal – an achievement unequalled in any team game.'

Dublin's domination of the championship was eventually ended by Antrim in 1967, inspired by the talent of Mairéad McAtamney. Wexford won their first title in 1968 and defended it a year later before Cork produced another great side to win four titles in a row. By then a new legend was growing and the game hasn't seen anything like it since.

Angela Downey was a fifteen-year-old schoolgirl who had already attracted notice in Kilkenny when she was called into the senior squad for the championship of 1972. A daughter of 1947 All-Ireland hurling winner Shem Downey, she had already acquired a reputation for her scoring prowess, skill and speed at club and school level.

Kilkenny reached the All-Ireland final for only the second time in the county's history but, as had happened in 1970, they lost to Cork.

Two years later, Angela travelled to training with her twin sister Ann, who had been called in at the start of 1974, and it was the beginning of a journey that lasted two eventful and very successful decades.

Kilkenny returned to the All-Ireland final that September and, once again, Cork appeared to be their nemesis. A last-minute point by Helena O'Neill earned Kilkenny a replay and on 6 October, Kilkenny won their first All-Ireland camogie title. Over the next twenty years, Angela and Ann were side by side for twelve All-Ireland successes.

That first success was hard-won. As journalist John Knox reported in the *Kilkenny People*: 'Once again it was the lion-hearted Angela Downey who ran herself into the ground that pulled the new champions out of the doldrums.'

Angela produced some incredible individual performances. In the 1977 championship, she scored 6–3 against Tipperary, four goals against Dublin and 2–3 in the All-Ireland final win against Wexford.

In a profile of the twins in the *Irish Independent*, GAA correspondent Colm Keys summarised what they brought to the game. 'They rewrote the rules and pushed out the parameters of a game that had trouble making an impression on the wider sporting public's psyche. But even if your interest in camogie was fleeting, there was still an awareness of who the Downeys were.

'They left that mark. To this day, with a new generation of stars in place, the Downey name remains instantly synonymous with the game.

'Angela was the first real superstar, with her lightning speed and assassin's instinct when the need was greatest. Her right to be considered camogie's greatest ever player is undisputed.'

The 1994 success was Kilkenny's last until they re-emerged in 2016 to win again. Ann was the manager, Angela one of her selectors. The legend lives on.

12 GAA GOES GLOBAL

The sun never sets on World GAA and this plan has the potential to provide more clubs, more teams, and more friends to the international Gaelic games family.
Larry McCarthy, then-president of the GAA, at the launch of the association's *World Strategic Plan*, February 2024.

Eugene McGee was not the type of man who exhibited great emotion. Whatever successes he enjoyed in life – and there were many in sport, journalism and business – McGee accepted it all quietly. He did not do excess.

So, when he stood on a makeshift platform in the shade of the stand at what was then known as Bruce Stadium in the Australian capital of Canberra, on a sunny November Saturday in 1990 and declared in front of 3,000 raucous Irish supporters that 'this is one of the best days of my life', you just had to stop and listen.

McGee, famed before then for guiding Offaly's footballers to All-Ireland glory in 1982, had presided over Ireland's emphatic second-test success against Australia, clinching the International Rules series with a test remaining.

But this was more than just a win in a football game. It was the sort of celebration of Gaelic football away from home that GAA officials had dreamed of when they pondered the possibility of some form of internationalisation of their games.

At that time, the Australian public was largely indifferent to this new game, which was a fairly random combination of the best features of Gaelic football and the Australian Rules version. And Canberra, not ranked as one of the party towns on any social calendar, on a late November weekend was hardly an ideal setting, especially since the locals preferred watching rugby league.

But on the night before the test, there was an invasion. The Irish came from Melbourne, Perth, Sydney and places beyond that even included New Zealand. They found their way to the team hotel, partied all night, and slept in corridors and conference rooms.

McGee might have despaired. Instead, he embraced the environment. He encouraged the players to mix with their fellow countrymen and women. He spoke to the supporters and told them to enjoy themselves. And then he ensured the players were well isolated so that they could enjoy a solid night's rest before the game.

With chants inspired by Jack Charlton's Republic of Ireland soccer team when they had lit up the Italia '90 World Cup – 'ole, ole, ole' and 'ooh, ahh Jack O'Shea' – the Irish in the 7,000 attendance made it feel like a home game.

McGee was visibly moved by the reaction of the supporters. To see what it meant for a largely young group of Irish emigrants, now living thousands of miles from home, touched something in him that he had not expected.

His captain Robbie O'Malley shared the emotion. 'To stand up after the game and see thousands of Irish people, living so far away from home, with huge smiles and singing joyfully was a great feeling. I'm very proud,' he told reporters.

Jim Stynes, the Dubliner who had moved to Australia and become one of the great exponents of their game, as well as a national hero, added: 'The victory last Friday in Melbourne [in the first test] was the proudest night of my life. This makes me even prouder. This is an unbelievable bunch of players. You would think we are a club team the way we play together.'

That weekend encapsulated everything that the GAA hierarchy had sought to achieve with an international dimension. There were other memorable games too, whether played before a packed Croke Park or a stadium in some Australian city, when the International Rules series showed exactly what could be achieved. There were also some lows, notably when games were marred by violence, but they could never take away from the reality that the 'compromise' game had real merit, a successful coming together of two codes from opposite sides of the world.

GAA leaders like Alf Murray, who as early as the 1960s had identified Australian Rules as a potential associate of the GAA in creating an external link, were not just looking for an international dimension: they were also seeking new ways to embrace the diaspora long before that became fashionable in the political world.

In cities throughout North America, especially New York, the GAA had thrived at the peak of emigration in Ireland. It prospered similarly in Britain. In Australia, the success of the GAA fluctuated with the state of the economy in Ireland.

As the world changed, so too did the needs of the GAA. Alf Murray's effort to link with Australia was a catalyst. The relationships that developed between the GAA units in Meath and Kerry, and interested parties in Australia like Harry Beitzel (a former player, umpire and broadcaster), had led to unofficial exhibition games being played in both countries under a variety of rules.

That ultimately led to the formation of a committee by the GAA at the beginning of the 1980s, led by Armagh's Gerry Fagan and consisting of Kerry footballer Jimmy Deenihan, the well-known referee John Moloney, and officials Pat O'Neill (Meath) and Dan Hanley (Dublin) to examine the possibility of formalising links with Australia.

Their report, issued in May 1983, gives a clear and valuable insight into GAA thinking at the time.

It is evident from the coverage on TV, radio and in newspapers that those sports which have an international dimension enjoy great prominence. This often is proportionally greater than might be warranted by the number of active or past-playing members who take/took part at national level.

Any weekend, one just has to watch television, which is becoming more and more the centrepiece of every home, to see the prominence given to sport of all descriptions. One only has only to stop and think, to realise what the TV series *Pot Black* has done to popularise snooker. The GAA is losing out badly in this area. With the increase in popularity of video our problems may increase.

Even the use of sports stars in commercial advertising on TV, in newspapers and magazines is weighted against the GAA. Such advertising serves to glamourise the games of those sports stars who are repeatedly seen.

The prominence and publicity given to soccer players and other international sportsmen and women have created superstars, such as Eddie Macken, Derek Daly, John Watson, Lester Piggott, Steve Cauthen, Kevin Keegan, Sebastian Coe, John McEnroe, Jimmy Connors, Daley Thompson, Barry Sheene, Niki Lauda, etc.

Introducing an international dimension to the GAA could affect media coverage in two ways. It could (1) reduce the coverage of club, county and provincial games; (2) it might increase the present level because of the extra dimension.

In Ireland the GAA once had a near monopoly on the sporting interests of boys and youths, but that is no longer the case. Leisure time and money have increased enormously and means of travelling have improved dramatically. In addition, methods of communication have become very sophisticated.

All these factors and media have contributed significantly to distracting the youth and turning them towards activities other than those of the GAA.

The GAA must compete for these boys. We need to win their allegiance and loyalty. The opposing forces are very formidable.

We have to use every public relations and promotional facility at our disposal and an international Gaelic football team could be a step towards retaining/regaining that interest. Many of us have witnessed children's bedrooms, the walls of which are covered with posters of their football [soccer] or pop idols, but how often does a GAA personality feature in these spontaneous pop-cult exhibitions?

The posters not only are propaganda for these people and organisations but are also a source of revenue and promotion for commercial and sports organisations. We, in the GAA, have suffered because we either do not have the personalities that appeal widely enough, or we do not promote them well enough over the 32 counties to attract commercial interests. We need 32-county superstars and the promotional and marketing know-how to promote our interests and to counter various other attractions presented to youth.

Where we have promotional material, we almost have to beg our own administrators and workers to distribute it, while others have commercial outlets doing the work for them. We are living in the age of cult idolatry. We have to promote our cult(ure) to the best of our ability and hopefully get onto the bandwagon in a much bigger way than at present.

The GAA needs something bigger; we need to capture the imagination of the youth of Ireland once again. The GAA needs to show more widely the high quality and manliness of its field games.

The establishment of international tours between the GAA and Australian Rules, which would bring about a competitive series of matches between two strong football organisations, would hopefully catch the imagination of the public. There would be the added advantage of tours coming to this country as well as going abroad.

The public and media in Ireland would have the opportunity of focusing their attention on the tour and the ensuing publicity would be a big help to the GAA and its many voluntary workers.

While that report, and what followed, displayed a new and forward-thinking GAA, it also highlighted the fears amongst leading officials that Gaelic games were facing a threat.

The introduction of All-Stars tours to the US in the 1970s had been a huge success, but by the 1980s the novelty was wearing off. Travel had become easier and going to New York or even San Francisco no longer held the attraction it once had.

The Ireland–Australia International Rules was different. As well as being attractive for Irish players to travel to Australia and vice versa, there was an intensely competitive element. Even the controversies, which almost exclusively centred on on-field violence, contributed to the success in that it attracted attention. It may not have been the sort of attention the GAA or AFL wanted, but it unquestionably added to attendances.

Through this period, the often-fractious relationship between the GAA authorities in Ireland and the powerful New York Board was mended. From the early days of the GAA, New York had been the mecca for many young footballers and hurlers when their seasons had run their course at home, but it was often run independently and sometimes contrary to the desires of the home association.

Central to this relationship was the mercurial figure of John 'Kerry' O'Donnell. He presided over Gaelic Park, the home of New York GAA, as his very own kingdom. He had sold some of the licensed premises he ran in the city in order to buy the lease for Gaelic Park in the 1940s and through contacts in the political and business worlds, as well as in the trade unions, O'Donnell remained in charge right up to the 1980s.

He fought with the GAA hierarchy on a regular basis and what was regarded as a rebellious streak endeared him to supporters in New York. The players imported from Ireland were well compensated and weren't complaining, even when Gaelic Park became a bit shabby during the 1970s.

But, with age, and faced with a new generation of men and women coming to the fore in the city, O'Donnell's power began to wane. Terry Connaughton, a native of Roscommon and an outspoken critic of O'Donnell, became New York president and negotiated a delicate peace with the GAA in Dublin, and New York officially affiliated to the Central Council. Connaughton's reward was the staging of the National Football League final in Gaelic Park in 1989, between 'home' winners Cork and New York, and the National Hurling League final a year later between Kilkenny and New York.

While the games continued to thrive throughout North America during the 1990s and the divisional boards there and in Canada became more organised, the GAA was beginning to discover new horizons. Toronto successfully staged two All-Stars tours in the city's Skydome.

A new All-Stars sponsor, the telecommunications company Eircell (later to be taken over by Vodafone), sought to inject new life into the scheme. The resumption of the All-Stars tours was proposed – they had halted during the 1990s – and new destinations were recommended. It opened up a whole new world.

Over the next twenty years, the All-Stars travelled to an exotic range of destinations, including Dubai, Hong Kong, Singapore, Buenos Aires, Kuala Lumpur, Shanghai and Abu Dhabi, as well as several cities in the US including Boston, New York, San Francisco, Phoenix, San Diego, Austin and Philadelphia.

In Asia, a new face of the GAA was emerging. While the games were driven by young Irishmen and women who were making successful lives for themselves away from home in new locations, they were also attracting players and officials from completely different backgrounds, who had known nothing of football or hurling.

There was a colour and vibrancy to the environment that was instantly attractive. Difficulties relating to gear, equipment and facilities were regarded as negotiable obstacles. The GAA was more than an athletic movement; it became a significant social and networking environment.

The visits by the All-Stars and the GAA hierarchy introduced the organisers in those far-flung places to the influencers and providers. The contacts made were crucial to the sustainability of what had already been organised and ensured that the GAA worldwide would grow.

In February 2024, the GAA launched its first *World Strategic Plan*, which was described by the then president Larry McCarthy as 'a roadmap to strengthen our existing roots internationally, and to encourage World GAA to boldly go in search of new territories where our magnificent games of hurling, football and camogie can have an inspirational impact'.

For the first time, World GAA had put together a comprehensive list of GAA clubs and regions. The Asian GAA Board now looks after twenty-three adult clubs, playing football, hurling, ladies football and camogie. Those clubs are spread through Malaysia, China, Korea, Japan, Vietnam, Cambodia, Thailand and Taiwan. This region has also seen the formation of ten youth clubs.

The Middle East Board, once under the auspices of Asia, became a separate unit in 2013. It has fifteen adult clubs, 1,000 affiliated members and 3,000 associate members in UAE, Oman, Saudi Arabia, Qatar, Bahrain and Kuwait.

Gaelic Games Europe, established in 1999, has 122 clubs in Poland, Slovakia, Austria, Czechia, Holland, Belgium, France, Spain, Germany, Slovenia, Switzerland, Finland, Sweden, Norway and Iceland.

While numbers and facilities in Asia and the Middle East mean that games are often eleven-a-side or nine-a-side, Europe has fifteen-a-side championships. The men's winners of this annual championship qualified for the Leinster junior football championship and the ladies' winners enter the All-Ireland junior championship.

In Galicia in Spain and Brittany in France, the PE curriculum in schools now incorporates Gaelic games. New initiatives have begun in Uganda, where Gaelic games are coached in some primary schools, in Kenya and in South Africa.

The former football All-Star Charlie Harrison from Sligo is the GAA's international manager. He is constantly fielding queries from around the world about the mechanics of forming a GAA club, the most recent coming from Mexico and Nigeria.

'The growth is exciting,' Harrison told the GAA website at the launch of the *World Strategic Plan*. 'It's also exciting to see where we're popping up all over the world in non-traditional international GAA hotspots.

> *You would have always considered cities like New York, Chicago, London and Sydney as the big ones, but we're popping up all over the world now in places like Argentina, Africa, all parts of Europe. And it's not just the expats anymore.*
>
> *It's well-documented the numbers that are leaving the Irish shores but there's a lot of non-Irish-born people taking up the games as well.*
>
> *What we're trying to do is stop the reliance on the island of Ireland, really. In the next five years, we want to be able to arm the units so they can cater for themselves in so many senses, but particularly in terms of games development.*
>
> *We'll be focusing on things such as getting coach developers trained up in the countries themselves. There's a target there of getting two new coach developers each year in each of the units.*
>
> *That would stop us flying people over and trying to do a quick fix. Instead, we'd have people in places like Australia who would be able to deliver coaching courses there.*

Traditionally in World GAA, it would have been from adult level that things would stem. But what we're seeing now is a big emphasis on child and youth development. Especially in the likes of Galicia, but also all around the world. In Dubai, you have a massive juvenile-only club there where they have 200–300 kids who train every week.

That wouldn't have traditionally been seen in the Middle East, where the playing cohort has generally been teachers that go over there. You have around 2,500 teachers going over there every year. There seems to be a trend now where people are staying over there and they want their kids to play.

The Strategic Plan *is designed to help international units complete the player pathway from child to youth to adult level and to provide enough meaningful games all along the pathway.*

Even this year we see USGAA joining the Junior All-Ireland championship for the first time, and that's the end goal for all of these units where they would have a pathway whereby their kids could play the whole way up from Go Games, Cúl Camps, tournaments, Féile, senior club, and then to have an opportunity if they wanted or were good enough to play in a senior All-Ireland competition.

It's probably a really ambitious plan, but I think strategic plans by their nature have to be that. You have to set out goals, you have to try to put some numbers on things. It's going to take a lot of hard work and dedication to try to hit some of those numbers, but I think they're useful to have as targets.

If anyone had any doubt about the growth of Gaelic games, an article in *The Guardian* newspaper – not an outlet noted for its coverage of GAA affairs – by its correspondent Rebecca Root dealt with the new phenomenon.

In a floodlit field, twenty women run the length of a pitch kicking, bouncing and passing the ball in a game of Gaelic football. Sweating it out, players with more experience 'buddy up' with new members to show them the basic skills before they take to the pitch.

It's a weekday training session much like any other, except that it's taking place in the humidity of Bangkok, where Gaelic games – including hurling, handball, rounders and camogie – are surging in popularity.

'I like the history aspect of it and how there's so much of a feel of love for your own community,' says Rajveer Chowdhary, a sports-science strength-and-conditioning consultant from India, who began playing Gaelic football with the Indian Wolfhounds in 2018 and now plays in Bangkok.

After the training, on a Tuesday evening, players hang back for a beer, catching up on the weekend's antics and enjoying the 'craic' as much as keeping fit.

The international reach currently enjoyed by the GAA is quite remarkable, but it's only a beginning. The progress made over the past thirty years – and in particular since 2000 – shows what's possible and the aim now it to build on the solid foundations, thereby increasing the GAA's imprint in all corners of the globe.

ACKNOWLEDGEMENTS

The motivation for writing this book came from a desire to mark the 140th anniversary of the founding of the GAA in 1884. It doesn't have the same historical significance as a 100th, 125th or 150th anniversary but it still maters. One-hundred and forty years and still prospering – perhaps even more so than at any time – it's quite an achievement.

Inspiration came from many sources. Principally for the authors, the greatest inspiration came from the efforts and achievements of generations of players who have provided, and continue to provide, the folklore, the magic, the high-quality performances, the great games, events and drama.

For half a century, we have been fortunate to have worked among those who make it all possible, experiencing at close quarters their skills, their driving forces, their many and varied personalities.

For the earlier periods of the GAA, we have relied mainly on the work of the great journalists and commentators of the past. That, in itself, was a valuable experience because it renewed a respect that

Acknowledgements

was always there for those people whose chronicles of the great matches and occasions are invaluable, not just for the GAA but as a key part of Irish sporting. cultural and social history.

While events between the white lines are the more glamourous pursuits, what happens in the committee rooms is important too. It shaped the GAA right from the start, helping to navigate a path that ensured the maintenance and growth of the association. We are all indebted to the many officials and volunteers without whom none of this could have happened.

The GAA president, Jarlath Burns, was an outstanding player with Armagh for many years and is now the association's leading official. His support for this project was a source of real encouragement and we are grateful to him for his backing.

Pulse of the Nation is the result of a chat over lunch during 2023 with two former colleagues – Alan Milton and Cian Murphy – who now hold senior positions in the GAA in Croke Park. We thank our friends for their input.

This book would not have happened without the enthusiastic support of the team at Hachette Ireland. We greatly appreciate the professionalism of Ciara Considine, Claire Rourke, Aonghus Meaney, Joanna Smyth and Stephen Riordan – they were brilliant to work with in every possible way.

And to our families who put up with our moods in the research and writing periods, a simple thanks. It wouldn't be possible without you.

Martin Breheny
Donal Keenan

IMAGE CREDITS

Plate Section 1
Page 1 (top): GAA Museum
Page 1 (middle): GAA Museum
Page 1 (bottom): GAA Museum
Page 2 (top left): GAA Museum
Page 2 (top right): GAA Museum
Page 2 (middle left): GAA Museum
Page 2 (middle right): GAA Museum
Page 2 (bottom): GAA Museum
Page 3 (top): Connolly Collection/Sportsfile
Page 3 (bottom left): Connolly Collection/Sportsfile
Page 3 (bottom right): Connolly Collection/Sportsfile
Page 4 (top): Ray McManus/Sportsfile
Page 4 (bottom left): Billy Stickland/Inpho
Page 4 (bottom right): James Meehan/Inpho
Page 5 (top left): Ray McManus/Sportsfile

Image Credits

Page 5 (top right): Ray McManus/Sportsfile
Page 5 (bottom left): James Meehan/Inpho
Page 5 (bottom right): Oliver McVeigh/Sportsfile
Page 6 (top left): Billy Stickland/Inpho
Page 6 (top right): David Maher/Sportsfile
Page 6 (bottom left): James Crombie/Inpho
Page 6 (bottom right): James Crombie/Inpho
Page 7 (top left): Inpho
Page 7 (top right): Billy Stickland/Inpho
Page 7 (bottom): Ray McManus/Sportsfile
Page 8 (top): Harry Murphy/Sportsfile
Page 8 (bottom left): Ray McManus/Sportsfile
Page 8 (bottom right): Billy Stickland/Inpho

Plate Section 2
Page 1 (top left): Billy Stickland/Inpho
Page 1 (top right): David Maher/Sportsfile
Page 1 (bottom): Ray McManus/Sportsfile
Page 2 (top): Lorraine O'Sullivan/Inpho
Page 2 (bottom): Patrick Bolger/Inpho
Page 3 (top left): Sportsfile
Page 3 (top right): Piaras Ó Midheach/Sportsfile
Page 3 (bottom): Ray McManus/Sportsfile
Page 4 (top): Ray McManus/Sportsfile
Page 4 (bottom left): Billy Stickland/Inpho
Page 4 (bottom right): Ray McManus/Sportsfile
Page 5 (top): Ray McManus/Sportsfile
Page 5 (bottom): Patrick Bolger/Inpho

Page 6 (top left): Ray McManus/Sportsfile
Page 6 (top right): Ray McManus/Sportsfile
Page 6 (bottom left): Pat Murphy/Sportsfile
Page 6 (bottom right): Seb Daly/Sportsfile
Page 7 (top left): Ryan Byrne/Inpho
Page 7 (top right): Piaras Ó Midheach/Sportsfile
Page 7 (bottom left): Ramsey Cardy/Sportsfile
Page 7 (bottom right): GAA Museum
Page 8 (top): Brendan Moran/Sportsfile
Page 8 (bottom left): Seb Daly/Sportsfile
Page 8 (bottom right): Ramsey Cardy/Sportsfile